THE
COPYWRITER'S
HANDBOOK

THE COPYWRITER'S HANDBOOK

*A Step-by-Step Guide
to Writing Copy That Sells*

ROBERT W. BLY

Dodd, Mead & Company
NEW YORK

This book is dedicated, with gratitude and affection, to my teachers, clients, and colleagues.

Published by Dodd, Mead & Company, Inc.
79 Madison Avenue, New York, N.Y. 10016

Distributed in Canada by
McClelland and Stewart Limited, Toronto

Manufactured in the United States of America

Designed by Berta Lewis

2   3   4   5   6   7   8   9   10

Library of Congress Cataloging in Publication Data

Bly, Robert W.
    The copywriter's handbook.

    Includes index.
    1. Advertising copy.   I. Title.
HF5825.B55   1985   659.13′22   84-18729
ISBN 0-396-08546-6
ISBN 0-396-08547-4 (pbk.)

Contents

Preface

This is a book for everyone who writes, edits, or approves copy—ad agency copywriters, freelancers, ad managers, account executives, creative directors, publicists, entrepreneurs, sales and marketing managers, and product and brand managers. It is largely a book of rules, tips, techniques, and ideas.

Many big agency copywriters and creative directors will tell you that advertising writers don't follow rules—that "great" advertising breaks the rules.

Maybe so. But before you can break the rules, you have to *know* the rules.

This book is written to give you guidelines and advice that can teach you to write effective copy—that is, copy that gets attention, gets its message across, and convinces the customer to buy the product.

Beginners will learn all the basics they need to know—what copy is, what it can do, how to write copy that gets results.

For people who have been in the business a few years, *The Copywriter's Handbook* will serve as a welcome refresher in writing clear, simple, direct copy. And, the book contains some new ideas, examples, and observations that can help these folks increase the selling power of their copy.

Even "old pros" will get some new ideas—or some old ideas that they can use profitably for their own clients.

My approach is to teach through example. Numerous case histories and sample ads, commercials, mailers, and brochures illustrate the principles of effective copy. Guidelines are presented as short, easy-to-digest rules and hints.

Perhaps the copywriters who don't know the rules *do* produce great advertising—one time out of one thousand. But the rest of the time, they create weak, ineffectual ads—ads that look pretty and read pretty but don't sell the product. (And the reason they produce bad ads is that they don't know what makes for a *good* ad!)

If you master the basics presented in this book, I can't guarantee that you'll go on to write "great" advertising or win prestigious advertising awards. But I *can* be fairly certain that you'll be writing good, clean, crisp, hardworking copy—copy that gives your customers reasons to dig into their wallets and buy your product. (And not someone else's!)

Here's how the book is organized.

Part I teaches you how to write copy that sells. You'll learn how to write to get attention . . . how to write to communicate . . . how to write to persuade . . . and how to prepare for a copywriting assignment.

Part II examines the tasks of the copywriter. It gives you specific guidelines for writing print ads, sales letters, brochures, catalogs, annual reports, TV and radio commercials, industrial films, slide presentations, press releases, feature articles, newsletters, and speeches.

Part III discusses the copywriting business. If you're a writer, you'll learn how to succeed as a freelancer and how to get a job at an ad agency. (You'll also learn everything a copywriter needs to know about presenting his or her ideas in visual form.) If you're a client, you'll learn how to hire a copywriter and evaluate his or her work.

Although I pretty much avoid jargon in this book, I

have included a glossary of advertising terms at the back of the book; beginners may find it helpful.

As you read *The Copywriter's Handbook*, you'll discover what you've suspected all along—that copywriters aren't "literary people" or creative artists. Copywriters are salespeople whose job is to *convince people to buy products.*

But don't be disappointed. When you begin to write copy that sells, you'll discover, as I have, that writing words that *persuade* can be just as challenging—and exciting—as writing a poem, magazine article, or short story.

And it pays a lot better, too.

Acknowledgments

I'd like to thank the following people and companies for contributing samples of their work for publication in this book:

Jim Alexander, *Alexander Marketing*
Len Kirsch, *Kirsch Communications*
Wally Shubat, *Chuck Blore & Don Richman Incorporated*
Brian Cohen, *Technology Solutions*
Len Stein, *Visibility PR*
Sig Rosenblum
Richard Armstrong
Herschell Gordon Lewis
John Tierney, *The DOCSI Corporation*
Sandra Biermann, *Masonry Institute of St. Louis*

I'd also like to thank my editor, Cynthia Vartan, for her patient and dedicated work on this project; my agent, Dominick Abel, for his usual fine job in finding a home for the book; and my wife, Amy, for her valuable editorial assistance.

Also, a tip of the hat to the folks who have encouraged and supported me in my freelance ventures—Gary, Eve, Amy, Fern, Mom, and Dad.

THE
COPYWRITER'S
HANDBOOK

PART I

HOW TO WRITE COPY THAT SELLS

1

An Introduction to Copywriting

"A copywriter is a salesperson behind a typewriter."

That quote comes from Judith Charles, president of her own retail advertising agency, Judith K. Charles Creative Communication. And it's the best definition of the word "copywriter" I've ever heard.

The biggest mistake you can make as a copywriter is to judge advertising as laypeople judge it. If you do, you'll end up as an artist or an entertainer—but not as a salesperson. And your copy will be wasting your client's time and money.

Let me explain a bit. When ordinary folks talk about advertising, they talk about the ads or commercials that are the funniest, the most entertaining, or the most unusual or provocative. Fast-talking Federal Express commercials, Wendy's "Where's the beef?" spots, and Michael Jackson's Pepsi extravaganzas are the ads people point to and say, "I really *like* that!"

But the goal of advertising is not to be liked—it is *to sell products*. The advertiser, if he is smart, doesn't care whether people like his commercials or are entertained or amused by them. If they are, fine. But commercials are a means to an end, and the end is increased sales—and profits—for the advertiser.

This is a simple and obvious thing, but the majority of copywriters and advertising professionals seem to ignore it. They produce artful ads, stunningly beautiful catalogs, and commercials whose artistic quality rivals the finest feature films. But they sometimes lose sight of their goals— more sales—and the fact that they are "salespeople behind typewriters," and not literary artists, entertainers, or filmmakers.

Being artistic in nature, advertising writers naturally like ads that are aesthetically pleasing, as do advertising artists. But the fact is, just because an ad is pretty and pleasant to read doesn't necessarily mean it is persuading people to buy the product. Sometimes, cheaply produced ads, written simply and directly without a lot of fluff, do the best job of selling.

I'm not saying that all your ads should be "shlock" or that shlock always sells best. I *am* saying that the look, tone, and image of your advertising should be dictated by the product and your prospects—and not by what is fashionable in the advertising business at the time, or is aesthetically pleasing to artistic people who deliberately shun selling as if it were an unwholesome chore to be avoided at all costs.

In a column in *Direct Marketing Magazine* (May 1983), freelance copywriter Luther Brock gave an instructive example of creativity versus salesmanship in advertising.

Brock tells of a printing firm that spent a lot of money to produce a fancy direct-mail piece. The mailing featured an elaborate, four-color, glossy brochure with a "pop-up" of a printing press. But, reports Brock, the mailing was less than effective:

They got plenty of compliments on "that unique mailing." *But no new business.* That's a pretty expensive price to pay for knocking 'em dead.

The next mailing the firm sent was a simple two-page sales letter and reply card. It pulled a hefty 8 percent response. Same pitch but no frills.[1]

should have worked then.

As a creative person, you naturally want to write clever copy and produce fancy promotions. But as a professional, your obligation to your client is to *increase sales at the lowest possible cost.* If a classified ad works better than a full-page ad, use it. If a simple typewritten letter gets more business than a four-color brochure, mail the letter.

Actually, once you realize the goal of advertising is selling (and Luther Brock defines selling as "placing 100 percent emphasis on how the reader will come out ahead by doing business with you"), you'll see that there *is* a creative challenge in writing copy that sells. This "selling challenge" is a bit different than the artistic challenge: Instead of creating aesthetically pleasing prose, you have to dig into a product or service, uncover the reasons why consumers would want to buy the product, and present those sales arguments in copy that is read, understood, and reacted to—copy that makes the arguments so convincingly the customer can't help but want to buy the product being advertised.

Of course, Judith Charles and I are not the only copywriters who believe that salesmanship, not entertainment, is the goal of the copywriter. Here are the thoughts of a few other advertising professionals on the subjects of advertising, copywriting, creativity, and selling:

My definition says that an ad or commercial has a purpose other than to entertain. That purpose is to conquer a sale by persuading a logical prospect for your product or service, who is now using or is about to use a competitor's product or service, to switch to yours. That's basic, or at least, it should be. In order to accomplish that, it seems to me, you have to promise that prospect an advantage that he's not now getting from his present product or service and it must be of sufficient importance in filling a need to make him switch.[2]

—HANK SEIDEN, *Executive Vice President*
Hicks & Greist, New York

For years, a certain segment of the advertising industry has been guilty of spinning ads out of whole cloth; they place a premium on advertising's appearance, not on the reality of sales. The result: too many ads and commercials that resemble third-rate vaudeville, desperately trying to attract an audience with stale jokes and chorus lines. . . .

On its most basic level, [the advertising] profession involves taking a product, studying it, learning what's unique about it, and then presenting that "uniqueness" so that the consumer is motivated to buy the product.[3]

—ALVIN EICOFF, *Chairman*
A. Eicoff & Company

Those of us who read the criticisms leveled at advertising around the world are constantly struck by the fact that they are not really criticisms of advertising as such, but rather of advertisements which seem to have as a prime objective finding their way into creative directors' portfolios, or reels of film.

Possibly the best starting discipline for any creative man [*professional*] in any country is the knowledge that the average housewife [*consumer*] does not even know that an advertising agency, creative director, art director or copywriter even exists.

What's more, she [*maybe*] couldn't care less if they do. She's [*they're*] interested in buying products, not creative directors.[4]

—KEITH V. MONK
Nestlé, Vevey, Switzerland

Of course, I have never agreed that creativity is the great contribution of the advertising agency, and a look through the pages of the business magazines should dramatize my contention that much advertising suffers from overzealous creativity—aiming for high readership scores rather than for the accomplishment of a specified communications task. Or, worse, creativity for self-satisfaction.[5]

> —Howard G. Sawyer, *Vice President*
> *Marsteller, Inc.*

When your advertising asks for the order right out front, with a price and a place to buy and with "NOW" included in the copy, that's hard-sell advertising, and it should invariably be tried before any other kind. . . .

Advertising is usually most beautiful when it's least measurable and least productive.[6]

> —Lewis Kornfeld, *President*
> *Radio Shack*

Viewers are turned off by commercials that try so hard to be funny, which is the present product of so many agencies. The question that comes to mind is, "Why do these people have to have characters acting like imbeciles for 30 seconds or more just to get the product name mentioned once or twice?" Are they afraid to merely show the product and explain why the viewer should buy it instead of another like product?

Possibly the most stupid thing advertisers do is allow their agency to have background music, usually loud, rock-type music, played while the person is trying to explain the features of the product. Frequently the music is louder than the voice, so the commercial goes down the drain. . . .

More and more people are relying on print ads for information to help them decide which product to purchase. The entertainment-type ads on tv are ineffective. . . .

> —Robert M. Snodell[7]

If there are two "camps" in advertising—hard-sell versus "creative"—then I side with the former. And so do the experts quoted above.

This first section of *The Copywriter's Handbook* is written to teach you how to write copy that sells. For copy to convince the consumer to buy the product, it must do three things:

• Get attention
• Communicate
• Persuade

Chapter 2 shows you how to write copy that gets attention. You'll learn to use both headlines and pictures as attention-getting tools. (And you'll learn to make them work *together*.)

Chapter 3 is a primer on writing to communicate. It provides rules for writing clear, concise, simple copy that gets your message across to the reader.

Chapter 4 presents guidelines on persuasive writing. It will teach you to be a salesperson as well as a writer.

And Chapter 5 presents step-by-step instructions that can help you prepare effectively for *any* copywriting assignment.

Now let's take a look at getting the reader's attention—the job of the headline.

2

Writing to Get Attention: The Headline

If you can come up with a good headline, you are almost sure to have a good ad. But even the greatest writer can't save an ad with a poor headline.

JOHN CAPLES
How to Make Your Advertising Make Money

YOUR AD MUST COMPETE FOR ATTENTION

When you read a magazine or a newspaper, you ignore most of the ads and read only a few.

Yet, many of the ads you skip are selling products that may be of interest to you.

The reason you don't read more ads is simple: There are just too many advertisements competing for your attention. And you don't have the time—or the inclination—to read them all.

This is why you, as a copywriter, must work hard to get attention for your ad or commercial. Wherever you turn—magazines, television, or the mail basket of a busy executive—there are just too many things competing for your reader's attention.

For example: The November 1983 issue of *Cosmopolitan* magazine contained 275 advertisements. A November 1983 issue of *The New York Times* ran 280 display ads and 4,680 classified ads. Each year, American companies spend more than $20 billion to advertise in popular magazines, newspapers, and trade publications.

Even worse, your ad competes with the articles published in these newspapers and magazines, as well as with all other reading material that crosses the reader's desk or is piled in her mail basket.

Let's say you are writing an ad to sell laboratory equipment to scientists. Your ad will compete with the dozens of other ads in the scientific journal in which it is published. And the scientist probably receives a dozen or more such journals every month. Each is filled with articles and papers he should read to keep up to date in his field. (John Naisbitt, author of *Megatrends*, estimates that 6,000 to 7,000 scientific articles are written *daily*, and that the total amount of technical information in the world doubles every five and a half years.)

This increased amount of information makes it difficult for any single piece of information to be noticed. According to Dr. Leo Bogart of the Newspaper Advertising Bureau, consumers are exposed to more than twice as many ads today as 15 years ago, but pay attention to only 20 percent more. Obviously, those ads that don't do something special to grab the reader's attention are not noticed and not read. Bob Donath, editor of *Business Marketing*, says the successful ad is one that is able to "pop through the clutter."

Direct-mail advertisers know that a sales letter has only *five seconds* in which to gain the reader's attention. If the reader finds nothing of interest after five seconds of scanning the letter, she will toss the letter in the trash. Similarly, an ad or commercial has only a few seconds to capture the prospect's interest before the prospect turns the page or goes to the refrigerator.

In advertising, getting attention is the job of the *headline*.

HOW HEADLINES GET ATTENTION

In all forms of advertising, the "first impression"—the first thing the reader sees, reads, or hears—can mean the difference between success and failure. If the first impression is boring or irrelevant, the ad will not attract your prospect. If it offers news or helpful information or promises a reward for reading the ad, the first impression will win the reader's attention. And this is the first step in persuading the reader to buy your product.

What, specifically, is this "first impression"?

In a print advertisement, it is the headline and the visual.

In a brochure, it's the cover.

In a radio or TV commercial, it's the first few seconds of the commercial.

In a direct-mail package, it's the copy on the outer envelope or the first few sentences in the letter.

In a press release, it's the lead paragraph.

In a sales presentation, it's the first few slides or flip charts.

No matter how persuasive your body copy or how great your product, your ad cannot sell if it does not attract your customer's attention. Most advertising experts agree that an attention-getting headline is the key ingredient in a successful advertisement.

Here's what David Ogilvy, author of *Confessions of an Advertising Man,* says about headlines:

The headline is the most important element in most advertisements. It is the telegram which decides the reader whether to read the copy.

On average, five times as many people read the headline as read the body copy. When you have written your headline, you have spent eighty cents out of your dollar.

If you haven't done some selling in your headline, you have wasted 80 percent of your client's money.

Ogilvy says that putting a new headline on an existing ad has increased the selling power of the ad tenfold.

What is it that makes one headline a failure and the other a success?

Many copywriters fall into the trap of believing that clever wordplay, puns, and "cute" copy make for a good headline.

But think a minute. When you make a purchase, do you want to be *amused* by the sales clerk? Or do you want to know that you're getting quality merchandise at a reasonable price?

The answer is clear. When you shop, you want products that satisfy your needs—and your budget. Good copywriters recognize this fact, and put *sales appeals*—not cute, irrelevant gimmicks and wordplay—in their headlines. They know that when readers browse ad headlines, they want to know: "What's in it for *me?*" The effective headline tells the reader: "Hey, stop a minute! This is something that you'll want!" As mail-order copywriter John Caples explains, "The best headlines appeal to people's self-interest, or give news."

Let's look at a few examples.

A classic appeal to self-interest is the headline "How to Win Friends and Influence People," from an ad for the Dale Carnegie book of the same name. The headline promises that you will make friends and be able to persuade others if you read the ad and order the book. The benefit is almost irresistible. Who but a hermit doesn't want more friends?

A recent ad for Kraft Foods appeals to the home-maker with the headline, "How to Eat Well for Nickels and Dimes." If you are interested in good nutrition for your family but must watch your budget carefully, this ad speaks directly to your needs.

The headline for a Hellmann's Real Mayonnaise ad hooks us with the question, "Know the Secret to Moister, Richer Cake?" We are promised a reward—the secret to moist cake—in return for reading the copy.

Each of these headlines offers a benefit to the con-sumer, a reward for reading the copy. And each promises to give you specific, helpful information in return for the time you invest in reading the ad and the money you spend to buy the product.

THE FOUR FUNCTIONS OF THE HEADLINE

Headlines do more than get attention.

The Dale Carnegie headline, for example, lures you into the body copy of the ad by promising useful infor-mation.

The Hellmann's ad also gets you interested in reading more. And it selects a specific type of reader—those peo-ple who are interested in baking cakes.

Your headline can perform four different tasks:

1. Get attention.
2. Select the audience.
3. Deliver a complete message.
4. Draw the reader into the body copy.

Let's take a look at how headlines perform each of these jobs.

1. Getting Attention

We've already seen how headlines get attention by appealing to the reader's self-interest. Here are a few more examples of this type of headline:

"Give Your Kids a   (Crest)
Fighting Chance"

"Why Swelter Through   (GE air conditioners)
Another Hot Summer?"

"For Deep-Clean, Oil-   (Noxzema moisturizer)
Free Skin, Noxzema
Has the Solution"

Another effective attention-getting gambit is to give the reader news. Headlines that give news often use words such as *new, discover, introducing, announcing, now, it's here, at last,* and *just arrived.*

"New Sensational Video   (exercise video tape)
Can Give You Thin
Thighs Starting Now!"

"Discover Our New   (Brim decaffeinated cof-
Rich-Roasted Taste"   fee)

"Introducing New   (Come 'N Get It dog
Come 'N Get It. Burst-   food)
ing With New Exciting
4-Flavor Taste."

If you can legitimately use the word *free* in your headline, do so. *Free* is the most powerful word in the copywriter's vocabulary. Everybody wants to get something for free.

(A *TV Guide* insert for Silhouette Romance novels offers free love in its headline, "Take 4 Silhouette Romance Novels FREE (A $9.80 Value) . . . And Experience The

Love You've Always Dreamed Of." In addition, the word FREE is used 23 times in the body copy and on the reply card.)

Other powerful attention-getting words include *how to, why, sale, quick, easy, bargain, last chance, guarantee, results, proven,* and *save.* Do not avoid these words because other copywriters use them with such frequency. Other copywriters use these words because *they work.*

Headlines that offer the reader useful information are also attention-getters. The information promised in the headline can be given in the copy or in a free booklet the reader can send for. Some examples:

"Free New Report on 67 Emerging Growth Stocks"   (Merrill Lynch)

"Three Easy Steps to Fine Wood Finishing"   (Miniwax Wood Finish)

"How to Bake Beans"   (Van Camp's)

Many advertisers try to get attention with headlines and gimmicks that don't promise the reader a benefit or are not related to the product in any way. One industrial manufacturer features a photo of a nude woman in his ads, with an offer to send a reprint of the photo to readers who clip the coupon and write in for a brochure on the manufacturer's equipment.

Does this type of gambit get attention? Yes, but not attention that leads to a sale or to real interest in the product. Attention-getting for attention-getting's sake attracts a lot of curious bystanders but precious few serious customers. When you write a headline, get attention by picking out an important customer benefit and presenting it in a clear, bold, dramatic fashion. Avoid headlines and concepts that are cute, clever, and titillating but irrelevant. They may generate some hoopla, but they do not sell.

2. Selecting the Audience

If you are selling life insurance to people over 65, there is no point in writing an ad that generates inquiries from young people.

In the same way, an ad for a $25,000 sports car should say, "This is for rich folks only!" You don't want to waste time answering inquiries from people who cannot afford the product.

The headline can select the right audience for your ad and screen out those readers who are not potential customers. A good headline for the life insurance ad might read, "To Men and Women Over 65 Who Need Affordable Life Insurance Coverage." One possible headline for the sports car ad is, "If You Have to Ask How Many Miles to the Gallon It Gets, You Can't Afford to Buy One."

Here are a few more headlines that do a good job of selecting the right audience for the product:

"We're Looking for People to Write Children's Books."	(The Institute of Children's Literature)
"A Message to All Charter Security Life Policyholders of Single Premium Deferred Annuities"	(Charter Security life insurance)
"Is Your Electric Bill Too High?"	(utility ad)

3. Delivering a Complete Message

According to David Ogilvy, four out of five readers will read the headline and skip the rest of the ad.

If this is the case, it pays to make a complete statement in your headline. That way, the ad can do some selling to those 80 percent of readers who read headlines only.

Here are a few headlines that deliver complete messages:

"Caught Soon Enough, Early Tooth Decay Can Actually Be Repaired by Colgate!"	(Colgate toothpaste)
"Gas Energy Inc. Cuts Cooling and Heating Costs Up to 50%"	(Hitachi chiller-heaters)
"You Can Make Big Money in Real Estate Right Now"	(Century 21)

Ogilvy recommends you include the selling promise and the brand name in the headline. Many effective headlines *don't* include the product name. But put it in if you suspect most of your prospects won't bother to read the copy underneath.

4. Drawing the Reader into the Body Copy

A few product categories—liquor, soft drinks, and fashion, for example—can be sold with an attractive photo, a powerful headline, and a minimum of words. But most items—automobiles, computers, books, records, telephones—require that the reader be given a lot of information. That information appears in the body copy, and for the ad to be effective, the headline must compel the reader to read this copy.

To draw the reader into the body copy, you must arouse his or her curiosity. You can do this with humor, or intrigue, or mystery. You can ask a question or make a provocative statement. You can promise a reward, news, or useful information.

A sales letter offering motivational pamphlets was

mailed to business managers. The headline of the letter was, "What Do Japanese Managers Have That American Managers Sometimes Lack?" Naturally, American managers wanted to read on and find out about the techniques the Japanese use to manage effectively.

A headline for an ad offering a facial lotion reads: "The $5 Alternative to Costly Plastic Surgery." The reader is lured into the ad to satisfy her curiosity about what this inexpensive alternative might be. The headline would not have been as successful if it said, "$5 Bottle of Lotion is an Inexpensive Alternative to Costly Plastic Surgery."

PFS Software begins its ad with the headline, "If You're Confused About Buying a Personal Computer, Here's Some Help." If you *are* confused about computers, you will want to read the ad to get the advice offered in the headline.

BREAKING THE RULES

It's only natural for a creative person to avoid formulas, to strive for originality and new, fresh approaches.

To the creative writer, many of the headlines in this chapter might seem to follow rigid formulas—"How to . . . ," "Three Easy Ways . . . ," "Introducing the New . . ." And to an extent, copywriters do follow certain rules, because these rules have been proven effective in thousands of letters, brochures, ads, and commercials.

Remember, as a copywriter, you are not a creative artist; you are a salesperson. Your job is not to create literature; your job is to persuade people to buy the product. As mail-order copywriter John Tighe points out, "We are not in the business of being original. We are in the business of reusing things that work."

Of course, John doesn't mean copywriters spend their time deliberately copying the work of other writers. The challenge is to take what works and apply it to your product in a way that is compelling, memorable, and persuasive. Certainly, the best copywriters succeed by breaking the rules. But you have to *know* the rules before you can break them effectively.

Here, then, are eight time-tested headline categories that have helped sell billions of dollars worth of products and services. Study them, use them well, and then go on to create your own breakthroughs in headline writing.

EIGHT HEADLINES THAT WORK

1. Direct Headlines

Direct headlines state the selling proposition directly, with no wordplay, hidden meanings, or puns. "Pure Silk Blouses—30 Percent Off" is a headline that's about as direct as you can get. Most retailers use newspaper ads with direct headlines to announce sales and bring customers into the stores.

2. Indirect

The indirect headline makes its point in a roundabout way. It arouses curiosity, and the questions it raises are answered in the body copy.

The headline for an ad for an industrial mixing device reads, "Ten Million to One, We Can Mix It." At first, this sounds like a wager—the company is betting ten million to one that its mixer can handle your mixing applications. But when you read the copy, you discover that the real significance of "ten million to one" is the mixer's ability to mix two fluids where one fluid is as much as ten million times thicker than the other. The headline has a double meaning, and you have to read the copy to get the real message.

3. News

If you have news about your product, announce it in the headline. This news can be the introduction of a new product, an improvement of an existing product ("new, *improved* Bounty"), or a new application for an old product. Some examples of headlines that contain news:

"The first transportable computer worth taking anywhere"	(Apple IIc)
"Introducing the New Citation II"	(Chevrolet)
"Finally, a Caribbean Cruise as Good as Its Brochure"	(Norwegian American Line)

The Norwegian American headline, in addition to containing news, has added appeal because it empathizes with the reader's situation. We've all been disappointed by fancy travel brochures that promise better than they deliver. Norwegian American gains credibility in our eyes by calling attention to this well-known fact.

4. How to

The words *how to* are pure magic in advertising headlines, magazine articles, and book titles. (There are more than 7,000 books in print with the words *how to* in their titles.) Many advertising writers claim if you begin with the words *how to*, you can't write a bad headline. They may be right.

"How to" headlines offer the promise of solid information, sound advice, and solutions to problems: "How to Turn a Simple Party Into a Royal Ball." "How to Write Better and Faster." "How to Stop Smoking in 30 Days . . . Or Your Money Back."

Whenever I'm stuck for a headline, I type "How to"

on the page, and what follows those words is always a decent, hard-working headline—good enough to use until something better comes along.

5. Question

To be effective, the question headline must ask a question that the reader can empathize with or would like to see answered. Some examples:

"When an Employee Gets Sick, How Long Does it Take Your Company to Recover?"   (Pilot Life Insurance)

"Is Your Pump Costing You More to Operate Than It Should?"   (Gorman-Rupp pumps)

"Do You Close the Bathroom Door Even When You're the Only One Home?"   (from a letter selling subscriptions to *Psychology Today*)

"Have You Any of These Decorating Problems?"   (Bigelow carpets)

Question headlines should always focus on the reader's self-interest, curiosity, and needs—and *not* on the advertiser's. A typical self-serving question headline used by many companies reads something like, "Do You Know What the XYZ Company Is Up to These Days?" The reader's response is "Who cares?" and a turn of the page.

6. Command

Command headlines generate sales by telling your prospects what to do. Here are a few command headlines:

"Try Burning This Coupon"	(Harshaw Chemical Company)
"Put a Tiger in Your Tank"	(Esso)
"Aim High. Reach for New Horizons."	(Air Force recruitment)

Note that the first word in the command headline is a strong verb demanding action on the part of the reader.

7. Reason-why Headlines

One easy and effective way of writing body copy is to list the sales features of your product in simple 1-2-3 fashion. If you write your ad this way, you can use a reason-why headline to introduce the list. Examples of reason-why headlines include "Seven Reasons Why You Should Join the American Institute of Aeronautics and Astronautics" and "120 to 4,000 Reasons Why You Should Buy Your Fur During the Next Four Days."

Reason-why headlines need not contain the phrase "reasons why." Other introductory phrases such as "6 ways," "7 steps," and "here's how" can do just as well.

8. Testimonial

In a testimonial advertisement, your customers do your selling for you. An example of a testimonial is the Publishers Clearing House commercial in which past winners tell us how they won big prize money in the sweepstakes.

Testimonials work because they offer *proof* that a business satisfies its customers. In print-ad testimonials, the copy is written as if spoken by the customer, who is usually pictured in the ad. Quotation marks around the headline and the body copy signal the reader that the ad is a testimonial.

When writing testimonial copy, use the customer's own words as much as possible. Don't polish his statements; a natural, conversational tone adds believability to the testimonial.

THE "CONCEPT": HEADLINES AND PICTURES WORKING TOGETHER

To rely on words alone to do your selling is to use only half the tools at your disposal. Pictures can work with headlines to create a unified sales concept more powerful than either words or pictures alone.

When advertising people speak of developing a "concept" for an ad, they mean a headline plus a visual. The concept comes first; body copy is not written until the concept is approved.

The best visuals complement the theme of the headline and catch the reader's eye. Let's look at a few examples:

RCA American Communications

RCA's headline, "Announcing a painless cut in defense spending," is a simple, effective statement that stands on its own. But by adding the visual—a shrinking army telephone photographed against a backdrop of an American flag—we immediately learn that lower phone bills are the cause of the cut in defense spending.

Crown Royal

The headline "How to turn a simple party into a royal ball" promises to tell us how to add a touch of class to an ordinary get-together. But instead of having to read copy to find the answer, a picture of the product tells us immediately that Crown Royal Whisky makes parties special. Color photography showing the whisky in glasses of fine crystal emphasizes the product's quality.

Ciba-Geigy

Ciba-Geigy uses a clever concept in its ad for a new low-temperature dye. The photo shows a group of white stuffed animals, and the headline tells us that "If these animals are exposed to 105° temperature, they'll dye." The body copy explains that the benefit of dyeing at low temperature is energy savings. Ciba's ad stops us with a headline/visual combination that arouses curiosity and leads us logically to an explanation of the benefits of using the product.

When my editor saw Ciba-Geigy's ad, she said to me, "I'm surprised you liked it. After all, the headline is a cute play on words, and you seem to be against that."

True, I don't like gimmicks for their own sake. But here, the cleverness enhances the selling message, because, in addition to being a pun, it relates directly to the problem that the product solves.

Diamond Walnuts

The main photo shows a luscious piece of walnut cherry cake, and the headline asks, "What Nut Did This?" For a second, you wonder why the advertiser would call anyone a nut for baking a cake; when you look at the secondary photo (a bag of Diamond Walnuts) and the body copy underneath, you see that the "nut" that makes the cake look so good is the Diamond shelled walnut. The copy is simply the recipe for the cake. This concept is a nice blend of an arresting headline and visual combined with informative body copy. Again, the headline is a pun, but it works because *the pun is relevant to the sales message.*

By now, you get the picture: A headline and visual working together can greatly increase an ad's attention-getting powers. English copywriter Alastair Crompton says that good headlines "should always work *with* the picture. Every good ad should be able to stand as a poster; the reader should never have to dip into the small print to understand the *point* of the story."

A CHECKLIST FOR EFFECTIVE HEADLINES

Here are a few points to consider when evaluating headlines:

- Does the headline promise a benefit or a reward for reading the ad?
- Is the headline clear and direct? Does it get its point across simply and quickly?
- Is the headline as specific as it can be? ("Lose 19 Pounds in Three Weeks" is a better headline than "Lose Weight Fast.")
- Does the headline reach out and grab your attention with a strong sales message, dramatically stated in a fresh new way?
- Does the headline relate logically to the product? (Avoid "sensationalist" headlines that lure you with ballyhoo and then fail to deliver what they promise.)
- Do the headline and visual work together to form a total selling concept?
- Does the headline arouse curiosity and lure the reader into the body copy?
- Does the headline select the audience?
- Is the brand name mentioned in the headline?
- Is the advertiser's name mentioned in the headline?
- Avoid blind headlines—the kind that don't mean anything unless you read the copy underneath. ("Give It a Hand" is a blind headline used in a recent ad for facial powder.)
- Avoid irrelevant wordplay, puns, gimmicks, and other copywriter's tricks. They may make for amusing advertising, but they do not sell products.
- Avoid negatives. (Instead of "Contains No Sodium," write, "100% Sodium-Free.")

TECHNIQUES FOR PRODUCING HEADLINES

No two copywriters have identical methods of producing headlines. Some writers spend 90 percent of their writing time coming up with dozens of headlines before they write one word of body copy. Others write the body copy first and extract the headline from this copy.

Many copywriters keep files of published ads and use headlines from these ads as inspiration for their own advertisements.

Copywriters who work at big agencies often rely on art directors to help them develop the concept. But I believe professional copywriters should be able to generate headlines, concepts, and ideas on their own.

Let me tell you how I go about writing a headline. You may find these techniques useful in your own work.

First, I ask three questions:

1. Who is my customer?
2. What are the important features of the product?
3. *Why* will the customer want to buy the product? (What product feature is most important to him?)

When I have my answer to question number 3, I know the key selling proposition I want to feature in the headline. Then, it's simply a matter of stating this benefit in a clear, compelling, interesting fashion—in a way that will make the reader take notice and want to know more about the product. Sometimes I'll use a "how-to" headline. Sometimes I'll use a question or a "reason-why" format. Other times I do something that doesn't fit in any of these categories. The point is, I don't try to force-fit the selling proposition into a formula. I start with a sales message and write headlines that do the best job of illuminating this message.

I usually come up with the right headline on the second or third try. Other copywriters I know write a dozen or more headlines for a single ad. If writing a lot of head-lines works best for you—fine. You can always use the discarded headlines as subheads or sentences in your body copy.

When writing a new ad for an existing product, I go through the file of previous ads to see what sales points were covered in these ads. Often, the sales message for my headline will be buried in the body copy of one of the existing ads.

Sometimes, when I am unable to produce a lively headline, I make a list of words that relate to the product. I then mix and match the words from this list to form different headlines.

One client asked me to write an ad on a new type of dental splint used to keep loose teeth in place. The old-type splints were made of stiff strips of metal; the new splint was made of braided wire that could more easily twist to fit the patient's teeth. My word list looked something like this:

Twist	Easy
Splint	Technology
Teeth	Invented
New	Revolutionary
Developed	Contour
Dental	Bend
Braided	Dentist
Wire	Introducing
Steel	Flexible
Fit	Loose

Mixing and matching words from this list produced half a dozen good headlines. The one I liked best was, "Introducing a New Twist in Splint Technology." (The client liked it, too.)

If you cannot come up with a headline, don't let it result in writer's block. Put it aside and begin to write the body copy. As you write the copy and go over your notes, ideas for headlines will pop into your head. Write them down as they come and go back to them later. Much of this material will be inadequate, but the perfect headline might just be produced this way.

A FINAL WORD ON HEADLINES

The headline is the part of the ad that gets attention. And getting attention is the first step in persuading your reader to buy your product.

Showmanship, clever phrases, and ballyhoo do not, by themselves, make for a good headline. Creating headlines that are wonderfully clever is worthwhile only if the cleverness enhances the selling message and makes it more memorable. Unfortunately, many copywriters engage in creativity for creativity's sake, and the result is cleverness that *obscures* the selling message.

If you have to choose between being clever and obscure or simple and straightforward, I advise you to be simple and straightforward. You won't win any advertising awards. But at least you'll sell some merchandise.

Jim Alexander, president of Alexander Marketing Services, also believes that headlines should sell. Here are a few of Jim's thoughts on the subject:

> We believe in dramatizing a product's selling message with flair and excitement. Those are important ingredients of good salesmanship in print. But simple statements and plain-jane graphics often make powerful ads.
>
> For example, the headline "Handling Sulfuric Acid" might sound dull or uncreative to you. To a chemical engineer who's forever battling costly corrosion, that simple headline implies volumes. And makes him want to read every word of the problem-solving copy that follows.

So before we let our clients pronounce an ad dull, we first ask them, "Dull to whom?" Dull to you, the advertiser? Or dull to the reader, our potential customer? It's easy to forget that the real purpose of an ad is to communicate ideas and information about a product. Too many ads are approved because of their entertainment value. That's a waste of money.

3

Writing to Communicate

Sometimes one has to say difficult things, but one has to say them as simply as possible.

G.P. HARDY
A Mathematician's Apology

WRITING THAT COMMUNICATES IS WRITING THAT SELLS

In an article published in the *Harvard Business Review* in 1965, Charles K. Ramond described experiments designed to measure advertising effectiveness. The experiments showed, not surprisingly, that advertising is most effective when it is easy to understand. In other words, you sell more merchandise when you write clear copy.

In theory, it sounds easy. Advertising deals, for the most part, with simple subjects—clothing, soda, beer, soap, records. But in practice, many advertisements don't communicate as effectively as they could. Here's an example from an ad that appeared in *Modern Bride* magazine:

THEY LOVED MY DRESS ON QUIRIUS 3

They smiled politely when Harry showed them our late model telestar, but when he opened the hood of our auto-drive one of their children burst into a shrill laugh and was boxed on his starfish-shaped ears. . . .

The students in my copywriting seminars call this one "What did she say?" This is an example of a "borrowed interest" ad: The writer didn't have faith in her ability to make the product interesting, so she hid behind a made-up scenario involving a conversation on the planet Quirius 3. The result? Maximum confusion and minimum communication.

"Borrowed interest" is a major cause of confusing copy. There are others—lengthy sentences, clichés, big words, not getting to the point, a lack of specifics, technical jargon, and poor organization, to name a few.

The following tips will help you write copy that gets its message across to the reader.

11 TIPS FOR WRITING CLEAR COPY

1. *The Reader Comes First*

In his pamphlet, "Tips to Put Power in Your Business Writing," consultant Chuck Custer advises executives to *think about their readers* when they write a business letter or memo.

"Start writing to *people*," says Custer. "It's okay that you don't know your reader! Picture someone you *do* know who's like your reader. Then write to him."

Think of the reader. Ask yourself: Will the reader understand what I have written? Does he know the special terminology I have used? Does my copy tell him something important or new or useful? If I were the reader, would this copy persuade me to buy the product?

One technique to help you write for the reader is to

address the reader directly as "you" in the copy—just as I am writing to *you* in this book. Copywriters call this the "you-orientation." Flip through a magazine, and you'll see that 90 percent of the ads contain the word "you" in the body copy.

The column at left shows examples of copy written without regard to the reader's interests. The column at right gives revisions that make the copy more you-oriented.

Advertiser-Oriented Copy	*You-Oriented Copy*
BankPlan is the state-of-the-art in user-friendly, sophisticated financial software for small-business accounts receivable, accounts payable, and general ledger applications.	BankPlan can help you balance your books. Manage your cash-flow. And keep track of customers who haven't paid their bills. Best of all, the program is easy to use—no special training is required.
The objective of the daily cash accumulation fund is to seek the maximum current income that is consistent with low capital risk and the maintenance of total liquidity.	The cash fund gives you the maximum return on your investment dollar with the lowest risk. And, you can take out as much money as you like—whenever you like.
To cancel an order, return the merchandise to us in its original container. When we have received the book in good condition, we will inform our Accounting Department that your invoice is cancelled.	If you're not satisfied with the book, simply return it to us and tear up your invoice. You won't owe us a cent. What could be fairer than that?

2. *Carefully Organize Your Selling Points*

The Northwestern National Bank in Minneapolis wanted to know if people read booklets mailed by the bank. So they included an extra paragraph in a booklet mailed to a hundred customers. This extra paragraph, buried in 4,500 words of technical information, offered a free ten-dollar bill to anyone who asked for it.

How many bank customers requested the free money? None!

Obviously, the organization of your material affects how people read it. If the bank had put "FREE $10!" on the brochure cover and on the outside of the mailing envelope, many customers would have responded to the offer.

When you write your copy, you must carefully organize the points you want to make. In an ad, you might have one primary sales message ("This car gets good mileage") and several secondary messages ("roomy interior," "low price," "$500 rebate"). The headline states the main selling proposition, and the first few paragraphs expand on it. Secondary points are covered later in the body copy. If this copy is lengthy, each secondary point may get a separate heading or number.

The organization of your selling points depends on their relative importance, the amount of information you give the reader, and the type of copy you are writing (letter, ad, commercial, or news story).

Terry C. Smith, a communications manager with Westinghouse, has a rule for organizing sales points in speeches and presentations. His rule is: "Tell them what you're going to tell them. Tell them. And then, tell them what you told them." The speechwriter first gives an overview of the presentation, covers the important points in sequence, and then gives a brief summary of these points. Listeners, unlike readers, cannot refer to a printed page to remind them of what was said, and these overviews and summaries help your audience learn and remember.

Burton Pincus, a freelance copywriter, has developed a unique organizational pattern for the sales letters he writes. Pincus begins with a headline that conveys a promise, shows how the promise is fulfilled, and gives proof that the product is everything the copy says it is. Then, he tells the reader how to order the product and explains why the cost of the product is insignificant compared to its value.

Before you create an ad or mailer, write down your sales points. Organize them in a logical, persuasive, clear fashion. And present them in this order when you write your copy.

3. Break the Writing into Short Sections

If the content of your ad can be organized as a series of sales points, you can cover each point in a separate section of copy.

This isn't necessary in short ads of 150 words or less. But as length increases, copy becomes more difficult to read. Breaking the text into several short sections makes it easier to read.

What's the best way to divide the text into sections? If you have a series of sections where one point follows logically from the previous point, or where the sales points are listed in order of importance, use numbers.

If there is no particular order of importance or logical sequence between the sales points, use graphic devices such as bullets, asterisks, or dashes to set off each new section.

If you have a lot of copy under each section, use subheads (as I've done in this book).

Paragraphs should also be kept short. Long, unbroken chunks of type intimidate readers. A page filled with a solid column of tiny type says, "This is going to be tough to read!"

When you edit your copy, use subheads to separate major sections. Leave space between paragraphs. And break long paragraphs into short paragraphs. A paragraph of five sentences can usually be broken into two or three shorter paragraphs by finding places where a new thought or idea is introduced and beginning the new paragraph with that thought.

4. Use Short Sentences

Short sentences are easier to read than long sentences. All professional writers—newspaper reporters, publicists, magazine writers, copywriters—are taught to write in crisp, short, snappy sentences.

Long sentences tire and puzzle your readers. By the time they have gotten to the end of a lengthy sentence, they don't remember what was at the beginning.

D. H. Menzel, coauthor of *Writing a Technical Paper,* conducted a survey to find the best length for sentences in technical papers. He found that sentences became difficult to understand beyond a length of about 34 words. And the consumer has far less patience with wordiness and run-on sentences than does the scientist studying an important report.

Rudolf Flesch, best known for his books *Why Johnny Can't Read* and *The Art of Plain Talk,* says the best average sentence length for business writing is 14 to 16 words. Twenty to twenty-five words is passable, he adds, but above 40 words, the writing becomes unreadable.

Because ad writers place a premium on clarity, their sentences are even shorter than Flesch's recommended 14- to 16-word average. Here's a list showing the average sentence length of some recent ads and promotions:

Sample	Average sentence length (number of words)
Velveeta cheese-spread ad	6.7
Lanier dictaphone ad	8.3
IBM PC software ad	10.6

Sample	*Average sentence length (number of words)*
Porsche 944 ad	10.6
INC. magazine subscription letter	12.2
3M/Audio-Visual Division brochure	13.6
IBM PC data-base communication ad	14.5
Jack Daniels ad	16.2

The average sentence length in these and dozens of other ads I measured ranges from 6 to 16 words. The average sentence length of *your* copy should also fall in this range.

Now, let's take a look at how you can reduce sentence length.

First, you should break large sentences into two or more separate sentences whenever possible.

Today every penny of profit counts and Gorman-Rupp wants your pumps to work for all they're worth.	Today every penny of profit counts. And Gorman-Rupp wants your pumps to work for all they're worth.
This article presents some findings from surveys conducted in Haiti in 1977 that provide retrospective data on the age at menarche of women between the ages of 15 and 49 years.	This article presents some findings from surveys conducted in Haiti in 1977. These surveys provide retrospective data on the age at menarche of women between the ages of 15 and 49 years.

Another method of breaking a long sentence is to use punctuation to divide it into two parts.

One purpose is to enable you to recognize and acknowledge the importance of people who handle people from company president right down to the newest foreman.

The outcome is presentations that don't do their job and that can make others wonder whether you're doing *yours.*

One purpose is to enable you to recognize and acknowledge the importance of people—from the company president right down to the newest foreman.

The outcome is presentations that don't do their job . . . and that can make others wonder whether you're doing *yours.*

Copy becomes dull when all sentences are the same length. To make your writing flow, vary sentence length. By writing an occasional short sentence or sentence fragment, you can reduce the average sentence length of your copy to an acceptable length even if you frequently use lengthy sentences.

Over 30 thousand aerospace engineers are members now. To join them, send your check for $46 with the coupon below and become a member *today.*

Now, discover the Splint-Lock System, a simply beautiful, effective, and versatile chair-

Over 30 thousand aerospace engineers are members now. Join them. Send your check for $46 with the coupon below and become a member *today.*

Now, discover the Splint-Lock System . . . a simply beautiful, effective, and versatile

| side splinting technique that helps you stabilize teeth quickly, easily, and economically. | chairside splinting technique that helps you stabilize teeth quickly. Easily. And economically. |

Train yourself to write in crisp, short sentences. When you have finished a thought, stop. Start the next sentence with a new thought. When you edit, your pencil should automatically seek out places where a long string of words can be broken in two.

5. Use Simple Words

Simple words communicate more effectively than big words. People use big words to impress others, but they rarely do. More often, big words annoy and distract the reader from what the writer is trying to say.

Yet big words persist, because using pompous language makes the reader or speaker feel important. Some recent examples of big words in action:

In his sermon, a Unitarian minister says: "If I were God, my goal would be to maximize goodness, not to eternalize evil."

In a cartoon appearing in *Defense News* (February 1980), a publication of the Westinghouse Defense Center, a manager tells his staff: "I want you to focalize on your optionalizations, prioritize your parametrics, budgetize your expendables, and then schedualize your throughput."

Fred Danzig, writing in *Advertising Age,* asks why an E.F. Hutton executive says the market might "whipsaw back and forth" when he could have said, "it will go up and down."

In advertising copy, you are trying to *communicate* with people—not impress them or boost your own ego. Avoid pompous words and fancy phrases. Cecil Hoge, the mail-order expert, says the words in your copy should be "like the windows in a storefront. The reader should be able to see right through them and see the product."

The column at left lists some big words that have appeared in recent ads, brochures, and articles. The column at right offers simpler—and preferable—substitutions.

Big Word	Substitute Word or Phrase
assist	help
automobile	car
container	bottle, jar, package
data base	information
diminutive	small
eliminate	get rid of
employ	use
facilitate	help
facility	building, factory, warehouse
finalize	finish, complete, conclude
garment	suit, shirt, dress
indicate	tell, say, show
obtain	get
operate	use
optimum	best
parameters	factors
prioritize	set priorities, rank
procure	get
perspiration	sweat
purchase	buy
substantiate	prove
select	pick
superior	best
utilize	use
terminate	end, finish
visage	face

Small words are better than big words whether you're writing to farmers or physicists, fishermen or financiers. "Even the best-educated people don't resent simple words," says John Caples. "But [simple words] are the only words many people understand."

And don't think your copy will be ignored because you write in plain English. In Shakespeare's most famous sentence—"To be or not to be?"—the biggest word is three letters long.

6. Avoid Technical Jargon

Industrial copy isn't the only writing that uses technical jargon. Here's a sample from a Porsche ad that ran in *Forbes:*

> The 944 has a new 2.5-liter, 4-cylinder, aluminum-silicon alloy Porsche engine—designed at Weissach, and built at Zuffenhausen.
>
> It achieves maximum torque of 137.2 ft-lbs as early as 3000 rpm, and produces 143 hp at 5500 rpm.
>
> The 944 also has the Porsche transaxle design, Porsche aerodynamics, and Porsche handling.

Like many *Forbes* readers, I'm not an automotive engineer. I didn't know that torque is achieved in ft-lbs, or that 3000 rpm is considered early for achieving it. I know hp is horsepower and rpm revolutions per minute, but I don't know whether 143 hp at 5500 rpm is good, bad, or mediocre.

The point is: Don't use jargon when writing to an audience that doesn't speak your special language. Jargon is useful for communicating within a small group of experts. But used in copy aimed at outsiders, it confuses the reader and obscures the selling message.

Computer people, for example, have created a new language—bits and bytes, RAMs and ROMs, CRTs and CPUs. But not everybody knows the vocabulary. A business executive may know the meaning of *software* and *hardware* but not understand terms like *operating system, applications package,* or *subroutine.* And even an experienced programmer may be baffled by a brochure that refers to *interprocess message buffers, asynchronous software interrupts,* and *four-byte integer data types.* When you use jargon, you enjoy an economy of words, but you risk turning off readers who don't understand this technical shorthand.

Computer experts aren't the only technicians who baffle us with their lingo. Wall Streeters use an alien tongue when they speak of *downside ticks, standstills, sideways consolidation,* and *revenue enhancements.* Hospital administrators, too, have a language all their own: *cost outliers, prospective payments, catchment areas, diagnostic-related groups, ICD-9 codes.*

Because advertisers are specialists, it is they—not their copywriters—who most often inflict jargon on the readers. One of my clients rewrote some brochure copy so that their storage silo didn't merely *dump* grain—the grain was "gravimetrically conveyed."

When is it okay to use technical terms, and when is it best to explain the concept in plain English?

I have two rules.

RULE #1: Don't use a technical term unless 95 percent or more of your readers will understand it. If your client insists you use jargon that is unfamiliar to your readers, be sure to explain these terms in your copy.

RULE #2: Don't use a technical term unless it precisely communicates your meaning. I would use *software* because there is no simpler, shorter way to say it. But instead of using *deplane,* I would just say, "Get off the plane."

7. Be Concise

Good copy is concise. Unnecessary words waste the reader's time, dilute the sales message, and take up space that could be put to better use.

Rewriting is the key to producing concise copy. When you write your first draft, the words just flow, and you can't help being chatty. In the editing stage, unnecessary words are deleted to make the writing sparkle with vigor and clarity.

One copywriter I know of describes her copy as a "velvet slide"—a smooth path leading the prospect from initial interest to final sale. Excess words are bumps and obstacles that block the slide.

For example, a writing consultant's brochure informs me that his clients receive "informed editorial consideration of their work." As opposed to *uninformed?* Delete *informed.*

Another such brochure refers to "incomplete manuscripts still in progress." Obviously, a manuscript still in progress is incomplete.

Make your writing concise. Avoid redundancies, run-on sentences, wordy phrases, the passive voice, unnecessary adjectives, and other poor stylistic habits that take up space but add little to meaning or clarity. Edit your writing to remove unnecessary words, phrases, sentences, and paragraphs.

Here are some examples of wordy phrases and how to make them more concise.

Wordy Phrase	*Concise Substitute*
at first glance	at first
the number 20	20
free gift	gift
whether or not	whether
a general principle	a principle
a specific example	an example
he is a man who	he

Wordy Phrase	*Concise Substitute*
they managed to use	they used
from a low of 6 to a high of 16	from 6 to 16
a wide variety of different models	a variety of models
approximately 17 tons or so	approximately 17 tons
expert specialists	specialists
simple and easy to use	easy to use
can help you	helps you
can be considered to be	is
most unique	unique
the one and only	the only
comes to a complete stop	stops
the entire issue	the issue
dull and boring	boring
on an annual basis	yearly
in the form of	as
exhibits the ability to	can
as you may or may not know	as you may know
a substitute used in place of	a substitute for
features too numerous to mention	many features
John, Jack, Fred, Tom, etc.	John, Jack, Fred, and Tom
feminine hygiene products for women	feminine hygiene products
children's toys	toys

Wordy Phrase	*Concise Substitute*
where you were born originally	where you were born
your own home	your home
a product that you can use	a product you can use
RAM memory*	RAM

----

* RAM stands for *random access memory*. So a RAM memory is a "random access memory memory."

8. Be Specific

Advertising persuades us by giving specific information about the product being advertised. The more facts you include in your copy, the better. Copywriters who don't bother to dig for specifics produce vague, weak, meaningless copy.

"If those who have studied the art of writing are in accord on any one point," write Strunk and White in *The Elements of Style,* "it is this: the surest way to arouse and hold the attention of the reader is by being specific, definite, and concrete. The greatest writers—Homer, Dante, Shakespeare—are effective largely because they deal in particulars and report the details that matter."

When you sit down at the typewriter, your file of background information should have at least twice as much material as you will end up using in the final version of your ad. When you have a warehouse of facts to choose from, writing copy is easy: You just select the most important facts and describe them in a clear, concise, direct fashion.

But when copywriters have little or nothing to say, they fall back on fancy phrases and puffed-up expressions to fill the empty space on the page. The words sound nice, but say nothing. And the ad doesn't sell because it doesn't inform.

Here are some examples of vague versus specific copy.

Vague Copy	*Specific Copy*
He is associated in various teaching capacities with several local educational institutions.	He teaches copywriting at New York University and technical writing at Brooklyn Polytech.
Adverse weather conditions will not result in structural degradation.	The roof won't leak if it rains.
Good Housekeeping is one of the best-read publications in America.	Each month, more than five million readers pick up the latest issue of *Good Housekeeping* magazine.

9. Go Straight to the Point

If the headline is the most important part of an ad, then the lead paragraph is surely the second most important part. It is this lead that either lures the reader into the text by fulfilling the promise of the headline, or bores the reader with uninteresting, irrelevant, unnecessary words.

The first piece of copy I ever wrote was a brochure describing an airport radar system. Here's the lead:

Times change. Today's airports handle a far greater volume of traffic than the airports of the late 1960's.

The radars of that era were not built with an eye toward the future and could not handle the rapidly increasing demands placed upon terminal air traffic control systems.

The air traffic handled by today's airports continues to increase at a tremendous rate. An airport surveillance radar must be built to handle not only today's airport traffic but also the more complex air traffic control requirements of tomorrow's airports.

All this is true, and as a layman, I found it interesting. But the person reading the brochure is in charge of air traffic control at a large or medium-size airport. Doesn't he already know that air traffic volume is increasing? If so, I am wasting his time by repeating the obvious.

Many novice copywriters fall into this trap. They spend the first few paragraphs "warming up" before they get to the sales pitch. By the time they do start talking about the product, most readers have fled.

Start selling with the very first line of copy. Here's how I *should* have written the lead to that radar brochure:

The X-900 radar detects even the smallest commercial aircraft out to a range of 145 miles. What's more, the system's L-band operating efficiency makes it 40 times more efficient than S-band radars.

If you feel the need to "warm up" as you set your thoughts on paper, do so. But delete these warm-ups from your final draft. The finished copy should sell from the first word to the last.

Here's another example of copy that fails to get to the point:

AIM HIGH. REACH FOR NEW HORIZONS.

It's never easy. But reaching for new horizons is what aiming high is all about. Because to reach for new horizons you must have the vision to see things not only as they are, but as they could be. . . .

What's the point of writing copy like this? The ad tries to be dramatic, but the result is empty rhetoric; the copy does not give a clue as to what is being advertised.

This copy appeared in an Air Force recruitment ad. The benefits of joining the Air Force are travel, vocational training, and the chance to fly jets. Why not feature these points right off?

10. *Write in a Friendly, Conversational Style*

Ann Landers is one of the most widely read columnists in the country. Why is she so popular?

"I was taught to write like I talk," says Ann. "Some people like it."

People enjoy reading clear, simple, easy-to-understand writing. And the simplest, clearest style is to write the way you talk. (The writing experts call this "conversational tone.")

Conversational tone is especially important in advertising, where the printed page is an economical substitute for a salesperson. (The only reason companies advertise is that advertising can reach more people at less cost than a traveling salesperson can.) A light, conversational style is much easier to read than the stiff, formal prose of business, science, and academia. And when you write simply, you become the reader's friend. When you write pompously, you become a bore.

For example, IBM's famous Charlie Chaplin ads and commercials have helped make the IBM PC a best-seller. This ad series is a model of friendly, helpful, conversational copy. Here's a sample:

> There's a world of information just waiting for you. But to use it, study it, enjoy it and profit from it, you first have to get at it.
>
> Yet the facts can literally be right at your fingertips—with your own telephone, a modem and the IBM Personal Computer.

Note the use of colloquial expressions ("a world of information," "at your fingertips") and the informal language ("just waiting for you," "you first have to get at it"). IBM seems to want to help us on a person-to-person level, and their copy has the sound of one friend talking to another. But here's how the copy might read if written in strictly technical terms:

Thousands of data bases may be accessed by individuals. These data bases provide information for business, educational, and leisure activities.

To access these data bases from your home, a telephone, modem, and IBM Personal Computer are required.

See the difference? When you write copy, you'll want to use conversational tone to make your ads glow with warmth, as IBM's do.

So how do you go about it? In an article in *The Wall Street Journal*, John Louis DiGaetani recommends this simple test for conversational tone: "As you revise, ask yourself if you would ever say to your reader what you are writing. Or imagine yourself speaking to the person instead of writing."

My former boss once wrote a sales letter that began, "Enclosed please find the literature you requested." I asked him, "If you were handing this envelope to me instead of mailing it, what would you say?"

"Well, I'd say, 'Here is the information you asked for' or 'I've enclosed the brochure you requested' or something like that."

"Then why not *write* it that way?" I replied.

He did.

And to help *you* write the way you talk, here are some tips for achieving a natural, conversational style:

- Use pronouns—*I, we, you, they*
- Use colloquial expressions—*a sure thing, turn on, rip-off, O.K.*
- Use contractions—*they're, you're, it's, here's, we've, I'm*
- Use simple words
- If you must choose between writing naturally and being grammatically correct, write naturally

11. *Avoid Sexist Language*

The day of the advertising man, salesman, and Good Humor man are over. Now it's the advertising *professional,* sales*person,* and Good Humor *vendor.*

Copywriters must avoid sexist language. Like it or not, sexist language offends a large portion of the population, and you don't sell things to people by getting them angry at you.

Handling gender in writing is a sensitive, as yet unresolved issue. Do we change *manpower* to *personpower? His* to *his/her? Foreman* to *foreperson?*

Fortunately, there are a few techniques for handling the problem:

• *Use plurals.* Instead of "the doctor receives a report on his patients," write, "the doctors receive reports on their patients."

• *Rewrite to avoid reference to gender.* Instead of "the manager called a meeting of his staff," write, "the manager called a staff meeting."

• *Alternate gender references.* Five years ago, I used *his* and *he* throughout my copy. Now, I alternate *he* with *she* and *his* with *her.*

• *Use "he and she" and "his and her."* This works in simple sentences. But it can become cumbersome in such sentences as, "When he or she punches his or her time-card, he or she is automatically switched to his or her overtime pay-rate."

When you use *he and she* and *his and her,* alternate these with *she and he* and *her and his.*

Do not use the awkward constructions *he/she* or *his/her.*

• *Create an imaginary person to establish gender.* For example: "Let's say Doris Franklin is working overtime. When she punches her time-card, she is automatically switched to her overtime pay-rate."

Finally, here's a helpful list of sexist terms and non-sexist substitutes:

Sexist Term	Nonsexist Substitute
anchorman	anchor
advertising man	advertising professional
chairman	chairperson
cleaning woman	domestic
Englishmen	the English
fireman	firefighter
foreman	supervisor
a man who	someone who
man the exhibit	run the exhibit
man of letters	writer
mankind	humanity
manpower	personnel, staff
manmade	artificial, manufactured
man-hours	work hours
Mrs., Miss	Ms.
newsman	reporter
postman	mail carrier
policeman	police officer
salesman	salesperson
stewardess	flight attendant
self-made man	self-made person
weatherman	meteorologist
workman	worker

A FEW TRICKS OF THE TRADE

Copywriters use a number of stylistic techniques to pack a lot of information in a few short paragraphs of smooth-flowing copy. Here are a few tricks of the trade.

End with a Preposition

Ending a sentence with a preposition adds to the conversational tone of the copy. And it's a perfectly acceptable technique endorsed by Zinsser, Flesch, Fowler, and most other authorities on modern writing. Some examples:

He's the kind of fellow with whom you love to have a chat.	He's the kind of fellow you love to have a chat with.
Air pollution is something of which we want to get rid.	Air pollution is something we want to get rid of.
For what are we fighting?	What are we fighting for?

Use Sentence Fragments

Sentence fragments help keep your average sentence length to a respectable number of words. And sentence fragments can add drama and rhythm to your copy.

Basic Eye Emphasizer does it all. It's the one eye makeup everyone needs. The only one.

Not one of the Fortune 1000 companies even comes close to our rate of growth. And no wonder. Computers are the hottest product of the 1980's, with no end to demand in sight.

It doesn't take much to block the door to success. A flash of an idea that slips your mind. A note that never gets written.

Begin Sentences with Conjunctions

Beginning a sentence with *and, or, but,* or *for* makes for a smooth, easy transition between thoughts.

Use these simple words instead of more complex connectives. *But* is a shorter, better way of saying *nevertheless, notwithstanding,* and *conversely.* And don't use such antiquated phrases as *equally important, moreover,* and *furthermore* when *and* will do just as well.

> The first lesson is free. But I can't call you. *You* have to take the first step.

> The choice is simple. Be a pencil pusher. Or get the Messenger. And move ahead at the speed of sound.

> ECS phones the first two numbers you've selected until someone answers. It announces the emergency. Gives your address. And repeats it.

Use One-Sentence Paragraphs

An occasional one-sentence paragraph provides a change of pace that can liven up a piece of copy. When all sentences and paragraphs are pretty much the same, the reader is lulled into a stupor, just as a driver can be hypnotized by a long stretch of straight road. A one-sentence paragraph is like a sudden curve in the road—it can shock your reader to wakefulness again. Here's an example from a sales letter pitching freelance copywriting services:

> For many ad agency people, industrial advertising is a difficult chore. It's detailed work, and highly technical. To write the copy, you need someone with the technical know-how of an engineer and the communications skills of a copywriter.

> That's where I can help.

Use Bullets, Breakers, and Numbers

Divide the copy into short sections, as in this book. It makes the copy easier to read (and easier to write).

Use Mechanical Techniques to Emphasize Words or Phrases in the Copy

When I was a student, I used a yellow marker to highlight sentences in my textbooks. This saved time in studying, since the highlights allowed me to reread only the important material and not the entire book.

Highlighting and underlining can make words and phrases stand out in print advertising and promotion as well as in schoolbooks. Many readers skim copy without reading it carefully, so an underline or highlight can be useful in calling out key words, phrases, paragraphs, and selling points.

Of course, underlines and other mechanical devices should be used sparingly. If you underline every other word in your sales letter, nothing stands out. On the other hand, if you underline only three words in a one-page letter, you can be sure most readers will read those words.

Here is a list of mechanical techniques copywriters use to call attention to key words and phrases:

underlines

capital letters

indented paragraphs

boldface type

italics

colored type

fake handwriting

arrows and notes in margins

yellow highlighting

reverse type (white type on black background)

boxed copy
call-outs
P.S. (in letters)

A COPYWRITER'S CHECKLIST

Before you release copy to the client or the art department, ask yourself these questions.

• *Does the copy fulfill the promise of the headline?* If the headline is "How to Win Friends and Influence People," the copy should tell you how to win friends and influence people. Copy that doesn't fulfill the promise of the headline cheats the reader . . . and the reader knows it.

• *Is the copy interesting?* Your copy can't generate enthusiasm for the product if the reader yawns as she reads it. Tell a story, give news, improve the reader's life. Make it *interesting*. You can't bore people into buying your product.

• *Is it easy to read?* When a person reads your copy, it is not his job to try and figure out what you mean. It is *your* job to explain what you mean in plain, simple English. Use short sentences, short paragraphs, small words. Be clear.

• *Is it believable?* Once a teacher said of a phrase I had written, "Bob, this has all the sincerity of a three-dollar bill." People mistrust advertising and advertising professionals. You must work hard to convince the reader that what you say is true. One way to establish credibility is to include testimonials from satisfied customers. Another is to offer a demonstration or scientific evidence that proves your claim. But the best way to get people to believe you is to *tell the truth*.

- *Is it persuasive?* Clear, readable prose is not enough. Your copy must *sell* as well as communicate. To sell, your copy must get attention . . . hook the reader's interest . . . create a desire for the product . . . prove the product's superiority . . . and ask for action. Chapter 4 covers the basics of salesmanship in print.

- *Is it specific?* To persuade people to buy, you have to give them specifics—facts, features, benefits, savings—reasons why they should buy the product. The more specific you are, the more informative and believable your copy.

- *Is it concise?* Tell the whole story in as few words as possible. When you are finished, stop.

- *Is it relevant?* Freelance copywriter Sig Rosenblum explains: "One of the rules of good copy is: Don't talk about yourself. Don't tell the reader what *you* did, what *you* achieved, what *you* like or don't like. That's not important to him. What's important to him is what *he* likes, what *he* needs, what *he* wants." Make sure your copy discusses facts that are relevant to the reader's self-interest.

- *Does it flow smoothly?* Good copy flows smoothly from one point to the next. There are no awkward phrases, no confusing arguments, and no strange terms to jar the reader and break the flow.

- *Does it call for action?* Do you want the consumer to switch to your brand, send for a free brochure, call your sales representative, send you a check? Find the next step in the buying process—and tell the reader to take it. Use coupons, reply cards, toll-free numbers, and other such devices to increase response.

4

Writing to Sell

"The object of advertising is to sell goods," said Raymond Rubicam of Young & Rubicam. "It has no other justification worth mentioning."[1]

For the beginning copywriter, this is new territory. If you've done other kinds of writing—magazine articles, news reporting, fiction, technical writing—you know how to express yourself in clear, simple English. You know how to write words that inform, and maybe even words that amuse or entertain. But now, you're faced with a new challenge: writing words that convince the reader to *buy your product.*

This puts most writers on uncertain ground. There are many choices you have to make, and unless you're experienced in sales or advertising, you don't know how to make them.

For example, should you write a lot of copy, or is it better to write short copy? (If you write a lot of copy, will people read it? Or is it true that people won't read ads with more than a couple of paragraphs?)

Do you need some clever gimmick, slogan, or sexy model to get the reader's attention? Or should you concentrate on the product when you write?

If your product has a minor advantage over the competition's, should you focus on that advantage? Or should you concentrate on the general benefits of using the product (which the reader gets from both your product and your competitor's)? What do you do if there is no difference between your product and the competition's?

How do you know whether what you're writing will be convincing or interesting to the reader? If you think of two or three ideas for an ad, how do you pick the best one?

Let's start finding out the answers to these questions.

FEATURES AND BENEFITS

The first step in writing copy that sells is to write about *benefits* and not about features.

A feature is a descriptive fact about a product or service. A benefit is what the user of the product or service gains as a result of the feature.

For example, I'm writing this book on a word processor. A *feature* of the machine is that it allows me to edit and revise what I'm typing electronically, so I can move a sentence or add a word without retyping the whole page.

The *benefit* of this feature is that I save a lot of time and can increase my productivity (and make more money) as a result.

Another example: A second feature of my word processor is that it has a detachable keyboard connected to the main unit with a coil cable. The benefit is that I can position the keyboard for maximum typing comfort.

In their pamphlet "Why don't those salespeople sell?" Learning Dynamics Incorporated, a sales training firm, cites poor ability to present benefits as one of ten reasons why salespeople fail to make the sale. "Customers don't buy products or services," the firm explains. "They buy what these products and services are going to *do* for them. Yet many salespeople describe only the features, assuming the customer knows the benefits. Salespeople need to know how to translate features into *benefits*, and then present them in a customer-centered language."

The same goes for copywriters. Novices tend to write about features—the facts, figures, and statistics at hand. Experienced copywriters turn those features into customer benefits—reasons why the reader should buy the product.

Here's a simple technique for digging out a product's benefits.

Divide a sheet of paper into two columns. Label the left-hand column "Features" and the right-hand column "Benefits."

In the left-hand column write down all the features of the product. Some of these you'll find in the background material you've collected on the product (Chapter 5 tells you what background material to collect). The rest you can learn by examining and using the product or by talking with people involved with the product—customers, salespeople, distributors, engineers.

Then, go down the list of features and ask yourself, "What *benefit* does this feature provide to the customer? How does this feature make the product more attractive, useful, enjoyable, or affordable?"

When you complete the list, the right-hand column will contain all the benefits the product offers the customer. These are the sales points that should be included in your copy.

Try this exercise with a common household product

that you have nearby. Below is my features/benefits checklist for a pencil. Can you add to this list or think of a stronger way to state the benefits?

FEATURES AND BENEFITS OF A #2 PENCIL

Features:	*Benefits:*
Pencil is a wooden cylinder surrounding a graphite core	Can be resharpened as often as you like to ensure clean, crisp writing
One end is capped by a rubber eraser	Convenient eraser lets you correct writing errors cleanly and quickly
Eraser attached with metal band	Tight-fitting band holds eraser snugly in place—no pencils ruined by eraser coming loose
Pencil is 7½ inches long	7½-inch graphite core ensures long writing life
Pencil is ¼ inch in diameter	Slender shape makes it easy to hold and comfortable to write with
Pencil is #2	Graphite core is blended for just the right hardness—writes smoothly yet crisply
Yellow exterior	Bright, attractive exterior—stands out in a pencil holder or desk drawer
Sold by the dozen	Sold in a convenient 12-pack so one stop to the store gives you enough pencils to last for months

FEATURES AND BENEFITS OF A #2 PENCIL

Features:	*Benefits:*
Also available in a box containing a gross	Sold by the gross to accommodate the needs of business offices and schools at a substantial savings over retail prices
Made in the U.S.A.	A quality product. (Also, buying American-made strengthens U.S. economy)

Now that you have a list of customer benefits, you must decide which sales point is the most important point—the one you will feature in your headline as the "theme" of the ad. You also have to decide which of the other points you will include and which you will not use. And, you have to arrange these points in some sort of logical order.

Let's take a look at a handy five-step sequence that can help you put your sales points in an order that will lead the reader from initial interest to final sale.

THE MOTIVATING SEQUENCE

Over the years many advertising writers have developed "copy formulas" for structuring ads, commercials, and sales letters.

The best known of these formulas is AIDA—which stands for Attention, Interest, Desire, Action.

According to AIDA, the copy must first get the reader's *attention*, then create an *interest* in the product, then turn that interest into a strong *desire* to own the product, and finally ask the reader to buy the product or take some other *action* that will eventually lead to a sale.

A second well-known formula is ACCA—Awareness, Comprehension, Conviction, Action. In ACCA, consumers are first made *aware* that the product exists. Then they must *comprehend* what the product is and what it will do for them. After comprehension, the readers must be *convinced* to buy the product. And finally, they must take *action* and actually make the purchase.[2]

A third famous formula is the four Ps—Picture, Promise, Prove, Push. The copywriter creates a *picture* of what the product can do for the reader, *promises* the picture will come true if the reader buys the product, *proves* what the product has done for others, and *pushes* for immediate action.

Lately, others have come up with their own versions, and I might as well join the crowd. The "motivating sequence" presented below is a five-step formula for writing copy that sells:

1. Get Attention

This is the job of the headline and the visual. The headline should focus on the single *strongest* benefit you can offer the reader.

Some copywriters try to hook the reader with clever phrases, puns, or irrelevant information, then save the strongest benefit for a big windup finish. A mistake. If you don't hook the reader with the strongest benefit—the most important reason why he or she should be interested in what you're selling—the reader won't get past the headline. (For a quick refresher on headline writing, go back and browse through Chapter 2.)

2. Show a Need

All products, to some degree, solve some problem.

A car solves the problem of getting to and from work. An air conditioner prevents you from sweltering in summer heat. Toothpaste with fluoride keeps your teeth from getting holes in them. And mouthwash saves you the embarrassment of having bad breath.

However, with most products, the need for the product may not be obvious or it may not be ingrained in the reader's mind. The second step of writing copy that sells, then, is to show the reader why he needs the product.

For example, many small-business owners do their own taxes and haven't thought about hiring an accountant. But an accountant, with his superior knowledge of taxes, can take advantage of the latest tax regulations and shelters and save the business owner hundreds or even thousands of dollars in income tax. So an accountant seeking small businesses as clients might run an ad with the headline, "Would You Pay $150 to Save $500 a Year or More on Your Taxes?" This headline does double duty by grabbing attention with a provocative question and hinting at the need for professional help at tax time. Body copy could go on to explain how an accountant can save you enough money to justify his fee several times over.

3. Satisfy the Need

Once you've convinced the reader that he has a need, you must quickly show him that your product can satisfy his need, answer his questions, or solve his problems.

The accountant ad might begin like this:

WOULD YOU PAY $150 TO SAVE $500?

Last year, a flower shop decided to hire an accountant to do their income tax returns. They worried about the seemingly high fee, but realized they didn't have the time—or the expertise—to do it themselves.

You can imagine how delighted they were when they hired an accountant who showed them how they could pay $500 less in income tax than they originally thought they would owe.

I am their accountant, and I'd like to tell you how the flower shop—and dozens of other firms whose taxes I prepare—

have saved $200 . . . $500 . . . even $1,000 a year or more by taking advantage of *legitimate* tax regulations, deductions, and shelters.

This copy isn't perfect. It needs some work. But it does get attention, show a need (the need to save money!), and show that the service being advertised can satisfy the need.

4. Prove Your Superiority—and Your Reliability

It isn't enough to *say* you can satisfy the reader's needs; you've got to *prove* you can. You want the readers to risk their hard-earned money on your product or service. You want them to buy from or hire *you* instead of your competitors. How do you demonstrate your superiority over the competition? How do you get the reader to believe what you say?

Here are a few proven techniques for convincing the readers that it's to their advantage to do business with you:

- Talk about the benefits of your product or service (use the features/benefits list as the source of your discussion). Give the reader reasons to buy by showing the benefits he'll get when he owns your product.

- Use testimonials. In testimonials, others who have used the product praise the product in their own words. This third-party endorsement is much more convincing than a manufacturer praising his own product.

- Compare your product to the competition's. Show, benefit for benefit, how you are superior.

- If you have conducted studies to prove your product's superiority, cite this evidence in the copy. Offer a free reprint of the study to interested readers.

- Show that your company is reliable and will be in business a long time. Talk about number of employees, size of distributor network, annual sales, number of years in business, growth rate.

5. Ask for the Order

The last step in any piece of copy should always be a call for action.

If the product is sold by mail, ask the reader to mail in an order. If the product is sold retail, ask the reader to clip the ad and bring it into the store.

If your ad doesn't sell the product directly, then find out the next step in the buying process—and tell the reader about it. For example, you might offer a free brochure on the product, a demonstration, or a sample. At the very least, encourage the reader to look for the product in the future if he is not going to buy it today.

Make it easy for the reader to take action. Include your company name, address, and phone number in every piece of copy you write.

If you're writing retail copy, include store hours and locations.

If you're writing copy for a hotel or tourist attraction, include easy-to-follow instructions on how to get there, along with a clearly drawn map of the area.

If you want the reader to send in an order or write for a free brochure, include a handy coupon he can clip and mail.

If you want the reader to call, highlight your toll-free number in large type. And, if you take credit-card orders, be sure to say so and indicate which cards you accept.

Put order forms in catalogs, reply cards in mailers, dealer lists in industrial sales literature. Make it *easy* for your reader to respond.

And, if possible, give the reader an incentive for responding *now*—a price-off coupon, a time-limited sale, a discount to the first 1,000 people who order the product. Don't be afraid to try for immediate action and sales as well as long-range "image-building." Ask for the order, and ask for it right away.

THE UNIQUE SELLING PROPOSITION

Rosser Reeves, author of *Reality in Advertising,* coined this term to describe the major advantage of your product over the competition's.

The idea is this: If your product is not different and better than other products of the same type, there is no reason for consumers to choose your product instead of someone else's. Therefore, to be promoted effectively, your product must have a Unique Selling Proposition—a major benefit that other products in its category don't offer.

Herb Ahrend, president of Ahrend Associates, Inc., says that "a copywriter has to create *perceived* value. He has to ask, 'What is the nature of the product? What makes the product different? If it isn't different, what attribute can you stress that hasn't been stressed by the competition?' "

The Unique Selling Proposition is the major benefit that is featured in the headline and as the "theme" of the ad or mailer. This benefit should be unique to your product, and it should be important to the consumer.

An ideal situation for the copywriter is to write an ad for a product that is clearly and significantly superior to all other products in the category. But this is rarely the case. Often, your product is only slightly better than the competition's (and in some ways, it may be worse). Or, there may be practically no difference between your product and the next fellow's. If that's the case, says Ahrend, you look for a benefit your competitors *haven't* stressed and make that your USP.

Malcolm D. MacDougall, president and creative director of SSC&B, says there are four ways to advertise seemingly similar products.[3]

1. Dramatize a Minor Product Difference

Once, a copywriter visited a brewery in the hopes of learning something that could set the brewery's beer apart from other beers. He was fascinated to discover that beer bottles—like milk containers—are washed in live steam to kill the germs. Although all brands of beer are purified this way, no other manufacturer had stressed this fact. So the copywriter wrote about a beer so pure that the bottles are washed in live steam, and the brew's Unique Selling Proposition was born.

Study your list of product features and benefits. Then look at the competition's ads. Is there an important benefit that they have ignored, one you can embrace as the Unique Selling Proposition that sets your product apart from all others?

2. Dramatize the Benefit

Radio Shack, for example, once ran a commercial showing two people using walkie-talkies, with each person standing on a different side of the Grand Canyon. Although most walkie-talkies work effectively over this distance, the Radio Shack commercial aimed to call attention to its product by demonstrating the walkie-talkie's range in a unique and dramatic fashion.

3. Dramatize the Name or the Package

Remember "Pez," the candy that came in plastic dispensers made to resemble Mickey Mouse, Pluto, and other cartoon characters? Pez was an ordinary candy, but the package made it special.

In the same way, the most unusual feature of L'Eggs pantyhose is not its design, fabric, or style but the egg-shaped package it is sold in.

And those old Maypo commercials never proved that Maypo was any better than other hot cereals. They simply made the name—"I want my Maypo!"—a household word.

Making your product name or package famous is one sure way to move merchandise off the shelves. But it's also expensive. Unless your client is a major marketer with a million-dollar budget, this tactic will be tough to pull off.

4. Build Long-Term Brand Personalities

Another tactic used by the manufacturers of major national brands is to create advertising that gives their brand a "personality." Thousands of Marlboro-man commercials have made Marlboro a "macho" cigarette. And, more recently, Don Meredith spots have drummed into the consumer's mind that Lipton Tea is "brisk" and "dandy tasting."

If you have millions to spend, you can use advertising to give your product a unique "personality" in the mind of the consumer. But if your advertising budget is not so grandiose, you can still use features and benefits to create a Unique Selling Proposition that sets your product apart from the rest.

KNOW YOUR CUSTOMER: THE KEY TO SALES SUCCESS

Psychology Today reported a recent study designed to uncover the characteristics of successful salespeople.

"The best salespeople first establish a mood of trust and rapport by means of 'hypnotic pacing'—statements and gestures that play back a customer's observations, experience, or behavior," wrote the author of the study. "Pacing is a kind of mirror-like matching, a way of suggesting: 'I am like you. We are in sync. You can trust me.' "[4]

In other words, successful salespeople *empathize* with their customers. Instead of launching into a canned sales pitch, the successful salesperson first tries to understand the customer's needs, mood, personality, and prejudices. By mirroring the customer's thoughts and feelings in their sales presentations, successful salespeople break down resistance to sales, establish trust and credibility, and highlight only those product benefits that are of interest to the customer.

Copywriters, too, must get to know the customer. Of course, as a copywriter, you can't create a separate ad or brochure for each individual prospect. But, by understanding the needs of the marketplace, you can tailor your presentation to specific *groups* of buyers—segments of the total market.

Understanding the customer and his motivation for buying the product is the key to writing copy that sells. Too much advertising is created in a vacuum. The advertiser and the agency write copy based on the product features that catch their fancy, not on the features that are important to the customer. The result is copy that pleases the agency and the advertiser, but leaves the customer cold.

In a recent survey published in *Mainly Marketing* (January 1984), advertising agencies and buyers of high-tech products were asked which product features they considered important.

The results showed that advertising agencies stressed features that were not important to buyers. The agencies also omitted information that was vital to the buyers. For example, both purchasing agents and engineers ranked price as the number two consideration when buying high-tech equipment. But the agencies said price was unimportant as a copy point. Agencies said high-tech ads should stress how the product saves the buyer time and money. But engineers and purchasing agents said this is far less important than product specifications and limitations.

When you write copy, don't write in a vacuum. Don't just sit down at the typewriter and pick the features and benefits that suit *your* fancy. Instead, find out which benefits and features your *readers* care about—and write about the sales points that will motivate readers to buy the product.

A good example of copy that "hits home" with the reader is a subscription letter I received from *INC.* magazine. Here's the opening of the letter:

```
A special invitation to the hero of
American business

Dear Entrepreneur:

You're it!

You're the kind of person free enterprise is
built on. The ambition, vision and guts of
small business people like yourself have
always been the driving force behind the
American economy.

Unfortunately, that's a fact which the general
business press seems to have forgotten. In
their emphasis on everything Big—
conglomerates, multinationals, oil companies
the size of countries—most business
publications pay very little attention to the
little guy.
```

The letter is effective because it speaks directly to the pride entrepreneurs feel in being "self-made." The letter writer has done a good job of empathizing with the reader and understanding how an entrepreneur thinks of himself.

You, too, must get to know your reader. One way of doing this is to start paying close attention to your own behavior as a consumer. The next time you start to write a TV commercial that uses dancing soup cans to sell canned soup, ask yourself if you want to be entertained when you buy soup . . . or if you're more interested in how the soup tastes, what it costs, its nutritional value, and where to find it in the supermarket. Once you start thinking as a consumer rather than a writer, you'll have more respect for your reader. And you'll write copy that provides useful product information and sales appeals rather than empty hype and ballyhoo.

Another way to know your reader—the consumer—is to observe consumers and be an active student of the marketplace. When you're in the supermarket, watch other buyers. Which type of person picks the sale items and which type goes for the name brand?

When you visit an automobile dealer, observe how the successful salespeople deliver their pitches and handle their customers. Listen to the pitch *you* receive—and think about why it did or didn't sway you.

Take an active interest in the world of commerce. When you receive a telephone solicitation, listen to the entire call to see what techniques you can use in your own copy. Attend trade shows to find out the nature of buyers in the various industries your clients deal in.

And *talk* to the business people you trade with—store owners, the plumber, your lawyer, the gardener, the person who repairs your hot-water heater—to find out the techniques they use to promote their services and products. People who are close to their customers—and most small business people are—know more about the reality of selling than most ad agency account executives or corporate brand managers do. Listen to these people, and you'll learn what makes the customer tick. Chapter 5 provides additional tips on getting to know your reader.

There's an old saying: "You can't be all things to all people." And it certainly applies to advertising and selling. You can't create one ad or commercial that appeals to everybody, because different groups of buyers have different needs. So, as a copywriter, you must first identify your audience—the segment of the market you are selling to—and then learn which product benefits interest these buyers.

You will tailor both the content and the presentation of your information to the group of customers you're selling to. Take frozen foods as an example. When you sell frozen foods to a homemaker, he or she is most interested in nutrition and price. But a young, single professional person is primarily interested in convenience—he or she doesn't want to spend too much time in the kitchen.

Price is not as much of a factor because he or she has more disposable income than the homemaker.

Take photocopiers as another example. The large corporation buying a copier wants a machine that is fast and offers a variety of features such as color copies, collating, and two-sided copying. But the self-employed professional who works at home has different needs. His budget is limited, so the copier must be inexpensive. And, since he's working from home, space is at a premium, so compactness is an important feature. But speed and capacity are not as crucial since the work-at-home professional makes fewer copies than the corporate user.

Sometimes, the benefits to stress to various groups of buyers are obvious. In other cases, you must ask the advertiser or his customers which features should be stressed. Once I had the assignment of selling a water purification system to two different types of customers: marine users (mostly commercial fishing vessels) and chemical-industry users (chemical plants). Same product, two different buyers. By talking with a few customers in each group, I discovered that marine users put a premium on reliable operation, since they can't afford to be without fresh water while at sea. Weight is also important, because the larger the equipment the more fuel the boat consumes in hauling the equipment around.

Chemical-industry buyers, on the other hand, don't care about weight, because the machine is placed on the plant floor. And, because they have many sources of water, reliability is not as crucial. The chemical-industry buyers— all engineers by training—were more interested in technical features. They wanted to know every product specification down to the last nut, bolt, pump, and pipeline. But I wouldn't have known these differences existed unless I *asked*. Which is why it's vital that you get to know your buyer.

A CHECKLIST OF COPY "MOTIVATORS"

As I've pointed out, different people buy products for different reasons. If I buy a car, I buy reliable transportation to get me where I want to go, and a used economy car suits me just fine. But the buyer of a Porsche or Mercedes Benz is buying more than transportation—he's buying status and prestige as well.

Before you write your copy, it's a good idea to review the reasons why people might want to buy your product. To help you, I've compiled the following checklist of "copy motivators"—22 motivations people have for making purchases. This list is not comprehensive. But it *will* get you thinking about who you're writing to and why you're writing to them.

Here, then, are 22 reasons why people might buy your product. Don't just read the list; *think* about each of the reasons and how it might apply to the products you handle.

- To be liked
- To be appreciated
- To be right
- To feel important
- To make money
- To save money
- To save time
- To make work easier
- To be secure
- To be attractive
- To be sexy
- To be comfortable
- To be distinct
- To be happy

- To have fun
- To gain knowledge
- To be healthy
- To gratify curiosity
- For convenience
- Out of fear
- Out of greed
- Out of guilt

Think about the things you buy—and why you buy them.

You buy cologne to smell nice. And you want to smell nice to attract the opposite sex.

You buy sports equipment to have fun. You join a spa to become healthy. You buy a gold-plated money clip to be distinct and to feel important.

You buy insurance to be secure. You buy slippers to be comfortable. You buy a refrigerator with an ice maker for convenience.

Once you understand what makes people buy things, you know how to sell—and how to write copy. The rest is just organization and good editing and a few simple techniques.

LONG COPY VERSUS SHORT COPY

The slogan from an old cigarette commercial was, "It's not how long you make it—it's how you make it long." And that's a good rule of thumb for determining the length of the copy you write.

In other words, the question isn't how many words should you write; it's how much information must you include for the copy to accomplish its sales mission?

In general, the length will depend upon three things:

the product, the audience, and the purpose of the copy.

First, consider your product. Is there a lot you can say about it? And will giving these facts help convince the reader to buy it?

There are some products that have a lot of features and benefits you can highlight in your copy. These include computers, stereos, cars, books, insurance policies, investment opportunities, courses and seminars, resorts and vacation trips, video recorders, software, cameras, typewriters, and home-exercise equipment.

There are many other products that don't have a lot of features and benefits, and there isn't too much you can say about them. These include soft drinks, fast food, designer clothes, candy, chewing gum, beer, wine, liquor, jewelry, lingerie, cologne, perfume, soap, laundry detergent, cosmetics, linens, pet food, and shampoo.

For example, there isn't much you can say about a new ginger ale, other than it tastes good and costs less.

But an automatic food processor has a lot of benefits you can highlight: the food processor saves time. It eliminates messy chopping and cutting. It makes cooking easier and more pleasant. It can slice, dice, mash, peel, whip, blend, chop, and crush virtually any food. You can use it for desserts, appetizers, salads, main courses, with fruits, vegetables, meats, nuts, cheeses.

So, the length of the copy depends on the product and what there is to say about it.

Second, the length of the copy depends upon the audience. Some customers don't need a lot of information and are not accustomed to reading long text. Others seek out all the facts they can get and will devour as much as you can provide.

The Playboy Book Club wanted to know how much copy to include in the direct mail package it used to get new members to join the club. They tested sales letters of various lengths—one, two, four, eight, and twelve pages. *The twelve-page letter pulled the most orders.* Why? One of the reasons is that people who will join a book club are *readers*—and they will read twelve pages of text if it interests them.

The third factor in determining copy length is the purpose of the copy. If you want your copy to generate a sales lead, then there's no need to go into complete detail, because you'll get a chance to provide more information when you respond to the lead. On the other hand, an ad that asks for the order by mail must give *all* the facts the reader needs to make a buying decision and order the product.

"This is all very nice," you say, "but how do I determine the length that's best for *my* product, *my* audience, and *my* purpose?"

Fortunately, there's an answer. I've formulated a rule of thumb—and I believe I'm the first to do this—for determining the length of your copy. And the rule is this:

The copy should contain enough information—no more, no less—to convince the greatest number of qualified prospects to take the next step in the buying process.

Note that I said "qualified prospects." You don't want to answer inquiries or waste time with people who are just curiosity seekers or browsers and not real prospects. You want your copy to select only the serious prospects and to weed out the rest.

For example, let's say you're writing a direct-mail piece aimed at getting business executives to participate in stress-control seminars. One way to increase inquiries would be to offer a free copy of your $9.95 book *How to Beat Stress and Take Charge of Your Life* to everyone who writes in for more information on the seminars.

But by offering a free book, you're inviting a lot of nonprospects to write in. Many have no intention of taking the seminar, but are glad to get a $9.95 book for free. And you're wasting time and money by attracting inquiries from these "freebie-collectors" and mailing them an expensive gift.

To prevent this, you can "qualify" prospects by structuring the offer so that they receive the book only after they've answered some questions about their company's stress-management needs and talked with your firm's representative. You can also require that they write their request for the book on their corporate letterhead. This makes it harder to respond and may reduce the number of inquiries as a result. But the people who *do* take the trouble to write a letter and spend time with your representative have proven their genuine interest in the seminars you are offering.

If the letter is used to generate inquiries, you just need enough information to whet the reader's appetite, arouse his curiosity, and get him to take the next step and ask for more information. A short one-page letter, centered around a major benefit of stress-management seminars (such as increasing executive productivity or reducing absenteeism) will do the trick.

If, however, the mailing asks for the order—asks the executive to register for a prescheduled public seminar— it must give more complete information. Since there will be no additional literature or salesperson calling to answer the reader's questions, the copy in the seminar mailing must anticipate the questions and provide the answers. (As mail-order copywriter Luther Brock points out, "When it comes to mail order, the more you tell, the more you sell.")

My rule is obviously a rough guideline only. The length of the copy—and the number of sales points to include— is something you, the copywriter, must decide for each project. However, I offer this piece of advice: *If you're unsure of how long to make the copy, you're better off including too much information than not enough information.*

There are many studies that confirm that, all else being equal, long-copy ads sell more effectively than short ones. For example, a recent survey of 72 retailers measured the "success ratio" of their ads against the number of merchandise facts each ad contained. Here are the results:

Number of merchandise facts	Success ratio
4	1
5	1.1
6	1.3
7	1.4
8 or more	1.5

As you can see, the more facts included, the more successful the ad. The study also revealed that whenever a store omitted any essential information from an advertisement, sales response was instantly reduced.[5]

Don't be afraid of long copy. Include as many facts as it takes to make the sale.

POSITIONING

Once, when I was shopping for a phone-answering machine, a salesman told me that a certain model was "the Rolls-Royce of phone-answering machines." The mention of "Rolls-Royce" connotes excellence, quality, value, and high price; by comparing his product to a familiar brand, the answering-machine salesman instantly created an image of the machine in my mind. This technique is called "positioning."

Jack Trout and Al Ries, authors of several articles and a book on positioning, write: "Today, positioning is used in a broader sense to mean what the advertising does for the product in the prospect's mind. In other words, a successful advertiser today uses advertising to position his product, not to communicate its advantages or features."

Here are a number of examples Trout and Ries give of using advertising to position a product:

• Seven-Up's positioning is defined by something it is *not*—a cola. Seven-Up is the "Un-Cola."

- Schaefer is positioned as a beer for the heavy beer drinker: "The one beer to have when you're having more than one."
- Avis is positioned as a hard-working underdog: "We're number 2 so we try harder."
- Tide makes clothes "white." Cheer makes them "whiter than white." Bold makes them "bright."[6]

Despite what Trout and Ries have written, positioning does not take the place of features and benefits and sales arguments; it *complements* them. If your product fills a special niche, positioning it against a well-known brand is a quick and effective way of establishing the product's identity in the consumer's mind.

But your copy must do more than get the consumer to think about the product; it must also persuade him to buy it. And you can't persuade consumers to buy unless you tell what the product can do for them and why the product does it better than other products can.

5

Getting Ready to Write

Helmut Krone—the art director who helped create such famous campaigns as Avis's "We Try Harder," Volkswagen's "Think Small," and Mennen's "Thanks, I Needed That"—has a basic approach to tackling advertising assignments:

"I start with a blank piece of paper and try to fill it with something interesting," says Krone.[1]

This chapter is about what the copywriter should do to prepare himself for facing that blank piece of paper.

What information do you need before you're ready to write your copy? How do you go about collecting this information? How do you develop advertising ideas?

This chapter provides answers to these questions and outlines specific techniques you can use to prepare for any copywriting assignment—from a one-page flyer to a multimillion-dollar corporate ad campaign.

THE WRONG WAY TO GET STARTED

Most copywriters approach their assignments backward.

When the client needs an ad or brochure, he calls his ad agency or freelance copywriter and says, "I have an assignment for you. Come on over for a meeting with our sales and technical people so we can get started."

This is the *worst* way to go about it.

What happens is that the copywriter sits down with a roomful of experts and spends hours listening to an outpouring of product specifications, advertising strategies, market research, and ad concepts. Since he's starting from ground zero, the copywriter spends the time frantically trying to write down and understand this flood of new information and ideas.

The roomful of executives and engineers, in turn, waste hours explaining the basics of their business to the writer. The writer can't really ask meaningful questions, because he's too busy trying to absorb all this new material. The writer grows confused and the technical experts grow impatient.

Then, at the end of the meeting, the ad manager, almost as an afterthought, hands the copywriter a stack of printed material and says, "Here are some brochures, article reprints, and other literature on the product. You might want to look these over before you write your copy."

This stack of literature contains 95 percent of the information the copywriter received at his briefing. Had he been given the material beforehand, the need for a lengthy meeting would have been eliminated—and time and money would have been saved as a result.

I cannot overemphasize the importance of getting all

printed literature on the product *before* you tackle the assignment. By reviewing this information first, you can at your leisure, become knowledgeable in the subject at hand. Which means the meeting can be used more productively as a question-and-answer session in which the advertising writer fills in whatever gaps the literature left in his product knowledge. Better still, the copywriter can fill in these gaps with a series of short phone interviews, eliminating meetings—and their consumption of time and money—in the process.

Unnecessary, time-wasting meetings are probably the thing I hate most about the advertising business. But the smart copywriter can eliminate 95 percent of these meetings by insisting that client and copywriter work primarily by mail and phone. Oh, you can have an occasional meeting to renew old acquaintances or discuss major ideas and strategies that aren't easily handled long distance. But the majority of assignments can be handled without long meetings that drag on and go nowhere.

Of course, convincing clients to work this way takes time. You have to educate them on the efficiency and economy of "copy by mail." You have to demonstrate that you can provide great copy and concepts *without* marathon meetings or the legendary three-martini lunches that Madison Avenue is famous for. Most importantly, you need to establish a procedure for handling assignments by mail and phone. My way of doing it is outlined below.

HOW TO PREPARE FOR A COPYWRITING ASSIGNMENT

Here's a four-step procedure you can use to get the information you need to write persuasive, fact-filled copy for your clients:

Step #1: Get all Previously Published Material on the Product

For an existing product, there's a mountain of literature the client can send to the copywriter as background material. This literature includes:

- Tear sheets of previous ads
- Brochures
- Annual reports
- Catalogs
- Article reprints
- Technical papers
- Copies of speeches and presentations
- Audiovisual scripts
- Press kits
- Market research
- Advertising plans
- Sales reports
- Letters from users of the product
- Back issues of promotional newsletters
- Files of competitors' ads and literature

Did I hear someone say the client can't send such material because their product is new? Nonsense. The birth of every new product is accompanied by mounds of paperwork you can give the copywriter. This paperwork includes:

- Internal memos
- Letters of technical information
- Product specifications, blueprints, plans
- Illustrations and photos of product prototypes

- Engineering drawings
- Business and marketing plans
- Reports
- Proposals

Insist that the client provide this background material *before* you attend any briefings or write the copy. One way to simplify this request for information is to create a checklist of the background material you need. Clients then simply mail in a completed checklist or copy "order form"—along with appropriate enclosures—for each copywriting assignment.

By studying this background material, the copywriter should have 90 percent of the information he needs to write the copy. He can get the other 10 percent by asking the right questions—either in a brief in-person conference or over the telephone. Steps 2 through 4 outline the questions the copywriter should ask about the product, the audience, and the objective of the copy.

Step #2: Ask Questions About the Product.

- What are its features and benefits? (Make a *complete* list.)
- Which benefit is the most important?
- How is the product different from the competition's? (Which features are exclusive? Which are better than the competition's?)
- If the product isn't different, what attributes can be stressed that haven't been stressed by the competition?
- What technologies does the product compete against?
- What are the applications of the product?
- What problems does the product solve in the marketplace?
- How is the product positioned against competing products?

- How does the product work?
- How reliable is the product? How long will it last?
- How efficient is the product?
- How economical?
- How much does it cost?
- Is it easy to use? Easy to maintain?
- Who has bought the product and what do they say about it?
- What materials, sizes, and models is it available in?
- How quickly does the manufacturer deliver the product?
- If they don't deliver, how and where can you buy it?
- What service and support does the manufacturer offer?
- Is the product guaranteed?

Step #3: Ask Questions About Your Audience

- Who will buy the product? (What markets is it sold to?)
- What exactly does the product do for them?
- Why do they need the product? And why do they need it *now?*
- What is the customer's main concern when buying this type of product? (price, delivery, performance, reliability, service, maintenance, quality, efficiency, availability)
- What is the character of the buyer? What type of person is the product being sold to?
- What motivates the buyer?
- How many different buying influences must the copy appeal to? (A toy ad, for example, must appeal to both the parent and the child.)

Two tips on getting to know your audience:

- If you are writing an ad, read issues of the magazines in which the ad will appear.

• If you are writing direct mail, find out what mailing lists will be used and study the list descriptions.

Step #4: Determine the Objective of Your Copy

This objective may be one or more of the following:

• To generate inquiries
• To generate sales
• To answer inquiries
• To qualify prospects
• To generate store traffic
• To introduce a new product or an improvement of an old product
• To keep in touch with prospects and customers
• To transmit news or product information
• To build brand recognition and preference
• To build company image
• To provide marketing tools for salespeople

Before you write copy, study the product—its features, benefits, past performance, applications, and markets. Digging for the facts will pay off, because in copywriting, *specifics sell.*

USING INTERVIEWS TO GATHER FACTS

Of course, collecting background material doesn't always give you *all* the answers to the questions listed above. At times, you must get additional facts from product experts employed by your client—engineers, designers, salespeople, product managers, and brand managers.

Journalists will tell you that a face-to-face interview is better than a phone interview. When you sit across the table from a person, you can observe their manner, their dress, their appearance. And you can learn a lot about a person from their surroundings.

But the kind of interview you conduct as a copywriter is different than the interview conducted by a reporter. You are not interested in the subject's colorful personality or history—you are only seeking straight facts and product information of a technical nature. Therefore, there's no need to get "up close" to the subject, and a telephone interview will serve your purpose just as well as an in-person conference.

Actually, there are a number of advantages to doing interviews by phone. First, although the experts have intimate knowledge of the product, advertising is usually not their area of responsibility, and since they are busy, they don't want to get involved with it. A phone interview takes less of their time and busy managers appreciate the efficiency of this method.

Second, it's easier to take notes by phone. Some people are made nervous by tape recorders; others get jittery when they see you scribbling on a pad (they peer over the note pad to make sure you are writing down exactly what they think you should write down). But these note-taking tools are invisible in a phone conference, and the subject can talk in a relaxed, natural manner without being aware that his words are being recorded.

Third, the copywriter eliminates a trip to and from the client's office. If you're billing by the job, this increases your profit on the assignment. If you're billing by the hour, the time saving is passed on to the client in less time spent on research. Either way, money is saved.

A frequent question beginning copywriters ask is, "Should I use a tape recorder or take notes by hand?" My answer is that it depends on the situation and on the assignment. (If you do decide to tape the interview, be sure you let the subject know your intention *before* you begin.)

At times, you will be forced to go to a briefing without much background material on the product or the market.

In this case, new information will be given to you at a frantic rate. It's best to use a tape recorder in these situations, because you can't write fast enough to get it all down on paper. And when you tape the interview, it leaves your pen free to jot down questions as they occur to you.

If, on the other hand, you have been thoroughly briefed and are familiar with the product, you should go into the meeting or the phone conference with a list of specific questions—gaps in your product knowledge that the background material didn't fill. Here, you are looking for short, specific answers, and taking notes with pen or pencil does the job. When in doubt about how much note-taking you need to do, have both a notepad and a tape recorder handy.

The method of note taking also depends on whether you need quotations from the subject. In writing testimonial copy, feature articles, speeches, press releases, newsletters, and case histories, you want the information in the person's own words, and you need a tape recorder to get it right. But if the interview is just for collecting information that you'll rewrite as copy for an ad, mailer, commercial, brochure, or catalog, use a pencil and pad instead.

In an article in *The Writer*,[2] author Dorothy Hinshaw Patent gives these tips for arranging and conducting a successful interview (the basic tips are Dorothy's, but I've added some elaboration to tailor them to the needs of the copywriter):

1. When you call a person to arrange an interview, immediately say who you are, who suggested you get in touch with the person, and why you want to interview them.

For example: "Jim Rosenthal? Good morning. My name is Bob Bly, and I'm handling the writing of the ground radar brochure for your ad agency, Anderson & Associates. Lansing Knight at the agency suggested I give you a call and says you know a lot about the design of the radar dish. I'd like to ask you a few questions, if that's convenient. . . ."

At times, you will encounter resistance from the person. Here are a few tactics to overcome this:

- *Explain that the interview won't take much time.* ("Well, I've got a small list of just six questions in front of me, and the interview will take but 10 minutes to complete. I know you're busy, but do you think we might chat for just 10 minutes sometime in the next few days?")

- *Flatter the subject—but be sincere.* ("I suppose I could talk to someone else in your department. But they told me you designed the antenna, and I'd really like to make sure I get the right information for this ad, since it's appearing in *Machine Design, Design News,* and *Electronic Digest.*")

- *Explain the importance of your assignment.* ("The article I'm putting together will be published in this year's annual report—so you can see why I'm trying to get the most accurate information possible.")

- *Use authority as leverage.* ("Shirley Parker, your department head, is working closely with the agency on this one and she felt it would be real important to get your input. . . .")

2. Let the subject select the time and date for the interview. Offer to do the interview in the morning, during lunch, after work, in the evening, or anytime that's convenient and comfortable for the person. Some people are too busy during office hours to talk with you, and would prefer to do it after 5 P.M., when they can relax. Others may find lunch the best time. Schedule the interview at the subject's convenience.

And, just as important, set a firm date and time for the interview, whether it's a face-to-face meeting or a phone call. If you're doing a phone interview, make sure the subject understands that you are setting aside time to be by your phone on that date; the phone interview should be considered as firm a commitment as a meeting.

3. Arrange for interviews well in advance of your deadline.

With advertising's short deadlines, this isn't always possible. So it's best to arrange interviews the day you get the assignment. That way, if a key interview subject is out of town or unavailable to meet, you can notify your client and work around it (by extending the deadline or finding someone else to take the subject's place).

4. Do your homework. Come prepared. Read all the background information *before* the interview. Know in advance specifically what you want to find out during the interview. Prepare a written list of questions you want to ask.

The subject's time—and your time—is money spent by the client. Don't waste it by asking your subject to give you an education in the basics. Instead, use this valuable time with the expert to get specific, detailed product and marketing facts the product literature and other background material didn't provide.

5. Be on time for the interview. Many business people are impatient types, and if you miss your appointment, you may never get a second chance. If you can't avoid being late, call in advance and explain the situation.

6. If you are taking notes, write down only the information you need to get the facts straight. This saves time when you type up your notes later on.

7. Establish a rapport with the subject. You two may not have a lot in common, but by showing an interest in and understanding of the subject's problems, you win him over as a friend. And friends give better interviews than hostile or indifferent subjects.

Maybe you really don't care how difficult it was to manufacture the world's first fiber-optic fishing pole. But the engineer you're interviewing does. So, when he turns to you and says, "Boy, you don't know the problems we had in adjusting tensile strength to the right length-to-diameter ratio," give an understanding nod and a smile. Maybe even say, "I can imagine the problems you've had. But it sure is a great fishing pole." This is just common courtesy, and it helps make the interview go smoothly.

8. Keep a list of the people you interviewed. Also save your notes until the copy is accepted and published. Refer to the list and notes if the client wants to know where you got your information or questions the accuracy of the copy.

9. Show your appreciation. Of course, you should always say "thank you" at the close of the interview. A short note in the mail is an even nicer way of showing your gratitude. A copy of the ad or brochure you've written (in its published form) is even better. You may not have time to do all these follow-ups, and it's not a necessity. But when you do follow-up, it will always be appreciated.

ORGANIZING YOUR INFORMATION

At this point, you've read mounds of product literature and have taken notes or underlined key passages—or both. You also have notes or tapes of interviews with product experts.

The next step in getting ready to write copy is to *type up your notes*.

There are two benefits to this. First, by filtering the information through your brain, to your fingers, and onto the typewritten page, you gain more familiarity with your facts.

In elementary school, teachers often assigned simple reports that could be based entirely on articles found in the encyclopedia. Not much research was involved, and as students, we thought we were pulling the wool over the teacher's eyes by cribbing from the *World Book* or *Encyclopaedia Britannica*.

But the teachers were smart. They knew that, by re-forming the encyclopedia essay in our own words, we would think through the ideas and come to our own con-clusions about the subject.

So it is with the copywriter. As you retype interviews and previous copy in your own words, you gain a per-spective on the product and generate your own ideas on how to sell it.

Now, to be fair, I know many copywriters who *don't* go through this step. All I can tell you is that it works for me, and I wouldn't tackle an assignment without first re-processing all the information I've collected through my brain and keyboard and onto the printed page.

The second advantage of typing your notes is that you have clean, typewritten sheets to work from. By single-spacing, you can reduce hours of interviews and mounds of old brochures and catalogs to three or four sheets of paper. Instead of searching through tapes and a pile of literature to find a key fact, you can quickly locate it on your typed notes. And you can use the notes as a check-list, checking off facts you have used in your copy, cir-cling those facts you must include but haven't yet, and crossing out information that will not be used in the copy. Also, looking at typewritten notes is a lot easier on the eye than trying to decipher page after page of your hand-writing.

Convenient as these notes are, I must tell you that, once you've gone through the process of typing your notes, the material will be so fresh in your mind that you will prob-ably be able to write the copy with only an occasional glance at the sheets to confirm a fact or search for a missing bit of data.

I've written complete ads and brochures without once looking at my notes. After the copy was finished, I used the notes as a checklist to make sure all important facts were included.

Some writers prefer index cards to 8½-by-11-inch

typewritten sheets of notes. They like cards because cards are easily rearranged in different order. The advantage of pages over cards is that you can see more information at a glance. With experience, you'll choose the method that works best for you.

I *do* use index cards if the project has many separate, distinct sections. This is the case with a catalog offering many products, a newsletter with many different articles, a press kit with four or five separate releases, or a product folder containing a number of inserts on different aspects or features of the same product.

Many copywriters debate the usefulness of preparing an *outline* before they write the copy. Again, this depends on your individual approach to writing, and you should make an outline only if it is helpful to you.

With most short pieces of copy—ads, sales letters, pamphlets—the number of separate sales points to be covered is small enough that I can hold the outline in my head. And so there's no need to commit it to paper. But if the copy has an unusually large number of sales points, or if an organizational scheme hasn't popped into my head (as it usually does), I will sit with pencil and paper and work up an outline.

For longer pieces—brochures, annual reports, feature articles, books—an outline is always helpful to me. I pin the outline to the bookcase next to my word processor and use it to guide me through the assignment. As first drafts of each section are completed, I check off the section on the outline. This gives me a sense of accomplishment and motivation to go on to the next step.

One warning: keep in mind that outlines are tools designed to help writers; they are *not* commandments etched in stone. If you discover that more information should be added to the copy, add it to the outline. If you think of a better way of organizing the information as you go along, change the outline.

This is why I do not usually like to submit outlines to

clients. The outline goes through a long, formal chain of approval, and then the copywriter feels locked into it and is inhibited from making changes that would improve the copy. If the client does ask for an outline, treat it as a working tool that can be changed, not a final version.

How do you organize your outline? The "sales sequence" presented in Chapter 4 is a general outline for all pieces of persuasive writing. Examples of organizational schemes for specific writing tasks—ads, brochures, catalogs, commercials, press releases, sales letters—are presented in Part II of this book.

THE WRITING PROCESS

Now comes the hard part—the actual writing of the ad, letter, commercial, or brochure.

Each writer has his or her own way of putting the words on paper, and you should use the method that's most productive for you.

Some writers start with a headline and rough drawing of the visual, then fill in the body copy. They cannot write a word of body copy until they have a headline and visual concept that pleases them.

Others write the body copy first. Then they extract the headline from the body copy or from their rough notes.

Some writers like to start with the longest or most difficult section of a brochure or annual report. Others prefer to "warm up" by typing up the easy sections first—the list of the board of directors, the company branch offices, the cover note.

However you approach copywriting, one thing you must realize is that you'll rarely get it right the first time. The key to writing great copy is *rewriting*— two, three, four, five, six, seven drafts, or as many as it takes to get it right.

Beginning copywriters tend to "freeze up" when faced with having to produce copy. They get nervous because they're afraid to write bad sentences or generate lousy ideas.

But nobody has to see your first efforts—and you don't have to get it right the first time. So don't be afraid to write down all the ideas, phrases, slogans, headlines, sentences, and fragments that come to you. You can always delete words that don't work. But, once you have an idea or think of a way to say something, it is lost unless you write it down.

Many copywriters write much more copy than they will need in the final version. This lets them trim the fat and save only the prime cut.

(In the same way, you should collect much more information than you will use in the final version. This lets you be more selective in the facts you include in your copy.)

Basically, copywriting can be divided into a three-stage process—although there may be several rewrites in each stage.

In the first stage, you "get it all down" on paper. Just let the ideas flow. Don't edit yourself; don't stop ideas from forming. Just write what comes to mind. Don't go back and fix up the words you've put on the page, but instead go on and keep writing as long as you have a flow of ideas and phrases you want to put down on paper.

Some writers have trouble letting their thoughts flow freely. They become inhibited and intimidated because they are "writing an ad," and that sounds like a difficult and challenging thing to do. If that's the case with you, try pretending you're writing a letter to a friend—a letter to convince this friend to buy a new product you've become excited about. This technique seems to work, perhaps because letter writing, unlike ad writing, is a familiar, everyday task.

In the second stage, you edit your work. You delete unnecessary words. You rewrite awkward phrases and sentences. You read the copy aloud to make sure that it flows smoothly. And you rearrange and reorder material into a more logical sequence.

Also, you read what you've written to see if it conforms to your criteria for effective, persuasive copy. If it doesn't, you rewrite to strengthen its selling power. This may involve more facts, a better headline, a stronger closing, or a different visual.

In the third stage, you "clean up" your copy by proofreading for spelling and grammar and checking the accuracy of your facts. Here's where you make sure you are consistent in your copy. For example, you don't want to write the company name as "GAF" in the headline and "G.A.F." in the body copy.

Skill in copywriting—and in any type of writing—comes only with practice. As you write copy, you will learn to overcome poor stylistic habits, become more comfortable with your writing, and gain greater control over the English language.

In the meantime, you will benefit greatly by reading books on writing. Three I recommend are:

On Business Communications by Rudolf Flesch. New York: Barnes & Noble Books, 1974.
On Writing Well by William Zinsser. New York: Harper & Row, 1980.
The Elements of Style by William Strunk Jr. and E.B. White. New York: MacMillan Publishing Co., Inc., 1979.

TECHNIQUES FOR PRODUCING ADVERTISING IDEAS

The copywriter's job is to come up with words and ideas that sell the product or service being advertised.

Where do these ideas come from? They come from an understanding of the product, the market, and the mission of the copy—which is to generate sales.

However, even the best copywriters get stuck for ideas at times. A number of techniques—some basic and common sense, some indirect and a bit "far out"—have been developed to help people dream up ideas.

In a series of articles published in *Success Unlimited*,[3] copywriter Don Hauptman offered these tips on coming up with ideas.

Get the Facts

Copywriters need to gather two types of facts: specific facts about the product and facts about people and things in general.

Just about every successful copywriter I know is a voracious reader and an avid collector of information. And you should be, too.

Read books, magazines, newsletters, flyers, posters, junk mail, product labels. Read advertising journals to learn about the advertising business. Read the journals your clients advertise in to learn about *their* business. Clip and save any articles of interest. You never know when this information may come in handy.

Also, talk to people. Take classes and seminars. Attend lectures. Attend meetings of professional societies and trade associations. Become an information collector.

Look for Combinations

"A new idea is simply a combination or synthesis of old elements," writes Hauptman. "All creativity is simply the rearrangement of existing materials." Many new business ideas—Pet Rocks, clock-radios, ice cream sodas, Pizza-Time Theatres—are simply the joining of two existing elements into a new combination.

Use a Checklist

This book, for example, provides you with a number of copywriting checklists—a checklist for headlines, a checklist for body copy, a checklist of reasons why people buy products. When stuck for an idea, you can use checklists to suggest possible strategies and directions.

Get Some Feedback

Show your rough ideas to others and get their comments. Or let someone else take a look at your finished copy and make comments on how it could be improved.

Team Up

Copywriters often team up with art directors. Composers team up with lyricists. Entrepreneurial types sometimes link up with corporate managers.

Your partner can expand upon your ideas to make them even better. Working with a partner also helps you sharpen your own thinking.

Incubation and Inspiration

Sleep on it. Put the problem aside and let your subconscious work on it awhile. During this incubation period, the idea you've been looking for may suddenly strike you "out of the blue."

MORE TECHNIQUES FOR PRODUCING ADVERTISING IDEAS

John Caples offers some additional techniques for producing advertising ideas in his book *How to Make Your Advertising Make Money.*[4]

- Write copy based on your own experience
- Write emotionally—"from the heart"
- Learn from the experience of others
- Talk with the manufacturer to get his ideas
- Examine the product
- Use the product
- Study past ads for the product
- Study the competition's ads

• Review customer testimonials
• See if you can create a new ad from a variation on a past ad

The tasks and procedures outlined in this chapter may seem like a tall order. But don't worry—it will come. Here's a comforting thought from Lou Redmond, a former Ogilvy & Mather copywriter.

> Advertising is one of the minor arts, so don't be intimidated by it. Try not to lose your sense of playfulness. Keep it fun.
> And remember, nobody writes as well as he would like to. We just write as well as we can.

PART II

THE TASKS OF THE COPYWRITER

Writing Print Advertisements
Writing Direct Mail
Writing Brochures, Catalogs, and Other Sales Literature
Writing Public Relations Material
Writing Commercials

6

Writing Print Advertisements

PRINT IS NOT DEAD

Many people hoping to become copywriters dream of having their words produced for television.

They believe television is more glamorous than print advertising, and that the "top" copywriters are the ones writing commercials for big-name national advertisers. They think that, in advertising, television is "where the action is."

They are wrong. In 1982, advertisers spent nearly $21.1 billion dollars to run ads in newspapers and magazines—more than television and radio *combined*.

Both print and television have their place and purpose in an advertising program. But television is primarily a medium of entertainment. Print is a medium of information. And it is information—not entertainment—that ultimately sells most products.

At first glance, it seems as if TV and other electronic media, and not print, are "hot." Everywhere you turn, you're reading about cable and direct-broadcast satellite and teletext and videotext and computers.

But print is still the preferred medium of consumers—and therefore of advertisers. If you don't believe it, consider these facts.[1]

- Book sales have gone up 51 percent in the last five years. More than five million books are sold in this country every day.

- Magazine circulation has increased at nearly double the rate of population growth over the last five years. *Standard Rate & Data Service* now lists 1,637 consumer magazines published in the United States—up 24 percent from five years ago—and more than twice as many business magazines.

- With a daily circulation of 63 million, more newspapers are published today than at any time since World War II.

- In 1982, J. Walter Thompson published a study showing that, for the first time ever, TV viewing by teenagers declined—by 14 percent. And a study by a firm specializing in advertising to students shows that less than half of college students watch more than an hour a day of TV. But two-thirds read a daily paper and three-quarters a weekly magazine.

All ad agency copywriters are expected to master print advertising before they are assigned work in television. Judging from the print ads appearing in the newspapers and magazines I read, many never do.

This chapter will teach you to write print ads that build

product awareness, generate sales leads, and bring in the orders.

TYPES OF ADS

Are all print advertisements basically the same? Or are there different techniques for writing ads in different media or ads designed to achieve different goals?

The *basics* of good print advertising are the same in all media, and the next section of the chapter outlines the nine characteristics of the successful ad. But the tone, content, and focus of the ad can vary with the purpose and the place of publication. Let's take a look at the different kinds of print ads you will be called upon to write.

First, an ad can have one of four basic missions:

• To sell products directly (mail-order advertising)
• To generate sales leads (ads that invite you to send for a free brochure or pamphlet)
• To build awareness of a product (ads for package goods and most consumer products of low unit cost)
• To build the company's image (corporate advertising)

How do these four categories differ?

Ads that ask for the order—that generate a sale directly—have to do a *complete* selling job. There is no salesperson, no showroom, no retail display, no explanatory brochure to add to the sales pitch. The ad must get attention, hook the reader, and then convince him to send in an order for a product he has never seen.

Mail-order ads are usually lengthy (800 words and up), because they must give complete information. They must answer all of the buyer's questions, lay his fears to rest, and overcome all his objections in order to close the sale. They must also devote space to the mechanism used in placing the actual order—a coupon, toll-free number, or other device. Among the most well-known mail-order ads are those for the Book-of-the-Month Club and the numerous "series" books produced by Time-Life.

Ads appealing to buyers in business and industry usually try to generate a sales lead—a response from an interested buyer asking for more information. This is because most products sold to business and industry cannot be sold directly, but require a company salesperson to give a presentation and close the sale in person.

Ads that generate leads may give a lot of information or a little, but they never give the full story. To get complete information, the reader must respond to the ad by writing, phoning, or mailing in a coupon. To write a successful lead-generating ad, you must understand the steps in the buying process and where the ad fits in.

Most consumer products are not sold by mail or by salespeople; instead, you can buy them at supermarkets, department stores, in automobile showrooms, and at fast-food chains. And, you usually buy them only when you need them—not when you read an ad about them. Therefore, the ads for these products don't sell them directly; they seek to generate an awareness of the product and a desire to use it. And the ad campaign builds this awareness and desire over an extended period. Burger King knows you don't rush out to buy a Whopper after viewing a Burger King commercial. The goal of their advertising is to make Burger King the first place you think of when you *do* want a hamburger—so you will eat their product instead of McDonald's or Wendy's.

Some ads promote companies instead of products. This type of advertising, known as corporate advertising, seeks to create a certain image of the company in the mind of the reader. Sometimes, these campaigns are aimed at the general public to clear up a misconception about a firm or promote the firm in a general sense. More often, they are aimed at stockholders, investors, and the business community. You can find examples of corporate advertising in any issue of *Forbes, Fortune, Business Week,* or *The Wall Street Journal.*

Ads also differ according to the type of publication in which they appear—newspaper, magazine, or directory.

Newspapers have long been the backbone of retail advertising campaigns. Retailers run what is called "price and where to buy" advertising—simple display ads that emphasize the price of the merchandise, and then direct local consumers to a nearby retail outlet to make the purchase. Such ads usually center around a storewide sale or price-off deal for certain items.

Of course, newspapers attract many other advertisers besides retailers—banks, insurance companies, real estate agents, theaters, restaurants, book publishers. Some use the simple price-and-where-to-buy format of retailers. Others run more sophisticated campaigns closer to magazine advertisements.

Magazines are different from newspapers in two important ways. First, newspapers are written for a general readership, while magazines are published for specialized audiences—women, teens, Christians, business executives, computer buffs, plumbing engineers, geologists, writers. As a result, magazines are effective for reaching small segments of the market, while newspapers are a medium of mass advertising.

Second, the reproduction quality of magazines is far superior to newspapers. Plus, magazines offer the advertiser the use of full color in their advertisements.

Manufacturers use magazines for campaigns that build product awareness and company image. Many consumer magazines also have special sections for mail-order advertisements.

But, whether it is published in a newspaper or a magazine, the ad has to work hard to get the reader's attention. The reader, after all, bought the publication for the articles—not for the ads. In most major newspapers, for example, your ad competes with hundreds of other ads. And most readers read only four ads in a typical magazine. So the headline and visual must stop the reader in her tracks with an attention-getting concept centered around a strong reader benefit or the promise of a reward.

Directory advertising is different. When the reader turns to the Yellow Pages or an industrial buyer's guide, he is searching for a supplier of a specific type of product or service. So, your ad doesn't have to convince him that he needs a limousine—it has to convince him to try *your* limousine service.

Naturally, the ads listed at the beginning of a category are the first ones read. But the order is alphabetical, so unless you change your company name, there is little chance of changing your position in the Yellow Pages.

Thomas Register, the major industrial product directory, did a study to show the effect of size on an ad's ability to generate response. The study showed that the biggest ad on the page gets 40 times the response of an ordinary one-line directory listing. You may not be able to afford the biggest ad, but the bigger your ad, the more response your ad will generate. Even a boldface listing generates twice the response of a listing in ordinary type.

Directory ads should immediately flag the reader with the benefit or special service he is looking for. For example, most people ordering a late-night pizza will pick the place that delivers for free. The winning ad in this section of the phone book will have, in big, bold type, the headline, "CRISP, HOT PIZZA—*FREE* DELIVERY!"

Think about what your prospects have in mind when they turn to the Yellow Pages to look for a pizza, limousine, exterminator, or whatever your business offers. Then make this important item the theme of your ad.

A New Jersey insurance agent reasoned that people with something to insure will respond to an ad that specifically refers to that type of insurance. He placed an ad with the headline "INSURANCE" run across the top in large bold lettering; underneath he simply listed 28 different types of insurance he offered—everything from aircraft and accident protection to trucks, trailers, and snowmobiles. His simple four- by five-inch ad pulls one or two phone calls every business day of the year.

The size of your ad also affects your approach to writing the copy. A full-page magazine or newspaper ad gives you great flexibility in the size of the illustrations and the amount of copy you use. (Although they are usually shorter, a full-page magazine ad consisting of solid text can contain nearly 2,000 words.) Smaller ads, of course, cannot contain as much artwork and copy. As a result, advertisers frequently use full-page ads as the "core" of their campaign for building image and awareness; smaller ads are used for generating sales leads. Many mail-order advertisers have also had great success with smaller ads.

STANDARDS FOR SUCCESSFUL ADVERTISING

The techniques used in different advertising situations— magazines versus newspapers, mail order versus image, business versus consumer—are important, to be sure. But the *basics* of good print advertising are pretty much the same no matter what medium you're writing for.

Here are nine criteria that an ad must satisfy if it is to be successful as a selling tool:

1. The Headline Contains an Important Consumer Benefit, or News, or Promises a Reward for Reading the Copy

An ad for RCA's satellite channel has the headline, "How to Cut Your Company's Long-Distance Phone Bill 50% Or More." The benefit and the reward are clear: You will find out how to cut your phone bill in half if you read the ad.

A savings or discount is one of the most powerful benefits you can feature in a headline. An example is the headline for a mail-order ad offering a set of cassette tapes on "assertiveness skills." The headline reads: "For $30 you can acquire the same Assertiveness Skills that are now being taught to Fortune 500 managers for up to $500 each."

Never mind that tapes are different from live seminars; this headline creates the impression that you can acquire new knowledge for $470 less than others have paid for it—a good bargain, simply but powerfully stated.

Century 21's recruitment ad for real estate agents is also direct: "You Can Make Big Money In Real Estate Sales Right Now." No clever copy. No puns. No fancy photography or special effects. Just an irresistible promise stated in plain, straightforward language.

2. The Visual (If You Use a Visual) Should Illustrate the Benefit Stated in the Headline

Note that I said "if you use a visual." Contrary to what some folks may tell you, it is the words—not the pictures—that do most of the selling in an advertisement. Hundreds of successful ads have used words alone to get their message across. Thousands of other successful ads are adorned only with simple photos, spot drawings, and plain-jane graphics.

If possible, the visual should illustrate the benefit stated in the headline. One of the most effective visual techniques for doing so is the use of before-and-after photos.

DuPont's ad for TEFLON explains how coating industrial-process equipment with TEFLON protects it from acid. There are two photos. One shows an uncoated mixing blade reduced to scrap by industrial acids. The other shows a TEFLON-coated blade used in the same corrosive chemicals; the TEFLON blade is in perfect condition. What better way to illustrate and prove the benefit of using TEFLON?

A Johnson & Johnson ad headline contains a strong

benefit: "Now, from Johnson & Johnson, Toys That Allow Babies to Master New Skills." The photo shows a toddler playing with—and obviously enjoying—one of the toys. The visual illustrates the benefit of the product and offers proof that babies like these toys.

A visual doesn't have to be elaborate to illustrate the benefit. An ad for a set of encyclopedias can show young children studying and using the books. An ad for homeowners insurance can show the safe, cozy home the insurance helped pay for after the family's first home burned down.

3. The Lead Paragraph Expands on the Theme of the Headline

A few examples:

THE WORSE YOUR CORROSION PROBLEMS, THE MORE YOU NEED DUPONT TEFLON.

In harsh, highly corrosive chemical process environments, fluid handling components lined or made with DuPont TEFLON resins and films consistently outlast other materials.

YOU CAN MAKE BIG MONEY IN REAL ESTATE SALES RIGHT NOW.

Business is booming at CENTURY 21. And so are careers. CENTURY 21 offices have helped more people to achieve rewarding careers in real estate than any other sales organization in the world.

NOW, FROM JOHNSON & JOHNSON, TOYS THAT ALLOW BABIES TO MASTER NEW SKILLS.

Your child is growing bigger. Brighter. More curious and eager to learn every day. That's why Johnson & Johnson Child Development Toys are designed to change and grow with your child. To encourage his skill development every step of the way.

A common error made by copywriters is to waste the lead paragraphs by telling the readers something they already know:

SPEEDWRITER—THE ONLY WORD-PROCESSING PROGRAM DESIGNED FOR THE PERSON WHO WRITES FOR A LIVING.

If you own a computer, you know that it's the software—not the hardware—that determines whether your machine is a great word processor. Or just a so-so one.

The word-processing program you now use is a general-purpose program—designed for a wide variety of computer users. It wasn't designed with the special needs of the professional writer in mind.

Introducing SpeedWriter—a word-processing package that can handle *all* the manuscript formats used by professional writers—from playwrights and TV writers, to novelists and poets, to publicists and copywriters.

It *sounds* okay—but think again. The ad is aimed at a person who is already using a computer and word-processing program in his work. Therefore, the ad writer wastes the first two paragraphs by explaining the importance of software—a subject with which the reader is already familiar. A more experienced copywriter would delete these paragraphs and go straight to the third paragraph, where the meat of the message begins.

4. The Layout Draws the Reader into the Ad and Invites Him to Read the Body Copy

Copywriters must consider the graphic elements of the ad and how these graphics will affect readership of their copy. Will the copy be broken up by subheads into many short sections? Will there be a coupon? Should the phone number be in larger type to encourage call-ins? Should the product or process be illustrated using a number of small secondary photos with captions? These are all the concerns of the writer.

The key to getting the ad read is a layout that is clean, uncluttered, and easy on the eyes. The layout should catch the reader's eye and move it logically from headline and visual to body copy to logo and address.

Chapter 14 covers graphics in detail. But here are some factors that enhance the readability and eye appeal of a layout:

- Use one central visual.
- Headline set in large, bold type.
- Body copy set underneath headline and visual.
- Body copy set in clear, readable type.
- Space between paragraphs increases readability.
- Subheads help draw the eye through the text.
- Copy should be printed black on a white background. Copy printed in reverse, on a tint, or over a visual is difficult to read.
- Short paragraphs are easier to read than long ones.
- The lead paragraph should be very short—less than three lines of type, if possible.
- Simple visuals are best. Visuals with too many elements in them confuse the reader.
- The best layout is a simple layout—headline, large visual, body copy, logo. Additional elements—a subhead, breakers, secondary photos—can enhance the ad's readability, but too many make it cluttered and unappealing to the eye.
- Many art directors believe that ads must have a large amount of "white space" (blank space) or else they will look cluttered and people won't read them. But, if your typography is clean and readable, you can set a solid page of text and people will read every word of it.

In the same way, there are certain visual techniques that make ads *unappealing* to readers. These techniques give ads an "addy" look and should be avoided. They include:

- Headlines and blocks of copy set on a slant
- Tinting of black-and-white photographs with a second color (usually blue or red)
- Tiny type (smaller than eight-point)
- Long, unbroken chunks of text
- Overuse of circles, bursts, arrows, and other techniques that call attention to the fact that the ad is an ad
- A long listing of company locations and addresses crammed in under the logo
- Type set in overly wide columns
- Poorly executed or reproduced artwork and photography

The look of your ad—its appearance, its layout, how the elements are set up on the page—won't make an ad with poor copy effective. But an unappealing layout can discourage interested consumers from reading brilliant copy that has a lot to offer them. Again, Chapter 14 covers the basics of what copywriters need to know about designing ads.

5. The Body Copy Covers All Important Sales Points in Logical Sequence

The effective ad tells an interesting, important story about the product. And, like a novel or short story, the copy must be logically organized, with a beginning, a middle, and an end.

If you are describing a product and its benefits, you will probably organize your sales points in order of importance, putting the most important point in the headline and taking the reader from the major benefits to minor features as you go through the body copy. In this format, the ad resembles the "inverted pyramid" style used by journalists in news stories.

If the sales points are not related in any way, you might prefer to use a list format, in which you simply number and list the sales points in simple 1–2–3 fashion.

If you are writing a case history or testimonial ad, you can use chronological order to relate the story as it happened. Or, you might use a problem/solution format to show how the product solved a problem.

6. The Copy Provides the Amount of Information Needed to Convince the Greatest Number of Qualified Prospects to Take the Next Step in the Buying Process

You remember this rule from Chapter 4: The *number* of sales points to be included in the copy depends on what you're selling, who you're selling it to, and what the next step is in the buying process.

Here are some observations on ad length that come from flipping through the March 1984 issue of *Good Housekeeping* magazine.

A full-page ad for Sophia perfume shows a color photo of the perfume bottle superimposed against a background of fireworks. The ad contains no body copy, just a headline and tag line.

SOPHIA IS DESIRE.

SOPHIA IS MYSTERY.

SOPHIA IS FANTASY.

SOPHIA BY COTY. WEAR IT WITH A PASSION.

Apparently, there is not a lot to say about perfume; it is sold on the mystique of what wearing perfume does to enhance your sex appeal.

An ad for Caltrate 600, a calcium supplement, contains a diagram, a chart, more than 400 words of body copy, and a straightforward headline announcing, "New Caltrate 600 Helps Keep Bone Healthy." Apparently, there is a lot to say about health products. The ad also invites the reader to write in for a price-off coupon for the product and a "calcium counter."

Many of the food ads contain recipes that center around the product being advertised. The food advertiser hopes the reader will like the recipe and, as a result, purchase the product every time he or she makes the dish.

The ads for more expensive items—blenders, telephones, flooring, a kit for pregnancy tests, real estate—all invite the reader to write or phone for additional information. The advertiser knows there is more to say about these products than can be put in a magazine ad; brochures and salespeople will have to augment the efforts of the ad.

When you sit down to write the ad, ask yourself: "What do I want the reader to do? And what can I tell him that will get him to do it?"

7. The Copy is Interesting to Read

"You cannot *bore* people into buying your product," writes David Ogilvy in *Ogilvy on Advertising*. "You can only *interest* them in buying it."

People will only read your ad as long as it is interesting to them. They will not read copy that is boring—in content or in style.

As a writer and a reader, you know when writing is interesting to read and when it is dull.

The style should be crisp, lively, and light. The copy should have rhythm and clarity.

But great style won't save an ad without substance. The copy must appeal to the reader's self-interest. It must contain benefits, or news, or it must solve the reader's problem. It cannot entertain for entertainment's sake; it must present compelling reasons why the product is desirable to the reader.

Here are a few things that add interest to advertisements.

- Copy that speaks directly to the reader's life, the reader's emotions, the reader's needs and desires
- Copy that tells a story
- Copy about people
- Copy written in a personal style, so that it sounds like a letter from a friend—warm, helpful, and sincere
- Testimonials from celebrities
- A free offer (of a gift, a pamphlet, a brochure, or a sample)
- Copy that contains important news
- Copy that addresses major issues—beauty, health, old age, parenting, marriage, home, security, family, careers, education, social issues
- Copy that answers important questions readers have in their minds
- Copy about a subject that interests the reader

Here are some things that make ads boring:

- Copy that centers on the manufacturer—that talks about the company, its philosophy, its success
- Copy that talks about how the product is made or how it works rather than what it can do for the reader
- Copy that tells readers things they already know
- Long-winded copy with big words, lengthy sentences, and large unbroken chunks of text
- Copy in which all sentences are the same length (varying sentence length adds snap to writing)
- Copy that gives product features instead of customer benefits

- Copy without a point of view—without a strong selling proposition or a cohesive sales pitch (such copy presents the facts without really showing the reader how these facts relate to his needs)
- Ads with cluttered layouts and poorly reproduced visuals look boring and turn the reader off

8. The Copy is Believable

"Cynicism and suspicion abound today," says Amil Gargano, "much of it with good reason. That's why advertising won't work unless it is trusted, no matter how clever it might seem. . . . And the way to be trusted is to be honest and sensitive to the people you want to reach."[2]

The copywriter's task is not an easy one. In addition to getting attention, explaining the product, and being persuasive, you must overcome the reader's distrust and get her to believe you.

We've already discussed a number of techniques for building credibility—testimonials, demonstrations, research tests. But these are just techniques. The key to being believed is to *tell the truth*.

This is not as radical as it sounds. Contrary to the image of advertising executives as slick hucksters, most are honest, professional business people who believe in the products they are selling. Most would not create advertising for a product they felt was harmful or inferior. And, although ethics plays a part, the real reason for this is a simple fact about advertising.

Clever advertising CAN convince people to try a bad product once. But it can't convince them to buy a product they've already tried and didn't like.

So, you see, there's no percentage in writing ads that tell lies. Besides being unethical, it's unprofitable for the agency and the advertiser and gives all advertising a bad name.

Few practitioners engage in such unethical behavior. The majority believe that the product they are advertising can do you a lot of good. When you believe in your product, it's easy to write copy that is sincere, informative, and helpful. And when you are sincere, it comes across to the reader and they believe what you've written.

9. *The Ad Asks for Action*

The ad should ask the reader to take the next step in the buying process—whether that step is to send in an order, call a sales office, visit a store, try a sample, see a demonstration, or just believe the advertiser's message.

You are already familiar with coupons, toll-free numbers, and other devices used to urge the reader to respond to the ad. Barry Kingston, Merchandising Director of *Opportunity Magazine,* offers these tips on getting the best response to your ad.

- Use a street address instead of a post office box number. A street address gives the impression that your firm is large, stable, and well established.
- If most of the magazine's readers qualify for your offer, use a toll-free phone number to increase response. But if you want to qualify your leads, use a regular company phone number.
- If the product can be ordered directly with a credit card, include a toll-free number.
- Use a company phone number for selling expensive items that involve inside salespeople.
- A coupon boosts response between 25 and 100 percent.
- Asking the reader to send in a letter reduces response but produces highly qualified leads (people with genuine interest in the product).

TO SLOGAN OR NOT TO SLOGAN

A slogan—also known as the tag line—is a phrase or sentence that appears beneath the company logo in an ad or series of ads. The slogan is used to sum up the central message of the ads, or to make a broad statement about the nature of the company.

Some well-known slogans:

WE'RE AMERICAN AIRLINES: DOING WHAT WE DO BEST

MAXWELL HOUSE: GOOD TO THE LAST DROP

LIKE A GOOD NEIGHBOR, STATE FARM IS THERE

NOTHING BEATS A GREAT PAIR OF L'EGGS

PRUDENTIAL: GET A PIECE OF THE ROCK

IF THEY COULD JUST STAY LITTLE TILL THEIR CARTER'S WEAR OUT

LONG DISTANCE: THE NEXT BEST THING TO BEING THERE

AMERICAN EXPRESS: DON'T LEAVE HOME WITH-OUT IT

These slogans have built consumer awareness of brand-name products because they are pithy, memorable, and because they sum up the nature of the product or service.

However, there are hundreds of slogans that have been used for a few months and then dropped from ads, never to be written or uttered again.

Should you use a slogan in your ad?

It depends on whether your product lends itself to this technique. In copywriting, the rule should be, "Form follows function." In other words, use a technique if it works and seems natural. But don't force-fit a copy technique in an ad where it doesn't belong.

Applying this rule to slogans, I'd say use a slogan if your product's key selling proposition or its nature can be summed up in a single, catchy statement. But if the essence of your product or business can't be captured in a one-liner, don't force it, or the result will be an artificial slogan that detracts from the ad and makes you, your ad agency, your employees, and your customers embarrassed and uncomfortable.

For example, let's say your company manufactures flypaper. The company president says, "Our slogan should be: The Leader in Quality Flypaper." But this slogan restricts you to a narrow product category. If you decide to expand and manufacture flyswatters, you'll have a hard time because people will think of you as a flypaper company only.

Then your ad agency says, "Let's think big. You're not just in flypaper; you're in 'pest control.' How about LEADERS IN THE SCIENCE OF PEST CONTROL as a slogan?" But this is too general—pest control can be anything from spraying termites to catching rats. And your company really doesn't plan to get involved in these areas.

So the danger with slogans is that some are too narrow and pigeonhole you in a specialty, while others are so broad-based that they lose any real meaning or applicability to your business.

AD CRITIQUES

Next to critiquing your own ads, which I can't do in a book, the best way to show you the principles of good ad writing in action is to critique some existing ads and see how they measure up.

Here, then, five recent ads—and my comments on their effectiveness.

1. *CBS Video Club*

CBS's ad for their Video Club is a textbook example of how to write effective mail-order copy.

The headline—"Own a Movie for Less than the Price of a Blank Tape. Just $4.95"—is a strong, straightforward promise of an important consumer benefit: money saved. A lazy copywriter would have been content just to say that

$4.95 is a bargain or a "low, low price." But the writer of this ad dramatizes the savings by pointing out how the cost of owning your favorite feature film is less than that of the tape it is recorded on.

The ad encourages response by making it *easy* to order. The 31 movies you can choose from are listed in a clear table for easy selection. The coupon offers the option of enclosing a check or paying by credit card, and there is enough space to write in the required information. Large, boldface type is used to call attention to the convenient toll-free number for telephone orders.

The copy covers all the information the reader needs to know about the Video Club—from what it takes to join, to how many tapes you have to buy, to how much the tapes cost and how much you save, to how you order by mail, to the money-back guarantee. The writing flows smoothly and is easy to read. Subheads help move the reader's eye through the text and highlight major benefits ("Save 50%," "Shop-By-Mail Convenience," "Try Us At No Risk").

If the ad has a fault, it is that it does not stress the benefits of owning your own videotapes vs. renting them or going out to the movies. This defect could be fixed by adding a section on the pleasure, status, and savings you get from owning a home library of your favorite feature films.

Other than that, a good ad: well written, cleanly designed, and hard-selling.

2. Colgate

Cavities in children's teeth are not a laughing matter. That's why Colgate's no-nonsense approach to toothpaste advertising is so effective.

This ad is a rarity in that it offers important product news of real concern to the consumer.

Wisely, Colgate puts the news up front in a headline set in big, bold type:

CAUGHT SOON ENOUGH,
EARLY TOOTH DECAY CAN ACTUALLY
BE REPAIRED BY COLGATE!

The importance and straightforward simplicity of this news-filled headline commands our attention. The exclamation point works here, adding excitement to the news. And I like the use of the word "actually"; it empathizes with our built-in skepticism of such claims and promises that this news is genuine.

The visual is an emotional appeal. It shows a child—much like our own child—who will suffer from the dentist's drill unless we heed Colgate's announcement and buy the toothpaste.

The body copy has the authoritative tone needed to convince us the news is true: "Now Colgate, and only Colgate, offers exclusive X-ray proof. Colgate helps prevent early tooth decay from becoming a cavity. . . . early tooth decay, when caught soon enough, can be repaired by Colgate. . . ."

I like the term "X-ray." Although *all* photos of cavities are taken with X-rays, there's something about "X-ray proof" that sounds scientific and irrefutable.

A box contains a set of before-and-after photos with its own headline (NEW PROOF: EXCLUSIVE X-RAY EVIDENCE!) and captions. The photos demonstrate the claim of the headline in a convincing fashion, and the captions explain it in plain, simple English.

This ad is proof that nothing sells like *news*. I can't imagine a humorous or entertaining ad that would provide parents with a stronger motivation to buy Colgate than the ad presented here.

3. *Johnson & Johnson Child Development Toys*

Like Colgate, Johnson & Johnson also captures our attention with a headline that presents important product news:

NOW, FROM JOHNSON & JOHNSON, TOYS
THAT ALLOW BABIES TO MASTER NEW SKILLS.

A large visual plus three secondary photos illustrate
how a single Johnson & Johnson toy continues to provide
fun and learning as the baby grows from a 6-month in-
fant to a 30-month-old child. The delightful expressions
on the children's faces are proof that kids do like (and learn
from) these toys.

The body copy restates what we've already learned
from the visuals, headline, and photo captions. But it is
incomplete. The "Balls In A Bowl" toy pictured in the ad
is obviously only one of a number of new toys from Johnson & Johnson, but the copy doesn't give any information
on what the other toys are or what they can teach your
child.

Maybe all the toys in the product line can't be described in a one-page ad. But more examples would have
given us a better idea of what makes the product line different and better. Or the company could invite readers to
request a catalog describing the Child Development Toys.
One way or the other, though, we need more information. And we don't get it from this ad.

4. DuPont TEFLON

DuPont's TEFLON ad illustrates effective use of the
before-and-after technique.

The headline makes a promise: that DuPont TEFLON
will help you solve your corrosion problems.

A photo at the top of the ad shows mixing blades de-
stroyed by corrosion. The caption tells us, "In two weeks,
aggressive acids and high temperatures turned this cast
iron pump impeller into scrap."

(Incidentally, I like using the word *scrap* to describe the
damaged blades. Scrap is a simple, strong word that gets
the message across quickly and forcefully. Many engineering writers would have weakened the ad's dramatic

appeal by writing, "The cast iron pump was corroded by exposure to acids and high temperatures.")

Underneath is a photo of blades protected by TEFLON. The caption reads: "After three months, an identical impeller encapsulated with TEFLON is hardly the worse for wear."

("Encapsulated" is a weak word; I'd use "coated" or "covered with" instead.)

The headline and visual make the point: Use TEFLON and your equipment won't be corroded by acid.

The copy backs up the selling point with supporting benefits, features, and technical specifications. And Du-Pont makes it easy for you to buy the product or request more information.

Excellent ad.

5. *The Institute of Children's Literature*

This ad for a home-correspondence course in writing selects the right audience with the headline, "We're looking for people to write children's books."

The ad is written as a letter from the dean of the institute to the reader.

The letter technique has two advantages. First, it builds trust. Readers are wary of home-study scams, but here's an accomplished writer (his credits are given in the lead paragraph and the photo caption) willing to put his reputation on the line for the school. (He's even showing us a picture of his face—and he sure does look honest.)

Second, the ad is *personal*. It's not a sales pitch from a faceless company; it has the friendly, helpful, reassuring tone of one writer talking to another.

There's no white space here: The entire page is filled with more than 1,200 words of copy. But, because it's well written, broken into short sections and paragraphs, and set in an attractive, readable typeface, aspiring children's-book writers will read every word. (I did, and I wasn't bored and didn't suffer the least bit of eyestrain.)

The copy is sincere and packed with reasons why you will profit by taking the course. Subheads guide the reader through the story and highlight the benefits. The copy includes testimonials from former students who praise the Institute and tell how it helped them become successful, selling authors.

At the end of the copy the reader is invited to send for a Writing Aptitude Test, which will be evaluated by the Institute at no cost and no obligation.

One of the biggest challenges this ad faced was overcoming readers' skepticism in study-by-mail writing courses. I think it succeeds admirably.

TYPING THE AD

Unless you already work in advertising, you've never seen an ad in its manuscript form. You only see the finished product in a newspaper, magazine, or directory.

There is no "official" manuscript format for submitting ad copy to your client. Different agencies all use slightly different formats. All of them are fine.

Some agencies and copywriters type their copy on special forms that have the word "copy" printed on them along with the name of the agency or the writer and room to fill in other information (client, date, word length, publication in which the ad will appear).

This is fine, but unnecessary. I type my copy on plain white paper, and so do many other writers. No client has ever asked me to do otherwise.

Copy should be typed double-spaced, with generous margins. You want to leave enough room for reviewers to pencil in comments and changes.

My format is to type double-space with four spaces between paragraphs (but only two spaces between a heading and the paragraph that follows). I do not indent at the beginning of paragraphs.

All copywriters include labels in their copy that indicate whether the text the reviewer is reading is for a headline, subhead, body copy, caption, boxed material, or the description of a visual. Some writers type these descriptions in parentheses in the left margin. I type them in capital letters flush against the left margin, with a colon following the label but with no parentheses. This way, my manuscript looks very neat because everything is flush with the left margin.

A sample page of manuscript is shown below.

```
ThermoPal ad—page 1

HEADLINE:
How to Keep Your Iced Tea on Ice.

VISUAL:
Tall glass of iced tea sitting next to an
open ThermoPal thermos.

COPY:
Nothing quenches thirst like a cold iced tea
on a hot summer's day.
But the tea in a can or a carton won't stay
cool in summer heat. And an ordinary thermos
won't fit in your briefcase, bag, or lunch-
pail.
Introducing ThermoPal, the pint-size thermos
that makes sure your cool summer drinks stay
cool . . . and is small enough to go where
you go.

SUBHEAD:
A big gulp in a tiny bottle

COPY:
ThermoPal is tiny enough to fit in the slim-
mest briefcase or in a tightly packed back-
pack.
```

But, it's big enough to hold a frosty 8 ounces of tea, lemonade, or fruit juice. That's as much as you get in a tall, cool glass at home or from a machine.

But by carrying your lunchtime drink in ThermoPal, your refreshment costs a few pennies instead of the better part of a dollar, as it would from a vending machine or fast-food stand. So ThermoPal pays for itself in just a few weeks . . . and brings big savings over the long, hot summer.

We know you'll be delighted with ThermoPal for years to come. If not, just send the lid back in the mail for a full refund—no questions asked.

To order ThermoPal, clip and mail the reply coupon. But hurry—supplies are limited, and we usually sell out by the middle of Spring.

COUPON:

<u>YES</u>, I want to keep cool. Please send me ____ ThermoPals at $8.95 each plus $1.00 each for shipping and handling. My check is enclosed. If not satisfied, I'll send back the top of the thermos for a full refund of my money.
Name_____
Address_____
City_____ State_____ Zip__

Mail coupon to:
ThermoPal
Box XXX
Anytown, USA XXXXX

A CHECKLIST OF ADVERTISING IDEAS

Copywriters don't sit down with an assignment and say "I want to do a testimonial ad" or "Let's make it a how-to ad." They first study the product, the audience, and the purpose of the advertisement. Then they use the technique that fits the assignment.

Still, it helps to be familiar with the various types of ads that have been successful over the years—how-to, testimonials, before-and-after, and others.

Below is a checklist of many of these categories. When you're stuck for an idea, a quick review of the list might give you inspiration; you might scan the list and say, "Hey, *here's* an approach that works with what I'm selling!" Turn to this checklist not as a crutch but as an aid in producing ideas.

THIRTY-TWO PRINT ADS YOU CAN USE

( )   QUESTION AD—asks a question in the headline and answers it in the body copy

( )   QUIZ AD—copy presents a quiz. Reader takes quiz. His answers determine whether he is a prospect for the product or service being offered.

( )   NEWS AD—announces a new product or something new about an existing product

( )   DIRECT AD—gives a straightforward presentation of the facts

( )   INDIRECT AD—has an obscure headline designed to arouse curiosity and entice the reader to read the body copy

( )   REWARD AD—promises a reward for reading the ad

( )   COMMAND AD—commands the reader to take action

( )   PRICE-AND-WHERE-TO-BUY AD—announces a sale. Describes the product, gives the price and discount, and tells where to buy it.

( ) REASON-WHY AD—presents reasons why you should buy the product

( ) LETTER AD—an ad written in letter form

( ) BEFORE-AND-AFTER—shows the improvements gained by using the product

( ) TESTIMONIAL—a user of the product or a celebrity speaks out in favor of the product

( ) CASE HISTORY—a detailed product success story

( ) FREE INFORMATION AD—offers free brochure, pamphlet, or other information. Ad concentrates on getting the reader to send for free literature rather than on selling the product directly.

( ) STORY—tells a story involving people and the product

( ) "NEW WAVE"—relies on far-out graphics to grab attention

( ) READER IDENTIFICATION—headline is used to select the audience

( ) INFORMATION AD—ad gives useful information relating to the use of the product in general rather than pushing the product directly

( ) LOCATION AD—features the product used in an unusual location to highlight its versatility, usefulness, convenience, or ruggedness

( ) FICTIONAL CHARACTERS—ad centers around a fictional character such as Mr. Whipple or the Green Giant

( ) FICTIONAL PLACES—ad centers around a fictional place such as Marlboro Country or Bird's Eye Village

( ) CARTOONS AND CARTOON STRIPS

( ) ADVERTISER IN AD—the advertiser appears in the ad to speak about his own product

( ) INVENT A WORD—the advertiser invents a word

to describe his product or its application (the term "athlete's foot" was invented by ad man Obie Winters to sell his client's product, a horse linament that could also cure ringworm of the foot)

( ) COMPARATIVE ADVERTISING—shows how your product stacks up against the competition

( ) CHALLENGE—challenges the reader to find a better product than yours

( ) GUARANTEE AD—focuses on the guarantee, not the product

( ) OFFER AD—focuses on the offer, the sale, and not the product

( ) DEMONSTRATION—shows how the product works

( ) PUN—headline attracts attention with clever wordplay. The pun is explained in the copy.

( ) CONTESTS AND SWEEPSTAKES

( ) TIE-IN WITH CURRENT EVENTS—to add timeliness and urgency to the selling proposition

7

Writing Direct Mail

THE DIRECT MAIL EXPLOSION

A recent article in *Forbes* told the story of Dr. Roger Breslow, a New York state internist who kept and crated every piece of junk mail he received in 1982. By December 31st of that year the crate tipped the scale at 502 pounds.

No doubt about it: Direct mail is more popular than ever before. According to the Direct Marketing Association, the amount of money spent on direct mail in the last seven years has more than doubled from $5 billion in 1975 to $11 billion in 1982.

Today, more than 50 billion pieces of direct mail pass through the post office each year. That averages out to about one piece of junk mail for every American every other mailing day.

There are a number of factors that account for direct mail's popularity as an advertising medium.

First, you can measure the results by counting how many order forms or reply cards come back. With print ads and broadcast commercials you usually don't know how effective your efforts have been. But direct-mail advertisers always know whether a mailing is profitable or not.

Second, direct mail can be targeted to select groups of prospects through the careful selection of the proper mailing lists. The copy for each mailing can be tailored to the needs of the various groups of prospects you want to reach. And, you can send as few—or as many—mailing pieces as your budget allows. Which makes direct mail cost-effective for both big corporations and smaller advertisers alike.

Third, direct mail gives you great flexibility in your presentation. Print advertising is limited by the size of the page, broadcast by the length of the commercial. Direct-mail writers can use as many words and pictures as it takes to make the sale. (I recently received a direct-mail piece that featured a *16-page* sales letter!) Your mailing can even include a sample of the product or a gift for the reader.

Because of these advantages, many advertisers use direct mail for a wide variety of applications:

- To sell products by mail
- To generate sales leads
- To answer product inquiries
- To distribute catalogs, newsletters, and other sales literature
- To motivate the sales force
- To keep in touch with former customers
- To get more business from current customers

- To follow up inquiries
- To tie in with other media such as telemarketing, print advertising, and broadcast (Publishers Clearing House, for example, runs TV commercials alerting consumers to look for the Clearing House sweepstakes offer in the mail)
- To invite prospects to attend seminars, conferences, hospitality suites, and trade show exhibits
- To renew subscriptions, memberships, service contracts, and insurance policies
- To get customers to come to the store
- To distribute information, news, product samples
- To conduct research surveys
- To build good will
- To announce a sale

THE WRITER'S APPROACH TO DIRECT MAIL

The main difference between direct mail and space advertising is that mail is a *personal* medium. A letter is a one-to-one communication from one human being to another. An ad appearing in a magazine will be seen by thousands or millions of other readers. But a letter is for your eyes only.

Now, it's true that most direct mail is mass-produced and distributed in bulk mailings to thousands of prospects. Still, the *reader* views mail as more personal than a magazine or newspaper. The trick is to take advantage of this—by creating direct mail that captures the best characteristics of personal mail.

Unlike an ad, a sales letter is signed. So the writer can use the first person—"I" writing to "you," the reader—to personalize the sale message.

The tone of the letter should also be personal. Successful direct-mail writers favor an informal, conversational style. They use contractions, colloquial language, and short, snappy sentences. Their letters brim with personality, enthusiasm, warmth, and sincerity.

Unlike print advertising, which is a new medium for the novice copywriter, direct mail should come easy; we all have experience in letter writing. But too many direct-mail letters sound like . . . well, like advertising. When you write direct mail, don't suppress your natural style. Let the words flow in your own voice. Write the direct-mail letter as if you were writing a letter to a friend.

Direct mail is almost always a response-oriented medium. It asks for the order (or at least for some type of action) *now*, not in a day or a week or a month from now. Direct-mail writers need to generate an immediate response from the reader. This is why most direct-mail packages include an order form, a reply envelope, and copy that tells you to "act now—don't delay—send in your order TODAY!"

As I mentioned, you have great flexibility in the elements you include in your mailing package. As the copywriter, *you* decide. Should the package contain a letter? a brochure? An order form? A reply card? A sample? A second letter? A second or third brochure?

The "classic" direct-mail package contains an outer envelope, a letter, a brochure, and a reply card. But knowledgeable direct-mail writers vary this format to suit their objectives. Of course, there's always the option of using a completely different format, such as a self-mailer or an invoice-stuffer.

The heart of the package is the sales letter. Most of the selling is done in the letter; the brochure is used to highlight sales points, illustrate the product, and provide technical information not appropriate to a letter. There's an old saying among direct-mail writers: "The letter sells; the brochure tells."

This chapter focuses on writing the sales letter. I'll also

talk about envelopes and order forms. Brochures are touched on briefly here and covered in more detail in Chapter 8.

HOW TO START A SALES LETTER

It's easy to begin an ad, because they all follow the same format: Headline first, visual that illustrates the headline, and lead paragraph that expands on the headline.

But the writer has more options with the start of a sales letter.

First, there's the choice of whether to personalize the letter with the individual recipient's name and address, or send out a form letter.

To personalize, you use a computer to generate customized letters for each person on the mailing list, and that's expensive. Personalized letters generally get a better response, as long as they look personally typed and *sound* personal in tone. Don't overdo it by repeating the person's name over and over in the letter (". . . so, MR. RAYMOND, we have reserved this special offer for you and the whole RAYMOND family . . ."). This technique sounds insincere; you wouldn't use the person's name that often if you were speaking face to face.

Also, avoid the old-fashioned "ink-jet" printing systems that produce letters in which the name is obviously inserted into a form letter. The letter should look as if it were typed by hand; you can achieve this effect with a word processor and letter-quality printer.

In most assignments, economy will require that you use preprinted letters. Some advertisers print form letters and then type in each prospect's name and address by hand (this is the "match and fill" technique). But match and fill is time-consuming, and mailing tests show that match-and-fill letters don't do any better than form letters with headlines running across the top.

Some advertisers set the headline in a large typeface. But it's not necessary. You can write the headline in the same typewriter type as the letter. (The body copy of the letter should be set in typewriter type, not in phototype, because the direct-mail letter should *look* like a personal letter, not like an ad or brochure.)

One technique is to type the headline across the top of the letter, either flush left or centered on the page.

A second technique is to type the headline in two or three short lines where the recipient's name and address would normally go (at the top left of the letter)—as I did in this letter promoting my copywriting services:

```
Thanks for your interest
in my copywriting services. . . .

Now, chances are you've never hired a
copywriter through the mail before. And,
maybe you responded to my ad out of curios-
ity. . . .
```

A third technique is to center the headline and put it in a box to call attention to it. Such a box is called a Johnson Box.

And in some letters, you may decide against a headline and simply start with the salutation: Dear Friend, Dear Reader, Dear Business Executive, Dear Friend of the Smithsonian Institute.

A salutation that identifies with the reader's special interest—Dear Farmer, Dear Lawyer, Dear Computer Enthusiast—is always better than Dear Sir, Dear Madame, or Dear Friend.

Sometimes you will use a salutation only. Sometimes, a salutation and a headline. In some cases, a headline without a salutation may be more appropriate.

15 WAYS TO START A LETTER

The first sentence of your letter is the most important one. This sentence signals whether there is something of interest in your letter or whether it is worthless junk mail to be thrown away without a second glance. The lead must hook the reader's attention, but it must also entice him to read further.

Over the years, letter writers have found that there are certain types of openings that are more effective in direct mail than other types. Here are samples of 15 of these leads. When you're struggling with your first letters, turn to these examples for possible ideas on how to structure your own opening.

1. *State the Offer*

The offer consists of the product for sale, its price, the terms of the sale (including discounts), and the guarantee.

If your offer is particularly attractive, you may make the offer—and not the product or its benefits—the theme of the letter.

Here's how the International Preview Society featured a free ten-day trial offer in a sales letter selling Beethoven records:

```
Yours FREE for 10 days—
the legendary music of Beethoven—
Nine Symphonies that epitomize the
beauty and harmony denied him in life.

Plus FREE Preview bonus.

Dear Music Lover,

Beethoven. The name alone calls to mind some
of the greatest music of the ages . . .
```

The letter writer figured that the reader already appreciated Beethoven, so there was no need to sell him on Beethoven's symphonies. And it's hard to sell one set of classical recordings over another based on the orchestra or conductor or the quality of the performance. So, he concentrated on the offer—a free trial plus a free bonus record just for accepting the trial offer.

The headline was typed in ordinary typewriter type and positioned where the reader's name and address would normally appear in a personal letter.

2. Highlight the Free Literature

Letters that seek to generate inquiries from potential customers usually offer the reader a free brochure, booklet, catalog, or other piece of sales literature. You can increase response by stressing the offer of free literature, and by centering the sales pitch on the benefits of the literature rather than those of the product or service.

Here's an example from a letter sent to me by The Mutual Life Insurance Company of New York:

```
Dear Friend:

We have reserved for you a free copy of
Prentice-Hall's TAX SAVING STRATEGIES, a
helpful book for Corporate Executives and
Professionals. It contains practical, timely
and useful ways for you to maximize the
value of your deductions and save dollars.
```

3. Make an Announcement

If you have something new to announce—a special offer, a new product, a new club, a one-of-a-kind event— start your letter with this important news.

From the publishers of *Encyclopaedia Britannica*:

Now . . . we've overcome the last reason
for not owning The New Encyclopaedia Britannica.

Money.

Dear Friend:

If money were no object, would you own
Britannica 3?

Of course. Most people would.

Well, now I'm happy to say that <u>you can acquire Britannica 3 for far less than you
thought possible.</u> You can do so . . . direct
from the publisher . . . at a substantial
Group Discount.

Another example, this one a letter from Calhoun's
Collectors Society:

In the world of U.S. stamps, there is only
one name older than that of the Federal Bureau of Engraving and Printing itself. The
revered house of <u>Scott</u>—known since 1863 as
the ultimate authority on American phi-
lately.

Now, for the first time ever, Scott's stamp
experts have selected the subjects to be
commemorated in a limited philatelic edition
that is unprecedented in collecting annals.

4. *Tell a Story*

Copy written in story format has great reader appeal.
First, it creates empathy with the reader. By telling a
story that relates to the reader's own situation, you build
a bridge between the reader's needs and your sales pitch.
Second, people are familiar with stories and enjoy
reading them. The news they get from newspapers, mag-

azines, and television is related to them in narrative form. Stories hold their interest and get them to read letters they might otherwise put aside.

A subscription letter for *INC.* magazine begins with the story of a man who quit his job to become an entrepreneur—a move many of us with corporate positions daydream of now and then:

```
Dear Executive,

Three years ago this month, a man I know—he
was then a vice president of a big corpora-
tion in Illinois—walked into his boss's of-
fice and handed in his resignation. Two
weeks later, he started his own company.

The man had everything going for him. He was
smart, he was energetic, he was dedicated,
and he knew his particular field inside out.

Almost from the start, the new company
caught on. It grew quickly, adding new cus-
tomers, new employees, new equipment.

But then, about a year ago, the picture be-
gan to change. Orders were still coming in,
but the company was stumbling. Things went
steadily from bad to worse until . . .

A week ago Friday, that man—who had started
out on his own with such high hopes just
three years before—was forced to go out of
business. His company closed its doors for
good.

What happened? What went wrong? Could it
have been avoided? How? . . .
```

This story holds our attention because it could happen to us someday. We want to know what went wrong—and how *INC.* magazine can help us avoid the same mistakes.

5. *Flatter the Reader*

One reason many people take a negative view toward direct mail is that they know it isn't really personal. They know they are just one of thousands of people whose names the advertiser obtained from a mailing list.

But you can turn this fact to your advantage by using flattery. Tell the reader, "Yes, I got your name from a list. Yes, you're part of that group. But that group is special—the people in it have superior characteristics that set them apart from the crowd. And you're superior, too. That's why I'm writing to you."

There is flattery in the opening of a letter from the Maserati Import Company, a seller of luxury automobiles:

```
Dear Mr. McCoy:

One of a kind. Is that phrase a little
trite?

I used to think so until I tried to find
you.

Now I know what ''one of a kind'' really
means.

The process of finding your name and address
was the advertising equivalent of panning
for gold. . . .
```

The letter goes on to offer the reader a free bottle of French champagne if he will test drive a Maserati luxury sedan.

6. *Write to the Reader Peer-to-Peer*

The logic here is that people in special-interest groups—and most direct mail is aimed at narrow groups of prospects—will be more receptive to a sales pitch from a peer than from an outsider.

So, a letter aimed at farmers should be signed by a farmer. And it should be written in the plain, straightforward language of one farmer talking to another.

With this approach, the writer can achieve empathy with the reader by saying, "Look . . . I am like you. I know your problems. I've been through them myself. And I've found a solution. You can trust me."

In a subscription letter for *Writer's Digest*, the pitch is made by one writer talking to other writers:

```
Dear Writer:

I don't have the great American novel in me.
I flunked Poetry 102 in college. My first,
last and only short story was rejected by 14
magazines. . . .
```

7. A Personal Message From the President

In direct mail, the owner or manager of a business can talk directly with his or her customers.

Customers like dealing with the person in charge. When the top person in your company signs the letter, it makes the reader feel important. And, having the owner's signature on the advertising adds a bit more credibility to the message. (I've often heard people say of such mail, "Well, he wouldn't sign it if it wasn't true.")

FutureSoft begins a brochure on its Quickpro software package with a letter from the company president:

```
Personal Message to Microcomputer Owners
from Joseph W. Tamargo, President of FUTURE-
SOFT . . .

I want to tell you why I have chosen to send
you an actual condensation of the Operating
Instructions of our exciting and unique
QUICKPRO, which writes programs for you.
```

Another example, this one from John L. Blair, president of the New Process Company, a mail-order clothing manufacturer:

```
Dear Mr. Bly:

A memo recently crossed my desk that said I
would have to RAISE MY PRICES--NOW--to off-
set our spiraling operating costs!

But I said, ''NO! NOT YET!''

I know that customers like you, Mr. Bly,
expect the BEST VALUE for their money when
they shop at NPC. And that's why I'm going
to hold the line on higher prices just as
long as I possibly can! . . .
```

8. Use a Provocative Quote

The quote should contain news, a startling statistic or fact, or say something outrageous. The quote must be like the lead of a news story—it must raise a question or arouse curiosity to make the reader want to read the body of the letter to find out more.

In a letter selling a new book on advertising, Prentice-Hall began with a quotation taken directly from the book itself:

```
''Advertising agencies and other consultants
score something on the order of a 9 on my
Least-Needed scale of 1-to-10 . . .''

. . . this is what Lewis Kornfeld has to
say, based on his extraordinary success as
Radio Shack's master marketer for over 30
years.
```

9. Ask a Question

Question leads are effective when the answer to the question is interesting or important to the reader, or when the question arouses genuine curiosity.

Here are a few examples of letters that lead with a question:

```
Dear Friend,

What do you think when you see a letter that
starts with ''Dear Friend'' . . . a letter
from someone you've never met?


WHAT DO JAPANESE MANAGERS HAVE THAT AMERICAN
MANAGERS SOMETIMES LACK?

How about workers with good attitudes?

Dear Mr. Blake:

Is freelance a dirty word to you?

It really shouldn't be . . .

Dear Mr. Bly:

What does it cost to create a brochure? De-
sign a booklet? Develop a newsletter? Pro-
duce a press party invitation? Prepare a
sales promotional flip chart?
```

10. *Make It Personal*

The most personal direct-mail piece I ever received began as follows:

```
Dear Friend,

As you may already know, we have been doing
some work for people who have the same last
name as you do. Finally, after months of
work, THE AMAZING STORY OF THE BLYS IN AMER-
ICA, is ready for print and you are in it!
```

This letter is highly personal for two reasons. First, my name appears several times in the body of the letter. Second, the product is designed especially for me, a Bly. (But

the letter is weakened by the stock opening "Dear Friend."
A better salutation is the more personal, "Dear Friend
Bly.")

Personalized mail usually gets more attention than form
letters. So whenever possible, make it personal. Insert the
reader's name in the copy once or twice (if your budget
allows for computer letters). And, more important, make
sure the copy speaks to the needs, interests, and ego of
the reader. (As a book called *The Amazing Story of the Blys
in America* has strong appeal to people named Bly.)

11. Identify the Reader's Problem

If your product or service solves a problem, you can
create a strong sales letter by featuring the problem in the
lead, then telling how the product or service solves the
problem.

There are two advantages to this technique. First, it
selects a specific group of readers for your letter. (Only
single people will respond to a letter that begins, "Are You
Sick and Tired of Paying Extra Taxes Just Because You
Aren't Married?")

Second, the format shows in a clear and direct manner how the product solves the reader's problem. When
you start with the problem, the natural next step is to talk
about the solution.

Manhattan dentist Dr. Brian E. Weiss used this technique in a letter inviting me in for an appointment:

```
Dear Mr. Bly:

You know how difficult it is to look your
best if dental problems are causing discom-
fort and pain or if the appearance of your
teeth needs improvement.

Have you been putting off a dental checkup
or consultation on an existing problem? This
note may encourage you to take the important
step to help yourself feel better by making
a dental appointment. . . .
```

Politician Jim Thompson used the technique in a campaign letter aimed at voters in Chicago:

```
Dear Mrs. Vanderbilt:

If you can't afford higher taxes.

If you're afraid to walk the streets at
night.

If you're sick and tired of corrupt govern-
ment officials.

If your children aren't getting the educa-
tion they deserve.

Then you don't need a Governor appointed by
Chicago's City Hall. . . .
```

12. Stress a Benefit

A straightforward presentation of a benefit can outpull other techniques if the benefit is significant and has strong appeal to the reader.

A sales letter from Prentice-Hall offering a new book on advertising began with the headline, "Just published . . . HOW TO MAKE YOUR ADVERTISING MAKE MONEY. A clear, concise guide to effective advertising . . ." The headline is effective because it's safe to assume that all advertising professionals who receive the letter want to create more effective advertising.

To get results, a benefit-oriented headline must appeal to the reader's self-interest. As Cahners Publishing points out in their booklet, *How to Create and Produce Successful Direct Mail,* "Don't tell your prospect about your grass seed, tell him about his lawn."

13. Use Human Interest

People enjoy reading about other people—especially about people who have anxieties, fears, problems, and interests similar to their own.

Some of the strongest sales letters center around powerful, dramatic human-interest stories. The readers get hooked because the events in the story relate somehow to their own lives. And, the letter leaves more of an impression because it deals with human emotions, not just technical product features or abstract sales arguments.

The publisher of *Cardiac Alert* newsletter used an autobiographical approach to add human interest to a sales letter asking for subscriptions to his publication. The headline read:

```
When I was 16,
my father died
of a heart attack. . . .
```

You can't help but be interested in the letter that follows.

14. *Let the Reader In on Some Inside Information*

When a customer sees your ad in a magazine, he knows he is sharing your message with tens of thousands of other people.

But he has no way of knowing whether you've sent the *sales letter* he received to thousands of prospects, or just a select few.

Direct mail is an excellent medium for appealing to the reader's need to feel special, important, exclusive. And nothing is more exclusive than revealing some inside information on a sale or product that others don't know about.

Here's exclusive news from a cover letter mailed along with a reprint of a magazine ad:

```
Here's a fresh-from-the-printer reprint
of our latest WALL STREET JOURNAL ad . . .

We'll be running the ad in June because we
want potential customers to know more about
our latest financial planning services.
```

```
But, as someone we've done business with
before, we consider YOU even more important
than the ''new business'' out there.

Which is why we're sending you our new ad
months before it will break in the press.

You see, we wanted you to be the first to
know about our new services which can save
you time and build your retirement nest
egg. . . .
```

The message is: We're telling you first because we think you're special.

And what reader of direct mail doesn't think he *is* special?

15. Sweepstakes

A sweepstakes can greatly increase the response to a direct-mail campaign.

One sweepstakes mailing I received began:

```
American Family Publishers Announces Ameri-
ca's First By-Mail GUARANTEED MULTI-MILLION
DOLLAR SWEEPSTAKES OFFER:

R BLY, A LOCAL NY RESIDENT, MAY HAVE ALREADY
WON ONE MILLION DOLLARS.
```

There are three ways of structuring a sweepstakes:

```
YOU MAY WIN . . .

YOU MAY HAVE WON . . .

YOU HAVE WON . . .
```

The "you have won" sweepstakes generates the most entries because the consumer is guaranteed a prize. This sweepstakes is expensive to run because you must award the consolation prize to everyone who claims it.

The "you may have won" is the second most effective sweepstakes. Here, the reader is told that the winning entry number has been preselected by computer . . . and that he just may hold that winning entry number in his hand.

These are just 15 common ways of starting your sales letter. There are others. Read the direct mail you receive and keep a file of effective direct-mail leads and letters you can use as a reference in your own work.

THE ENVELOPE: TO TEASE OR NOT TO TEASE?

The outer envelope is the first thing the reader sees when he receives your mailing package. It is here the selling starts. If the outer envelope fails to entice the reader to open the letter, or worse, if it prompts him to throw the letter away, the brilliant copy of your sales letter will be wasted.

There are two basic approaches to outer envelopes.

The first is to start your sales pitch right away with headlines and copy printed on the outer envelope. This copy, known as "teaser copy," is designed to entice the reader to open the envelope by arousing his curiosity or promising a strong reward for reading the package.

The problem with this strategy is that teasers are labels that instantly identify the package as containing advertising matter. Large headlines and copy lines printed on an envelope shout at the reader, "This is advertising . . . junk mail . . . it's worthless . . . throw it away!"

My rule is: Use a teaser only if it contains an irresistible message that will compel the reader to open the envelope. But don't feel you *must* use a teaser—a weak teaser can actually reduce response versus a package with a plain envelope!

We know that people always open their personal mail before their junk mail. We also know that many people throw away every "teaser" envelope they receive without a second glance.

Teasers are effective only when the message is compelling. For example, I'd have a hard time ignoring an envelope with the teaser, "Inside—The Secret to Living Longer and Feeling Better . . . Without Dieting or Special Exercise."

On the other hand, you'd probably save yourself the trouble of opening an envelope that began, "Sawyer Life Insurance Announces its 50th Year of Operation . . . Quality Service to the Community for over Half a Decade."

Teasers can take many forms. You can have a headline only. Or a headline plus copy.

You can use an envelope with a window so the teaser is copy that shows through the window.

You can mail the package in a clear plastic bag so the whole package shows through to tease the reader.

You can even print illustrations, graphics, and photos on the outer envelope.

However, most teasers seem to follow one of three basic formats: [1]

A. THIS IS THE BEST WIDGET EVER MADE
B. THIS WIDGET MAY SAVE YOU UP TO $500
C. ENCLOSED IS YOUR *FREE* WIDGET

The third teaser, C, works best because it promises a reward for opening the envelope. (The promise of a prize inside has sold millions of dollars worth of Cracker Jacks and breakfast cereals.) Even though you know you hold advertising material in your hands, teaser C overcomes your resistance to junk mail by making you wonder what's inside.

Teaser A is the worst. It's pure boasting, and the

reader's reaction to the smug claim will be to throw the mailing away.

Teaser B, though not as effective as C, is still an improvement over A because it makes the promise of a benefit. This promise says to the reader, "Yes, you hold junk mail in your hands. But it might be worth your while to open the envelope and see what we can do for you."

Often a blank envelope—one with no teaser—is more effective than one with a teaser. The idea behind the no-teaser approach is to make the direct-mail package resemble personal mail. When the reader sees the envelope, he's not sure whether the envelope contains personal mail or advertising material—and so he opens it, just to be sure. Once the mailer is opened, the battle is half won; if the letter contains a strong, compelling lead, you will hook the prospect and get him to read the body copy.

When using the no-teaser approach, take pains to make the letter look like personal mail. Use a plain white or off-white envelope. Don't let any brightly colored sales literature show through the window, if there is one. And don't embellish the envelope with a company logo; just have the return address set in plain type.

THE FLYER TELLS, THE LETTER SELLS

Many direct-mail packages do an effective selling job with a letter and reply form only.

Every direct-mail package should contain a letter; flyers and brochures are optional. As the writer, you must decide whether a flyer is needed.

Here are some helpful suggestions:

Use a flyer when you are selling products that are colorful or visually impressive: subscriptions to colorful magazines, flowers, fruit, fine foods, coins, collectibles, sports equipment, consumer electronics.

Some products are most effectively sold through demonstration. But you usually can't demonstrate by mail. The next best thing is to take step-by-step photos of a demonstration and put them in a flyer to be included in the mailer.

Sometimes, the offer is so strong that the writer decides to devote the letter solely to the benefits of the sale. The benefits of the product itself can then be covered in an accompanying flyer.

Use a flyer for transmitting technical data or product information that is too detailed to be explained or listed in the letter.

In writing direct mail to sell books, I list a detailed table of contents in a flyer separate from the letter. This way, the small percentage of readers interested in some esoteric topic can scan the contents to see if it is included. And if it is, the flyer will have tipped the odds in favor of a sale.

You are not limited to one flyer or one letter or one order form. You can include whatever you think it will take to make the sale.

HOW TO INCREASE RESPONSE TO YOUR MAILINGS

In direct mail, response is the name of the game.

Maintaining a dignified image or getting people to remember your message is not important. The only thing that counts is how many sales or inquiries your mailing generates. The more responses, the more successful the mailer.

Reaching the right audience with the right offer and the right copy is the key to successful direct mail. But there are a number of response-increasing techniques that have little to do with copywriting skill or common sense. Here are a few that you can use:[2]

- Always include a response mechanism. This can be a business reply card, reply envelope, order form, or toll-free 800 number.

- Use self-addressed, postage-paid envelopes and reply cards (known as *business reply envelopes* and *business reply cards*). They generate more response than cards or envelopes that require a postage stamp from the prospect.

- Order forms and reply cards with tear-off stubs or receipts generate more response than those without.

- The letter should be the first thing the reader sees when he opens the envelope. The package should have a natural flow from outer envelope to letter to flyer to reply card.

- Offer a premium—a gift to prospects who respond to the mailing. The premium should be something that they want, and it should relate to the product or the offer.

- Offer something of value in return for responding to the letter—a free brochure, booklet, catalog, demonstration, survey, estimate, consultation, or trial offer.

- Allow for a negative response. And turn it into a positive. The reply card for a letter promoting my freelance copywriting services gives the reader the option of checking off a box that reads, "Not interested right now. But try us again in_____." Even if the reader doesn't
  (month/year)
  need my services now, he can still respond to the mailing.

- Use physical objects in the mailing. An envelope that feels bulky almost always gets opened. These objects can include product samples, premiums, 3-D pop-ups, and other gimmicks. (In the last year or so I've received direct-mail packages that contained instant coffee, chili powder, a set of coasters, a calendar, pens, pencils, a flashlight, and a magnifying glass.) Although costly, mailings with objects enclosed can really stand out from a mailbox or in a basket full of flat envelopes containing regular letters and flyers.

- Put a time limit on the offer. Once the reader puts the letter aside, he probably won't come back to it, so you'll get the most response if you urge him to act *now* . . . by putting a time limit on the offer.

- You can put a real date limit on the offer ("Remember, Beethoven's Violin Concerto is yours to keep just for taking advantage of this offer within the next 10 days").

- You can hint that the offer won't last forever ("But hurry—supplies are limited").

- Or, you can add a sense of urgency to your call for action ("Remember—the time to buy insurance is *before* tragedy strikes. Not after").

- Make the outer envelope resemble an invoice, telegram, or other "official-looking" document. People almost always open such envelopes.

- Use a plain outer envelope with no copy, not even a return address. The mystery of such a mailing is irresistible.

- Use a P.S. in the letter to restate the offer or reemphasize a sales point; 80 percent of readers will read a P.S.

- Guarantee the offer. When you sell by mail, make a money-back guarantee good for 15, 30, 60, or even 90 days.

- When you are generating leads, tell the prospect that he's under no obligation and that no salesman will call (unless he wants one to).

- Envelopes addressed with labels are as effective as envelopes individually typed with the recipient's address. Addressing envelopes by hand reduces response, perhaps because it looks amateurish.

- If your mailing list contains titles but not names, print a description of the person you're trying to reach on the outer envelope ("Attention Buyers of Electronic Components . . . Important Information Inside").

- A preprinted postage permit or postage-metered envelope outpulls an envelope with stamps.

- An order form printed in color, or designed as an elaborate certificate, or printed with a lot of information outpulls a clean, ordinary-looking order form.

- Letters with indented paragraphs, underlined words, and portions of the text set in a second color outpull plain letters.

- Letters with a lot of "bells and whistles"—arrows, fake handwritten notes in the margins, spot illustrations, highlighting—can increase response when mailed to low- and middle-status consumer audiences. Avoid these techniques when writing to business executives or upper-class consumers.

- A form letter with a headline is just as effective as a form letter with the recipient's name and address typed in by hand.

- A package with a separate letter and brochure does better than a combination letter/brochure.

- Repeat the offer on the reply card.

- Use action words in the first sentence of the reply card and restate the offer in the body copy. ("YES, I'd like to know how I can cut my phone bill in half. Please send literature on your long-distance service. I understand I'm under no obligation and that no salesman will call.")

- Avoid intimidating, legal-type wording. State your offer, terms, and guarantee in plain, simple English.

- Make it simple to respond to the mailing. This means having a simple offer and an easy-to-complete order form. And be sure to leave enough space on the form for the reader to fill in the required information (a surprising number of reply cards and coupons don't).

- Keep in mind the buyer's level of interest in your product so you don't oversell or undersell. (Prospects whose names were taken from the *Popular Computing* mailing list probably have a greater interest in video games than the subscribers of *Field and Stream.*)

Writing sales letters is the best education I can recommend for both novice and experienced copywriters alike. Within a few weeks of your mailing, you know whether your copy is successful or not. No other form of copywriting yields such immediate—or such precise—feedback on your work.

8

Writing Brochures, Catalogs, and Other Sales Literature

Promotional literature has been around for a long time. According to *Ripley's Believe It or Not,* the first brochure was written by Hernan Cortez 465 years ago. It was circulated as a broadside to the people of Spain by Charles the Fifth, and it advertised a sale on turkeys.

Today, few businesses operate witout some kind of printed sales literature to hand out to customers and prospects. Travel agents, supermarkets, department stores, industrial manufacturers, consultants, insurance agents, colleges, and dozens of other types of organizations depend on brochures, circulars, fliers, catalogs, and other printed advertising matter to help make the sale.

Advertisers need sales literature for two reasons. First, credibility: People expect a "real" company to have printed product literature. Anyone can spend $50 on letterhead and business cards and call themselves a corporation. But a brochure proves you are in business and shows you're more than a fly-by-night operation.

Second, the brochure is a time-saving device. People want printed information they can take home with them and study at their leisure. But it would take too much time to type individual letters of information to every prospect that asked about your product. The solution is to collect your basic product information in a single, mass-produced brochure. The brochure gives prospects most of the information they need to know; the rest can be filled in by letter, phone, or a visit to the store.

Brochures support advertising and direct-mail programs. They are also used as sales tools by salespeople and distributors. Brochures are a handy way of quickly communicating the essentials of your business to new customers, prospects, employees, and dealers.

Brochures are primarily a medium of information. They tell prospects what the product is and what it can do for them. Your brochure should also explain how the product works, why people should buy it, and how they can order.

But a good sales brochure does more than explain and inform. It also *persuades*. Remember, the brochure is a sales tool, not an instruction manual. Good brochure copy does more than list facts or product features; it translates these facts and features into customer benefits—reasons why the customer should buy the product.

A good brochure does more than tell. It *sells*.

11 TIPS ON WRITING BETTER BROCHURES

Here are 11 tips on writing brochures that tell the reader what he wants to know—and sell him on buying the product.

1. *Know Where the Brochure Fits into the Buying Process*

Unlike package goods you buy off a supermarket shelf (soap, shampoo, canned beans, cigarettes), products that require a brochure are seldom sold in a single step. Computers, cars, vacation trips, insurance, telephones, financial services, seminars, club memberships, real estate, and dozens of other products and services require several meetings or contacts between buyer and seller before the sale is closed.

For most of these products and services, a brochure comes in somewhere between initial contact and final sale. But where? Do you write the brochure for the uninformed buyer who shows initial interest in the product? Or is the brochure used to build credibility and answer questions as you get closer to closing the sale?

The answer is: It depends on the product, the market, and the advertiser's individual approach to making the sale. Some advertisers might even use a series of brochures to guide the buyer through the steps of the buying process.

I make my living as an advertising copywriter. I get sales leads from many sources—ads I run in advertising journals, direct mail, publicity from articles and speeches I give, word of mouth, and referral from other clients.

When a lead comes in, I chat with the caller to determine his level of interest. By asking a few questions over the phone, I can quickly determine whether the caller is a likely potential customer for my service.

Once I qualify the lead by phone, the next step is to send a comprehensive package of sales literature. It contains seven or eight separate pieces including a biography, client list, 4-page sales letter, reprints of articles I've written, samples of my copy, a price list, and a form the prospect can use to order copy by mail. In short, it contains everything the prospect needs to know about my freelance copywriting services.

From this material, the prospect should be able to decide whether to hire me. There may be a follow-up call or a mailing of more samples of my work, but the basic literature package allows the client to order the service directly, by mail. No additional information or sales visits are required.

On the other hand, a friend of mine who is a management consultant mails very little information to prospects. He sends a brief cover note along with a slim booklet that presents his services in concise outline form. The reason he sends incomplete information is that the next step in *his* sales sequence is a meeting with the prospect. If he sent a package as weighty as mine, there would be nothing left to follow up with. But by sending less, he whets the reader's appetite with key sales benefits of his service, while raising questions that can only be answered if the reader requests a face-to-face meeting with the consultant.

Here are some of the ways brochures can fit into the buying process:

- *As leave-behinds.* A leave-behind is a brochure you leave behind after a meeting with a potential customer. The leave-behind brochure should summarize your sales pitch and contain a fairly complete description of the product and its benefits.

- *As point-of-sale literature.* Point-of-sale literature is literature displayed at the point of sale. A travel agent's office, for example, contains racks of brightly colored pamphlets on faraway places. The cover of the point-of-sale literature should have a catchy headline and visual that team up to make passersby stop, pick up, and keep the brochure.

- *To respond to inquiries.* An inquiry is a request for more information about your product. The person making the inquiry became interested in you through your advertising, publicity, or referral, and represents a "hot" sales lead—someone much more likely to buy than a prospect who has not contacted you.

The inquiry fulfillment package should contain enough information to answer the prospect's questions and convince him to take the next step in the buying process. The hot prospect has already expressed interest in your product, so don't hesitate to load your inquiry fulfillment package full of facts and sales points.

· *As direct mail.* As mentioned in Chapter 7, brochures and flyers are used to add information to direct-mail packages. The sales letter does the selling; the brochure provides additional sales points, lists technical features, and contains photos and drawings of the product. In the interest of keeping mailing costs down, this type of brochure is usually slim (and is designed to fit in a standard mailing envelope).

· *As a sales support tool.* Many products—hospital supplies, office equipment, life insurance, industrial equipment—are sold by salespeople who visit the prospect at his home or office. These salespeople use brochures as selling aids in their sales pitches (and also as leave-behinds). Such brochures have large pages, big illustrations, and bold headlines and' subheads that lead the salesperson and prospect through the pitch. Sometimes, a standard product brochure is adapted for use as a sales aid and printed as separate panels in a three-ring binder or self-standing easel that sits on the prospect's desk.

Whatever your application—leave-behind, point-of-sale, inquiry fulfillment, direct mail, sales support—let the advertiser's particular method of selling be your guide in writing and designing the brochure. The best brochures contain just the right amount of product information and sales pitch to lead the prospect from one step of the buying process to the next.

One additional tip on designing sales literature: Think about how the reader will use and file the brochure. A small pocket-size brochure may be ideal for direct mail or point-of-sale display, but it will be lost in a file folder or on a bookshelf of full-size literature (8½ by 11 inches)—the kind your competition is probably publishing.

In the same way, a brochure of unconventional shape or size may stand out from the crowd, but might be thrown away because it won't fit in a standard file cabinet. And a brochure aimed at purchasing agents will probably be punched for a three-hole binder, which means part of your copy will be punched out unless you leave margins for binding.

2. Know Whether the Brochure Stands Alone or is Supported by Other Material

In some selling situations, the brochure stands alone. Aside from the salesperson, it is the only sales tool the company has.

Other firms use a brochure to supplement their promotional campaign, which may consist of print advertising, radio and TV commercials, direct mail, publicity, trade shows, seminars.

Some companies have one product—and one brochure. Others use a series of brochures, each describing one product in their product line, or one segment of the total market they sell to.

The brochure writer must know whether his brochure stands alone or is supported by other material, because the existence of other material determines the content of his brochure.

For example, I would normally devote half a page of an eight-page product brochure to a description of the manufacturer and his capabilities and resources as a major corporation. But, if the manufacturer already had a separate "corporate capabilities brochure," I wouldn't need to do that. Instead, we could mail both brochures—product and company—to prospects requesting more information.

Another example: A client asked me to write a sales

brochure on an industrial mixer. He wanted to include detailed calculations on how to determine the energy consumption of the mixer.

Although some engineers might be curious as to how the calculation is done, such an elaborate mathematical treatment is wasted space in a selling piece. The solution was to talk about energy savings without showing the calculation in the sales brochure, and create a separate "technical information sheet" that showed the detailed calculation.

Find out the environment in which your brochure will be working. Is it a stand-alone brochure or part of a series? Is it supported by print ads, direct mail, publicity? Has the advertiser also published an annual report, corporate capabilities brochure, catalog, or other general brochure describing the corporation? Are there article reprints, fact sheets, or other pieces of literature that can be mailed along with the main brochure?

Form should follow function. Recently I was asked to write sales literature describing a system of modular software. For this modular product, I wrote a modular brochure. The main piece is a four-page folder. Copy giving the reader an overview of the system is printed on the left inside page; the right page is a pocket containing 16 sheets, each describing a different software module.

This approach allows salespeople to use the sheets as separate flyers for presentations and mailings. In addition, the brochure is easy to update. When a new modular program is added to the package, we just add a flyer to the brochure.

3. Know Your Audience

We've already seen that a brochure must fit into the right step in the buying process.

Your brochure must also fit the informational needs of your audience.

Think about the reader and what he expects to get out

of the brochure. Ask yourself, "How can I use the brochure to convince the reader to buy the product?"

Let's say you are writing a brochure selling alfalfa seeds to farmers. The farmer probably isn't interested in the history of alfalfa (or the history of your company). And he doesn't much care about alfalfa's biological structure or the chemical composition of the seed.

The farmer wants to know that your seeds are plump and healthy . . . that they're free of weeds . . . that they'll yield a good, healthy crop of alfalfa . . . and that the price is right.

How do you convince him? One way is to show the results. Put two photos of alfalfa fields on the cover of your brochure. The one on the left shows weed-infested, scrawny alfalfa. The one on the right shows a field of lush, healthy plants. The headline tells him the field on the right was planted with your seeds—seeds he can learn more about by reading the brochure.

The brochure can go even further. Why not attach a sample bag of seed to the brochure and mail it to the farmer? The brochure copy can begin, "Our alfalfa is clean, healthy, practically weed-free. But don't take our word for it. See for yourself."

Know your reader. Farmers don't want hype or a scientific treatise; they want straightforward talk that shows them how to run their farms more profitably. Scientists are most comfortable with charts, graphs, and tables of data, so include plenty of them in a brochure aimed at scientists.

Engineers are at home with diagrams and blueprints. Accountants understand tables of financial figures. Human resource managers will probably be interested in photos of people.

Also, the *length* of your copy depends not only on the amount of information you have, but on whether your customer is someone who will read a lot of copy. A brochure selling a new microfilm system to librarians can be long, because librarians like to read. A brochure aimed at busy executives should probably be shorter, because most executives are pressed for time. A brochure offering a new cable TV service will probably contain mostly pictures, because people who watch a lot of TV would rather look at pictures than read.

4. Put a Strong Selling Message on the Cover

The first thing the reader sees when he pulls your brochure out of an envelope or off a display rack is the cover.

If the cover promises a strong benefit or reward for reading the copy, the reader will open the brochure and read it (or at least look at the pictures, captions, and headings).

If the selling message on the cover is weak, or worse— if there is no selling message on the cover—the reader has no motivation for opening the brochure. It is just junk mail, something to be thrown away.

A surprising number of brochure covers contain no headline or visual, just the product name and company logo. This is like running an ad without a headline: It wastes a valuable selling opportunity.

Let's look at a few examples.

A brochure from The Prudential Insurance Company of America has the headline, "Now . . . you can enroll in this AARP Plan of Group Hospital Insurance—Designed to help pay expenses your other insurance does not cover!" The cover is illustrated with a drawing of a retired couple enjoying a life of leisure.

This brochure cover is effective because it offers a strong, solid benefit, simply stated—"Designed to help pay expenses your other insurance does not cover!" What gimmick or clever cover design could do a better selling job than this promise? My only complaint with the headline is the use of the abbreviation "AARP." I didn't know what it meant and was annoyed that I had to search through the copy to find out.

Sometimes, the visual communicates the benefit more strongly than the headline. My favorite summer retreat is Montauk, Long Island, and no words can make me long for a weekend on the Island as much as a beautiful color photo of the waves rolling in and lapping against the soft sands of the shore. If you own a hotel on the Montauk beach, put such a photo on the cover, and I'll be sold!

Occasionally, a brochure writer attempts to lure the reader into the brochure with a gimmick that doesn't relate to the product. In front of me is a brochure whose cover features a drawing of a church and a diamond ring and the headline, "Forget about marriage . . . why not just 'get engaged.' "

This caught my eye years ago, when I was engaged. But when I opened the brochure, I was given a sales pitch on why it's better to rent cars instead of buying them. The brochure had nothing at all to do with engagement or marriage. I was more than disappointed—I felt cheated. I'm sure other folks felt the same and doubt that this brochure sold many car-rental contracts.

The traditional brochure cover contains a headline and graphic only, with no text; body copy begins inside. But you can get people to start reading your sales pitch by breaking this tradition and beginning your body copy on the front cover. The reader's eye will automatically go to the lead paragraph, and if it's strong enough, they'll be hooked.

5. Give Complete Information

Give as much information as it takes to get the prospect to take the next step in the buying process.

The average brochure contains a lot of words. Certainly more than you read in most ads or hear in TV commercials.

But remember that the brochure is a medium of *information*. Ads, commercials, and direct mail may be an unwanted interruption in the reader's life. But the reader has *asked* for the brochure, and he is interested in the information it contains.

Don't be afraid to make the brochure as long as it has to be. Don't be afraid to include all the necessary information—prices, product specfications, ordering information, guarantees, descriptions. The reader who represents a serious potential customer will read every word of the copy—as long as it is interesting and engaging. The minute you write boring copy, or copy that doesn't give useful information, you'll turn the reader off.

There is a ridiculous tendency among brochure designers to use a large amount of "white space" (blank area) on the page and very little copy. I've seen 8½- by 11-inch brochures where each page had only one or two paragraphs in small type in the upper corner. The rest of the page was mostly blank and decorated by some graphic design—stripes, color patterns, lines, shapes.

This is a waste of space and printing costs. Your customer doesn't send for your brochure to look at fancy designs; he sends for it because he wants information.

Some designers hold dear to the "white space myth"— the belief that people won't read text unless it is surrounded by blank space on all sides. If you want proof that this myth is untrue, take a look at your daily newspaper—pages and pages of sold text and photos. No white space, no graphic "design elements." Just information that the reader wants and has paid for.

Of course, not every page in your brochure should be solid type to the edges. Margins and space between paragraphs help increase readability. Photos, illustrations, captions, and subheads break up the text and help tell the story. But to think your brochure should be largely blank space is folly. Don't be afraid to write and print all the words it takes to make your sales pitch. Give the reader *complete* information.

6. Organize Your Selling Points

People read brochures in much the same way they read paperback novels. They look at the cover first, maybe take a quick peak at the back cover, and thumb through the book once. Then, if it looks promising, they open to page one and start reading.

Your brochure, like a paperback novel, should have a logical structure to it. A good brochure tells a story—a *product* story—with a beginning, a middle, and an end.

The organization of a brochure is dictated both by the product story you want to tell and by the informational needs of the reader.

For example, my in-laws have a business in which they buy books from publishers and resell them to corporations. This is a rather unusual service, one the corporate librarian may not have thought about before, so my in-laws began their brochure with a summary of the service they offer and why corporate librarians find it useful.

Next, they go into the six major benefits of using the service. These benefits are listed in simple 1–2–3 fashion so the reader can quickly see how he can come out ahead by doing business with the book-buying service.

Finally, the brochure tells the reader the technical details of how the service works and gives instructions for placing orders.

Let the organization of your brochure be dictated by what your customer wants to know about your product. If you own a computer store, and you find that customers coming in off the street seem to ask the same questions over and over, you might write a booklet titled, "Six Important Questions to Ask Before You Buy A Computer." The booklet would present computer shopping tips in a simple question-and-answer format.

If your company designs and decorates offices, your brochure could be organized as a walking tour of the modern office. At each point of the tour, from the copier to the water cooler, the copy could point out how redesigning that section of the office can make the office a better place to work and improve productivity.

There are many ways to organize a brochure—alphabetical order, chronological order, by size of product, by importance of customer benefit, question and answer, list of customer benefits, by product line, by price, by application, by market, by steps in the ordering process. Choose the approach that best fits your product, your audience, and your sales pitch.

7. *Divide the Brochure into Short, Easy-to-Read Sections*

As you organize your brochure, you'll come up with a scheme, an outline that breaks the topic into a number of sections and subsections.

You should keep this organizational scheme in the final copy. Write the brochure as a series of short sections and subsections, each with its own headline or subhead.

There are a number of benefits to this approach.

First, the use of headings and subheads allows the reader to get the message even if he only scans the brochure. Many people won't read all the copy, but a series of heads and subheads gives them the gist of the sales pitch at a glance.

Be sure to write headings and subheads that tell a story. Avoid headings that are just straight description or clever plays on words. Instead of "Hitachi plays it cool," write, "Hitachi chiller-heaters cut cooling costs in half."

Second, breaking the copy into short sections makes the brochure easier to read. People are intimidated and tired by long chunks of text; they prefer to read a short section of copy, stop, take a rest, and absorb the information before going on to the next section. (This is why novels are divided into chapters.)

Third, short sections make the brochure easier to write. You just follow your outline and put the information in your notes under the appropriate section. If you uncover new facts that don't fit anywhere in the outline, you can simply add a new section to the brochure. And, like your reader, you can rest after writing one section before you go on to the next.

When you write your brochure, think about how the sections will appear on the pages of the published brochure. For example, you might like the clean look and feel of having a six-page brochure with four sections (one on each page), a headline on the front cover, and the company logo and address on the back cover.

Some brochure writers design their brochures so that each page contains a complete section or two. Other writers claim that a good way of getting the reader to turn the page is to have the sections run off one page and continue on the next. Both techniques have their merits, and the choice is really a matter of taste. But you should be aware of how organization and layout work together.

If your brochure is folded or designed in an unusual format, make a mock-up out of scrap paper. Use the mock-up (called a "dummy") to show the layout and how the copy flows from page to page. Make sure that the reader will see the various sections of text in the same order you wrote them in the manuscript.

8. Use Hard-Working Visuals

Photos in brochures are not ornaments. They are included to help sell the product by showing what it looks like, how it works, and what it can do for the reader.

The best brochure photos demonstrate the product's usefulness by showing it in action. Putting people in these photos usually adds to the visual's appeal (people like looking at pictures of people).

Photos make the best visuals because they offer *proof* that a product exists and works. But artwork is also useful for many purposes.

A drawing can illustrate a product or process that is

not easily photographed (such as the inner workings of an automobile engine).

A map can show where something is located.

A diagram can show how something works or how it is organized. An organizational diagram, for example, uses arrows and boxes to show how the divisions and branches of a company are organized.

A graph is used to tell how one quantity changes as another quantity changes. In a brochure on air conditioning, a graph could show how your electric bill goes up as you lower the temperature setting on your air conditioner.

Pie charts show proportions and percentages (for example, the percentage of your company's annual income spent on research and development). Bar charts demonstrate comparisons among quantities (this year's sales versus last year's). And tables are a handy way of listing a body of data too large to include in the text of the brochure.

Use visuals when they can express or illustrate a concept better than words can. If the visual doesn't improve on the written description, don't use it.

Popular brochure visuals include:

- Product photographs
- Pictures of the product photographed next to other objects to give a sense of the size of the product. (A brochure on semiconductors might show a photo of a chip on a postage stamp to dramatically convey the smallness of the integrated circuit.)
- Photos of actual installations of the product
- Photos of the product in use
- Photos of the product being manufactured
- Tables of product specifications
- Tables summarizing product features and benefits
- Photos of technical reports and studies done on the product

- Photos of items made with (or from) the product
- Photos of the company headquarters, manufacturing plant, or research laboratories
- Photos of the product packed and ready for shipping
- Photos of the product being tested by company scientists
- Photos of people who are enjoying the use of the product
- Photos of people who attest to the product's superiority
- Tables listing the various models and versions of the product
- Graphs presenting scientific proof of the product's performance (heat tests, ability to stand up under pressure, longevity of operation, etc.)
- Photos of available parts and accessories
- A series of photos demonstrating the product's performance or how to use it
- Diagrams explaining how the product works or how it is put together
- Sketches of planned product improvements, forthcoming new products, or planned applications

Always use visuals that illustrate your key selling points. In an automobile brochure that extolls the benefits of rack-and-pinion steering, it would be helpful to have a diagram that shows how rack-and-pinion steering works. But if rack-and-pinion steering was not a selling point, there would be no reason to include a picture of it.

Label all visuals with captions. Studies show that brochure captions get twice the readership of body copy. Use captions to reinforce the body copy or make an additional sales point not covered in the copy.

Make captions interesting and informative. Instead of labeling a photo, "Automatic wiring device," write "A tape-controlled, fully automatic wiring device (above left) makes approximately 1,000 wire-wrap connections an hour. Such automatic devices provide increased reliability and a significant savings in manufacturing costs."

9. Find the Next Step in the Buying Process—and Tell the Reader to Take it

Do you want your reader to buy pasta from your gourmet shop?

Enroll for membership in your health spa?

Visit your factory?

Or test-drive a new luxury sedan?

A brochure moves the customer from one step in the buying process to the next.

To do this successfully, the brochure must identify this next step and tell the reader to take it.

Typically, this "call for action" appears at the end of the brochure. The copy urges the reader to call or write for more information, or to take some other action.

Make it easy for the reader to respond by using such devices as reply cards, self-addressed stamped envelopes, order forms, toll-free 800 numbers, and listings of local dealerships and distributors.

End the brochure with copy designed to generate an immediate response. Use action words and phrases: "Give us a call today." "For more information, write for our FREE catalog." "Please complete and mail the enclosed reply card." "Visit our store nearest you." "Order today—supplies limited."

Here's an effective closing from a brochure for an advertising agency:

THE NEXT STEP

Now that you know something about us, we'd like to know a little bit more about you.

Send us your current ads, sales literature, and press releases for a free, no-obligation evaluation of your marketing communications program.

If you'd like to meet with us, give us a call. We'll be glad to show you some of the work we've done for our clients, and take a look at what we can do for you.

This closing is persuasive for three reasons: 1) it's personal; 2) it asks for specific action ("Send us your current ads," "give us a call"); and 3) it offers the reader something for free ("a no-obligation evaluation of your marketing communications program").

Always ask for the order in your brochure. Or at least for action that will lead to an eventual sale.

10. Don't Forget the Obvious

Sometimes you get so wrapped up in the creative aspects of copywriting that you forget to include basic information—phone numbers, directions, street addresses, store hours, zip codes, and guarantees.

When you write a brochure, don't forget the obvious. Often, seemingly minor details can mean the difference between a sale and a no-sale.

For instance, one company forgot to include its second telephone number in a direct-mail brochure. As a result, its phone was frequently busy when prospects called in to order the product, and many sales were lost.

When you're proofreading your brochure copy, be sure you've included the following items:

- Company logo, name, address, and phone number
- Street address in addition to box number
- Directions ("located on the corner of Fifth and Main off I-95")
- Prices, store hours, branch locations
- List of distributors, dealers, or sales reps
- Instructions for placing orders by phone or mail
- Credit cards accepted

- Product guarantees and warranties
- Shipping and service information
- Trademarks, registration marks, disclaimers, and other legal information
- Form numbers, dates, codes, copyright lines

Also, be sure to proofread for errors in spelling, punctuation, and grammar.

These details are important. For instance, mail-order firms know their sales can double when they add a toll-free number and "major credit cards accepted" to their brochures.

11. *Make the Brochure Worth Keeping*

When the customer receives your brochure, he can do one of three things:

Respond to it—by placing an order or asking for more information.

File it for future reference.

Or throw it away.

You want the first two things to happen. You want the customer to respond to your brochure. And you want him to save it for when he needs the product again in the future.

To get someone to save your brochure, you must write a brochure that is worth keeping.

Brochures that are worth keeping are valuable because of the information they contain. This information may be directly related to the product. Or it may be service information of a general nature that is indirectly related to the product.

For example, a brochure for a resort hotel in Montauk might print a detailed map of the town on the back cover. Travelers will save the brochure because of the map.

The literature package I mail to potential clients for my freelance copywriting services includes a reprint of an article I wrote ("Ten Tips For Writing More Effective Industrial Copy"). The reprint includes my picture, name, address, and phone number. Even if the prospect throws away the promotional part of my package, he is likely to keep the article because it contains information that may be useful to him in his work.

Most people don't have a good idea of how the stock market works. So if a broker published a booklet titled, "A Layman's Introduction to the Stock Market . . . and How to Play It," people would be likely to save this booklet. Later, when they accumulate enough money to invest in stocks, they would find the brochure in their files and call the broker to have him handle their business.

So, if you want your brochure to keep selling for you, make your brochure worth keeping.

HOW TO ORGANIZE YOUR BROCHURE

This is an oversimplification, but basically, there are only three type of brochures:

• Brochures about a product
• Brochures about a service
• Brochures about a company (known as "corporate" brochures or "capabilities" brochures)

The content and organization of every brochure is unique, because every selling situation and product, service, or company is unique.

However, many brochures share common characteristics. Most brochures describing consulting services, for example, include a list of the consultant's clients.

Below are three outlines for "typical" product, service, and company brochures. These will give you a rough idea of what to include in the sales literature you write for your clients.

For a Product Brochure

- Introduction—a capsule description of what the product is and why the reader of the brochure should be interested in it.

- Benefits—a list of reasons why the customer should buy the product.

- Features—highlights of important product features that set the product apart from the competition.

- "How it works"—a description of how the product works and what it can do. This section can include the results of any tests that demonstrate the product's superiority.

- Types of users (markets)—this section describes the special markets the product is designed for. A wastewater plant, for example, might be sold to municipalities, utilities, and industrial plants—three separate and distinct markets, each with its own special set of requirements.

  This section might also include an actual list of names of well-known people or organizations that use and endorse the product.

- Applications—descriptions of the various applications in which the product can be used.

- Product availability—lists of models, sizes, materials of construction, options, accessories, and all the variations in which you can order the product. This section can also include charts, graphs, formulas, or other guidelines to aid the reader in product selection.

- Pricing—information on what the product costs. Includes prices for accessories, various models and sizes, quantity discounts, and shipping and handling.

- Technical specifications—electrical requirements, power consumption, resistance to moisture, temperature range, operating conditions, cleaning methods, storage conditions, chemical properties, and other characteristics and limitations of the product.

· Questions and answers—answers to frequently asked questions about the product. Includes information not found in the other sections.

· Company description—a brief biography of the manufacturer, designed to show the reader that the product is backed by a solid, reputable organization that won't go out of business.

· Support—information on delivery, installation, training, maintenance, service, and guarantees.

· "The next step"—instructions on how to order the product (or on how to get more information on the product).

For a Brochure Describing a Service

· Introduction—outlines the services offered, types of accounts handled, and reasons why the reader should be interested in the service.

· Services offered—detailed descriptions of the various services offered by the firm.

· Benefits—describes what the reader will gain from the service and why he should engage the services of your firm instead of the competition.

· Methodology—outlines the service firm's method of doing business with clients.

· Client list—a list of well-known people or organizations who have used and endorse the firm's services.

· Testimonials—statements of endorsements from select clients. Testimonials are usually written in the client's own words, surrounded by quotation marks, and attributed to a specific person or organization.

· Fees and terms—describes the fees for each service and the terms and method of payment required. Also includes whatever guarantee the service firm makes to its clients.

- Biographical information—capsule biographies highlighting the credentials of the key employees of the service firm.
- "The next step"—instructions on what to do next if you are interested in hiring the firm or learning more about their services.

For a Corporate Brochure

The corporate brochure should contain information about:[1]

- The business or businesses the company is engaged in
- The corporate structure (parent company, divisions, departments, subsidiaries, branch offices)
- Corporate "philosophy"
- Company history
- Plants
- Geographical coverage
- Major markets
- Distribution system
- Sales
- Ranking in its fields relative to competition
- Extent of stock distribution
- Earnings and dividend records
- Number of employees
- Employee benefits
- Noteworthy employees
- Inventions
- Significant achievements (including industry "firsts")
- Research and development

- Quality control practices
- Community relations (environmental programs, contributions to public welfare, charitable activities, support of the arts, etc.)
- Awards
- Policies
- Objectives, goals, plans for the future

The above outlines are suggestions only, not mandatory formats. Mold them to suit your needs; let your product, audience, and sales objectives be your primary guide to content and organization of the copy.

CATALOGS

Catalogs are similar to brochures but with two important differences:

1. Brochures usually tell an in-depth story about a single product. Catalogs give short descriptions of many products. Because each item is given limited space, descriptions must be terse. Catalog copy is often written in a clipped, telegram-like style, with sentence fragments that convey a great deal of information in the fewest possible words.
2. The brochure's mission is usually to provide enough information to take the reader to the next step in the buying process. Most catalogs are mail-order vehicles from which you can order the product directly; salespeople are rarely involved. (The exception is the industrial product catalog.) As a result, a great deal of the copywriter's time is spent designing an order form that is easy to use and encourages the reader to send in an order.

Catalog writing is a separate art from brochure writing. The basics are the same but the mechanics are different. Here are a few tips to help you write successful catalogs:

Write Snappy Headlines

Even if space requires that your catalog headlines be short, you can still add selling power to them. Don't be content to simply describe the product in the headline; add a snappy phrase, a strong benefit, a descriptive adjective that hints at the product's distinct qualities.

In its order-by-mail book catalogs, Boardroom Books turns mundane book titles into strong, hard-selling catalog headlines. Instead of the "The Book of Tax Knowledge," they write, "3,147 Tax-Saving Ideas." For a book titled "Successful Tax Planning," the catalog description reads, "Did your tax accountant ever tell you all this?" And a book on how to buy computers is advertised with the provocative headline, "What the computer salesmen *don't* tell you."

Include a "Letter From the Manufacturer"

Many catalogs include a "personal" letter from the company president, either printed on letterhead and bound into the catalog or printed directly on one of the pages in the front of the catalog. In the letter, the president talks about the quality of the products in the catalog, the firm's commitment to serving its customers, and the manufacturer's guarantee of customer satisfaction. The letter may also be used as an introduction to the company's product line, or to call attention to a particular product or group of products that is especially noteworthy or attractively priced.

Here's a homey paragraph from a letter in an L.L. Bean catalog:

"L.L." had a simple business philosophy. "Sell good merchandise at a reasonable profit, treat your customers like human beings and they'll always come back for more." We call this "L.L.'s" golden rule. Today, 72 years later, we still practice it.

You can't help but be won over by the good sense of this honorable business philosophy and the sincerity of its statement. Putting a letter in your catalog adds warmth and a human quality to an otherwise impersonal presentation of product facts, specifications, and prices.

Give All the Facts

A catalog description must give the reader all the information he needs to order the product. This includes sizes, colors, materials, prices, and styles. The copy should also give the reader a concise but complete description of the product, so he can make a decision as to whether he wants to buy it.

Give the Most Space to Your Best Sellers

Devote a full page or half page to your best-selling items and list them up front. Less popular items get a quarter page or less and appear toward the back of the catalog. Items that don't sell should be dropped altogether.

Use Techniques that Stimulate Sales

These include toll-free phone numbers . . . credit card orders accepted . . . a gift to the customer for placing an order . . . two-for-one offers . . . arrows, stars, bursts, and other graphic devices used to highlight special discounts within the catalog . . . last-minute items added as a special insert sheet or printed on the order form . . . volume discount for large orders ("10% off when your order exceeds $25") . . . gift packaging available for merchandise ordered as gifts . . . special sale items featured on the order form.

Order Form Designed to Increase Response

Make the order form simple and easy to fill out. Give the customer sufficient space for writing in his order. Print step-by-step instructions for ordering right on the form. Print the guarantee in large type and set it off with a border. Provide a business reply envelope in which the customer can enclose his check.

If the Item Is Discounted, Indicate It in the Copy

One way of doing this is to write, "25% Off! Was $11.95—Now $8.95." Another is to cross out the old price and write in the new price—"~~$11.95.~~ $8.95."

OTHER TYPES OF SALES LITERATURE

Brochures and catalogs account for most of the sales literature published in the world.

Still, there are a few other types of sales literature you may be asked to write.

Annual Reports

Annual reports are summaries of the company's performance for the past year. They combine the company information found in "capabilities brochures" with financial data on the company's sales, profits, revenues, and dividends. Annual reports are usually lavish affairs, printed on glossy stock and featuring expensive four-color photography, sophisticated graphics, and stylish copy.

Flyers

Flyers are sales literature printed on one or two sides of an unfolded 8½- by 11-inch piece of paper. Visuals, if used, are limited to simple line drawings. Flyers are used as handouts at conventions and trade shows or as bulletins posted around the neighborhood. Many small businesses find flyers an inexpensive way of reaching new customers.

Broadsides

Broadsides are flyers folded for mailing. Companies that maintain mailing lists of customers often send monthly broadsides announcing sales, new products, or other news of interest to their customers.

Invoice Stuffers

Invoice stuffers are small pieces of promotional literature designed to fit in #10 envelopes. They are mailed to customers along with the monthly bill or statement and used to announce a sale or solicit mail-order sales of a special item. The advantage of using invoice stuffers is that they get a "free ride" in the mail because they're sent with routine correspondence rather than in separate mailings.

Circulars

Circulars are printed advertising sheets that are mailed, inserted in packages or newspapers, or distributed by hand. They are usually four to eight pages long, printed in color, and contain price-off coupons for products sold in local retail outlets.

Pamphlets

Also called booklets, pamphlets are similar to brochures, except they usually contain useful information of a general nature while brochures describe the features and benefits of specific products and services.

9

Writing Public Relations Material

"Do you also write press releases?"

Although public relations is a different discipline than advertising, they overlap, and every copywriter is asked to write press releases or other public relations materials at some point.

To the copywriter trained in hard-sell persuasive writing, the soft-sell touch of PR writing takes some getting used to.

Advertising reaches the reader directly and makes a blatant, undisguised pitch to part him from his money.

Press releases are sent to *editors*, not advertising departments, in the hopes the editors will publish them in their magazines or papers.

Once you send out a release, you have no control over when it will appear, in what form it will appear, or even whether it will appear. The editor can publish the release as is, rewrite it or cut it as he pleases, use it as the basis for a different story, or ignore it altogether.

The editor has total control, and, unlike the publication's advertising department, has no interest in helping you promote your firm.

The editor's only concern is publishing a magazine or paper filled with news and information of interest to his readers. If your press release contains such news or information, he is likely to use it. If the release is just a warmed-over ad, he will recognize it as such and trash it.

Companies new to public relations ask me, "Do editors really use press releases?" The answer is that they do. *The Columbia Journalism Review* surveyed an issue of *The Wall Street Journal* to find out how many of the stories were generated by press releases. The survey revealed that 111 stories on the inside pages were taken from press releases, either word for word or paraphrased. In only 30 percent of these stories did reporters put in additional facts not contained in the original release.[1]

There are no figures on how many press releases are generated each year, but my guess is that it runs into the hundreds of thousands—maybe even the millions.

One reason why press releases are so popular is that they are inexpensive. To print a one-page release and mail it to a hundred editors costs less than $30.

If an editor picks up your release and runs it as a short article in his magazine, your firm receives the space free. Running an ad of the same size could cost hundreds or even thousands of dollars.

What's more, publicity is more credible than paid advertising. The public has a built-in skepticism for advertising but is trained to believe almost everything they read in the paper or hear on TV. They do not realize that most of the news they read and hear is generated by press releases—releases sent out by the same firms that run ads and commercials.

But there is no *guarantee* that a press release will be picked up by the media or, once picked up, will generate much interest or new business.

Some releases are ignored; others generate spectacular results. When Leisure Time Ice, a trade association of ice manufacturers, sent out a press kit claiming that packaged ice is clearer and purer than homemade ice, the head of the association was interviewed by at least 25 editors and appeared on 15 radio and TV talk shows. *The Wall Street Journal, The New York Times, Los Angeles Times,* United Press International, and Associated Press all ran feature stories on Leisure Time Ice. The association's membership increased by 10 percent. And sales of manufactured ice went up.[2]

More and more firms are using publicity to promote their products and services. Even professionals who traditionally look down at public relations—doctors, lawyers, architects, engineers, management consultants—are now writing releases, placing stories, and appearing on radio and TV talk shows. (A recent survey of 523 members of the American Bar Association revealed that 20 percent of these lawyers use publicity to promote their practices.[3])

WHAT, EXACTLY, IS A PRESS RELEASE?

A press release is a printed news story prepared by an organization and distributed to the media for the purpose of publicizing the organization's products, services, or activities.

Here's a sample of an effective release typed in the proper press-release format:

```
FROM:  Kirsch Communications, 226 Seventh
Street, Garden City, N.Y. 11530
      For more information please call: Len
            Kirsch, 516/248-4055
```

FOR: Pinwheel Systems, 404 Park Avenue
South, New York, N.Y. 10016
   Contact: John N. Schaedler, President,
                   212/684-5140

                         FOR IMMEDIATE RELEASE
11/4/77

INTRODUCTORY KIT FOR NEW ''RUFF-PROOFS''
COLOR COMPS OFFERED BY PINWHEEL SYSTEMS

A special Introductory Kit of watercolor
dyes and other supplies which can be used
with its new ''Ruff-Proofs'' do-it-yourself
coloring system has been developed by Pinwheel Systems, New York, it was announced
today by John N. Schaedler, president of the
company.

Ruff-Proofs are latent-image prints made
from black and white artwork. They can be
transformed into multi-color art for layout
and design comps, packaging, flip charts and
other graphics, Schaedler said, merely by
applying watercolor dyes or markers. (Patents are pending on the process.) The prints
are delivered in sets of four to give the
artist an opportunity to experiment with
different colors and explore varying color
combinations. They are available from fran-
chised Pinwheel Studios.

The Introductory Kit has a retail value
of $45.00, Schaedler said, and is being of-
fered to artists and designers for $20.00
with the purchase of Ruff-Proofs. It contains a complete set of coloring materials:

• A 36-bottle assortment of Dr. P.H. Mar-
  tin's Synchromatic Transparent Watercolor
  Dyes, with a swatch card of actual color
  chips

- A 30-cup palette for mixing colors, squeeze-
  bottle dispensers for water and clean-up
  solution, plus absorbent tissues and cotton
  swabs used in the coloring process.

  More information about the kits and the
Ruff-Proofs process is available from John
Schaedler at Pinwheel Systems, 404 Park Avenue South, New York, N.Y., telephone
212/684-5140.

Len Kirsch, author of the above release, gives these 12
tips on press-release format and content.

1. What you say is more important than using fancy
   printed PR letterheads or layouts. Clarity and accuracy are critical.
2. When an outside public relations firm writes the
   release for you, its name and your own should appear as the sources for the release. If you wrote
   the release yourself, you become the source for
   more information. Either way, be sure to include
   names and phone numbers so the editor can get
   more information if he needs it.
3. The release can be dated with a release date or with
   the phrase "For Immediate Release." Date one day
   in advance of the actual mailing to make it timely.
4. Leave as much space as possible between the release date and the headline (to give the editor room
   to write instructions to his typesetter).
5. The headline should sum up your story. Maximum length: two to three lines. This tells a busy
   editor, at a glance, if the story is worth considering.
6. The lead contains the "who, what, when, where,
   why and how." If the editor chops everything else,
   at least you've gotten the guts of your story across.

7. Include a person to be credited if there's something worth quoting or if you make any claims. Editors don't want to take the position *they* are claiming something . . . they'd rather hang it on you. The personal credits often get deleted, but it's wise to put them in where needed.

8. The body of the story picks up the additional facts. Lay off the superlatives and complimentary adjectives. "We're dealing with news space, not advertising where you can say anything you want as long as it isn't indecent, immoral, or fattening," says Len.

9. Length: Shoot for a single page, no more than two pages. Beyond that, reading becomes a burden for the editor. If you go to a second page, put the word "more" at the bottom of page 1 to let the editor know that there is more to the story (in case the pages get separated). Put an abbreviated version of the headline (one or two words) and the page number in the upper left-hand corner of the second page.

10. When the reader might need it, include the name, address, and phone number of someone to contact for more information (this usually appears in the last paragraph of your story). Also indicate the end of the story by writing "-END-," "###," or "-30-" after the last line of the text.

11. If you use photos, type up a photo caption on a separate piece of paper and attach it to the back of the photo with transparent tape. Be sure to include your sources, contacts, and release date on the caption sheet.

12. Keep the release simple, straightforward, newsy. If you need only two paragraphs, don't write ten. Excess verbiage turns editors off.[4]

"YES, BUT WHAT'S NEWSY?"

Len and I have been saying that editors look for press releases containing *news*.

Like a good ad, the headline of the press release must instantly transmit the news to the reader. Editors are flooded with press releases and don't have time to wade through your release and dig for the real story. (Pamela Clark, Editor-in-Chief of *Popular Computing*, says her staff receives 2,000 press releases a month.[5]) The release must telegraph the news in the first five seconds of reading.

But what makes for a news story? It depends on your industry and your audience.

Forbes and *Fortune* would not consider publication of your new ball-bearing catalog to be news. But the editors of *Machine Design, Design News,* and other trade magazines whose readers use ball bearings might very well run a short news release on the catalog and a picture of its cover.

One thing that is *not* news is advertising and promotion. Editors will not publish descriptive stories about your product, service, or organization unless the story tells them something new, or provides service information useful to the publication's readers.

A press release with the headline, "Ajax Dry Cleaners Provides Top Quality Cleaning at Reasonable Prices" will probably not generate any coverage. But if Ajax sent out a release titled "Ajax Dry Cleaners Offer Expert Advice on How to Remove Tough Stains," the editor of your local paper's home section might reprint the advice as a how-to article. Ajax gets publicity by being listed as the source of the expert advice. (And Ajax can also use reprints of the article as fliers or direct mail.)

Here is a list of possible topics for news releases about your company. They all hold interest because they contain either news, or useful information, or both.

You can write a press release about:

- A new product
- An old product with a new name or package
- A product improvement
- A new version or model of an old product
- An old product available in new materials, colors, or sizes
- A new application of an old product
- New accessories available for an old product
- The publication of new or revised sales literature—brochures, catalogs, data sheets, surveys, reports, reprints, booklets
- A speech or presentation given by an executive
- An expert opinion on any subject
- A controversial issue
- New employees
- Promotions within the firm
- Awards and honors won by your organization or its employees
- Original discoveries or innovations (such as patents)
- New stores, branch offices, headquarters, facilities
- New sales reps, distributors, agents
- Major contracts awarded to your firm
- Joint ventures
- Management reorganization
- Major achievements, such as number of products sold, increase in sales, quarterly earnings, safety record
- Unusual people, products, ways of doing business
- Case histories of successful applications, installations, projects
- Tips and hints ("how-to" advice)
- Change of company name, slogan, or logo
- Opening of a new business

- Special events such as a sale, party, open house, plant tour, contest, or sweepstakes
- Charitable acts or other community relations

The only type of press release that does not need to contain news is the "background release" or "backgrounder." Backgrounders present a brief (three to five pages) overview of your company. They are not mailed alone but are included with other releases when editors want background information on your company.

Even though the backgrounder is not, strictly speaking, a news story, you should try to put *something* new, or at least some little-known fact or startling piece of information in the backgrounders you write. This will grab an editor's interest more strongly than a bland summary of your organizational chart.

Another special type of press release is the "fact sheet." Fact sheets contain detailed information, usually in list form, too lengthy to be included in the body of the main release.

A press release announcing the opening of a new gourmet food store might be mailed with a fact sheet listing recipes for three or four of the store's specialties. A fact sheet for a consulting firm could contain a list of clients or brief biographies of the firm's principals.

QUESTIONS AND ANSWERS ABOUT PRESS RELEASES

Here are some questions I'm frequently asked by companies who are just getting into public relations:

What's the Best Length for a Press Release?

For a new product release, one to two pages. If you have a lot to tell, three pages is acceptable. But certainly no longer than that.

Case histories and backgrounders usually run longer—three to five pages is average.

If it takes more than five pages to tell your story, make it a feature article, not a press release.

Should I Print the Release on My Stationery or on a Special PR Letterhead? Or Can I Just Use Regular Paper?

Some companies design special forms for their news releases. But this doesn't increase the release's chance of being published. You are better off printing on plain white paper.

Some novices print their releases on purple, pink, or other brightly colored paper, hoping this will make the release stand out from the crowd. It has the *opposite* effect; editors are turned off by this gimmicky approach to serious news-gathering.

Is There One "Right" Format for Typing the Release?

Formats vary, and there's no "official" format you must follow. Just make sure your release is typed double-spaced, neatly, and with no misspellings or typos. The format in Len Kirsch's release for Ruff-Proofs is a good one to follow.

Should I Enclose a Letter with the Release?

No. It's not necessary. The editor is accustomed to receiving releases and knows what to do with yours. If you feel a need to explain the content of your release, you haven't done a good job writing the story.

Is it Better if the Release Comes from a PR Firm or Straight from the Company?

What counts is not who wrote the release, but whether the release contains interesting news clearly presented.

Some people have a theory that editors are wary of dealing with public relations people and prefer to go straight to the source. I know a few editors who do feel this way. But the majority don't.

How Do I Reproduce the Release?

Offset printing is best and doesn't cost very much (about $5 per 100 copies of a one-page release). Photocopies are acceptable if they are crisp, sharp, and free of smudges or streaks.

Do I Need to Send a Photo Out With My Release?

It's helpful but not mandatory. An interesting photo of a product, person, plant, process, or package will heighten the editor's interest. Remember, most magazines and papers publish pictures as well as words.

Photos should be glossy, black-and-white, and 8 by 10 inches. Color is better, but expensive. To save money, take both color and black-and-white; then mail out the black-and-white and write "color photos available upon request" at the end of the release. This way, you'll be sending costly color prints only to those magazines that ask for them.

WRITING A FEATURE STORY

Copywriters also get called upon to "ghostwrite" full-length feature stories for trade and business publications.

Take a look at *Byte, Chemical Engineering,* and other trade journals.

They contain many articles written by outside contributors—scientists, engineers, managers, and other professionals employed by companies.

These contributors write not for pay (most trade journals pay a small honorarium or nothing at all) but to promote their own careers as well as the companies they work for.

Many companies have a regular, scheduled program

of placing feature articles in magazines. And they hire professional writers to ghostwrite these articles.

Although each article is different, there are four basic types of articles that magazines publish:

1. Case Histories

A case history article is a product "success story." It tells the story of how a product, service, or system was helpful to a specific customer.

"Case history reporting derives its effectiveness from the principle that what works for one customer company might work for others," explains Jim Hayes, a writer-photographer specializing in case histories. "Case histories are effective, too, because they're credible. They deal in specifics rather than in claims or generalities. Finally, case histories are an inherently story-telling approach to selling."

Here's how a typical case history article gets started:

A telephone manufacturer installs a new office phone system in a sales office. The office manager finds that the new system has increased the productivity of the sales force 25 percent and cut phone bills in half.

When the telephone manufacturer gets wind of this, he asks the office manager if he can write up this success story and place it with an appropriate trade journal. If the office manager agrees, the telephone maker hires a writer.

The writer interviews the office manager at the sales firm and writes the story. After it is approved, it is submitted to the magazine and published. The byline may be that of the manufacturer, the office manager, or the writer. It depends on the nature of the article.

2. How-to Articles

These provide useful information that helps the reader do something better ("How to Choose the Right Computer for Your Small Business," "Seven Ways to Cut Energy Costs," "A Guide to Ball-Bearing Selection").

How-to articles are also known as "tutorials," perhaps because they tutor the reader in a new skill or area of knowledge.

The how-to article does not discuss your product directly (your company shouldn't even be mentioned, except in the byline). Instead, it promotes you indirectly by establishing your firm's reputation as a leader in the field.

Readers tend to clip and save "how-to" articles. So, although your article may not generate immediate business, people will keep it for years and call on you when the need arises.

3. Issue Articles

In issue articles, industry experts speak out on some topical, controversial, or technical issue of the day. These articles help strengthen your company's image as a leader in its field.

4. News

News articles are usually prepared by staff editors and reporters, not outsiders. Occasionally, though, a corporation with big news to report—a merger, an acquisition, a revolutionary new invention—will work with a reporter to develop a feature story. The reporter gets a scoop, while the company gets good press.

QUERY LETTERS

The first step in getting a feature story published in a magazine is to get an editor interested in the article topic.

This means first suggesting the topic to the editor, either in a phone conversation or by letter.

Some editors will listen to your pitch over the phone. Most want to see the idea written up in a short proposal known as a "query letter."

The query letter is a one- or two-page outline, in letter form, of the article you propose to write.

The query letter explains what the article is about, what your "angle" is, why the magazine's readers will be interested in the article, and what makes you qualified to write it.

The letter is also a demonstration of your writing style. Boring query letters rarely result in an article assignment, because the editor assumes your article will be as boring as your letter.

Here is a sample of a query that got me an assignment to write an article for *Amtrak Express:*

March 24, 1983

Mr. James A. Frank, Editor
AMTRAK EXPRESS
34 East 51st Street
New York, NY 10022

Dear Mr. Frank:

Is this letter a waste of paper?

Yes—if it fails to get the desired result.

In business, most letters and memos are written to generate a specific response—close a sale, set up a meeting, get a job interview, make a contact. Many of these letters fail to do their job.

Part of the problem is that business executives and support staff don't know how to write persuasively. The solution is a formula first discovered by advertising copywriters—a formula called AIDA. AIDA stands for Attention, Interest, Desire, Action.

First, the letter gets attention . . . with a hard-hitting lead paragraph that goes straight to the point, or offers an element of intrigue.

Then, the letter hooks the reader's interest. The hook is often a clear statement of the reader's problems, his needs, his desires. If you are writing to a customer who received damaged goods, state the problem. And then promise a solution.

Next, create desire. You are offering something—a service, a product, an agreement, a contract, a compromise, a consultation. Tell the reader the benefit he'll receive from your offering. Create a demand for your product.

Finally, call for action. Ask for the order, the signature, the check, the assignment.

I'd like to give you a 1500-word article on ''How to Write Letters That Get Results.'' The piece will illustrate the AIDA formula with a variety of actual letters and memos from insurance companies, banks, manufacturers, and other organizations.

This letter, too, was written to get a specific result—an article assignment from the editor of AMTRAK EXPRESS.

Did it succeed?

Regards,

Bob Bly

P.S. By way of introduction, I'm an advertising consultant and the author of five books including TECHNICAL WRITING: STRUCTURE, STANDARDS, AND STYLE (McGraw-Hill).

Editors usually respond to query letters within a month or so. (If a month goes by and you haven't heard, follow up with another letter or a phone call.)

A positive response to a query is, "Your proposed article idea interests us. Send a manuscript."

This means the editor wants to see the article. It doesn't mean he has promised to publish it. He won't make that decision until after he's read it. *A positive response to a query letter is no guarantee that your article will be printed.*

If the editor turns down your proposal, you can retype the query letter and send it to other publications. Few article ideas are restricted to one magazine only. Most are appropriate to at least half a dozen publications or more.

HOW TO WRITE A SPEECH

Business executives don't always express themselves by writing articles. Sometimes they make speeches. And, as with article writing, executives often hire ghostwriters to write their speeches for them.

When I got my first speech-writing assignment, I was paralyzed with fear because I had no idea how long—in minutes or words—a speech should be.

Now I do. The average speaker speaks at a rate of 100 words a minute. It follows that a 20-minute speech should be 2,000 words long (about eight double-spaced, typewritten pages).

The best length of time for a speech is 20 minutes. Less seems insubstantial. More can get boring. No speech, no matter how important, should last more than an hour.

Every speech should have a clear-minded purpose. Most speeches are given to entertain, to teach, to persuade, or to inspire.

Speeches are effective at getting across ideas, opinions, and emotions. They are less effective at transmitting a large body of facts (print is the appropriate medium for that).

Here are some additional tips for writing speeches that accomplish their goals without boring the audience to tears.

1. Find Out What the Speaker Wants to Say

Few writing assignments are as personal—or as idiosyncratic—as writing someone else's speech. You'll avoid headaches if you take the time to know the speaker's requirements before you sit down to write.

"You have to ask the right questions of your client to prepare a speech that he'll deliver as if he really means it," writes freelancer Nancy Edmonds Hanson. "Sometimes a lengthy discussion of the topic is necessary before the client himself clarifies his position on it. Your job is to probe, to ask him to carry his own thoughts a little further until he's worked the topic through in his own mind."[6]

Interviews with the client reveal the basic thrust of the speech and provide most of the facts. Information gaps can be filled in through library research or by browsing through the client's private files on the subject.

2. Know Your Audience

Learn as much as you can about the group you'll be speaking to. This will help you tailor your talk to their specific interests.

For example, a speech on videotext should be geared toward the professional interests of the audience. Engineers are interested in the technology—how it works. Advertising executives want to know more about videotext as an advertising medium. Bankers are curious as to whether banking by interactive television will become a reality.

3. Write a Great Opening

The first sentence uttered by the speaker is like the headline of an advertisement or the lead paragraph of a direct-mail piece. An engaging opening grabs attention and gets the audience enthusiastic about your topic. A bland opening is a turn off.

4. Then, There's Humor

Speechwriters are always uncertain when it comes to using humor. They know that humor can quickly warm an audience to the speaker. But a joke that bombs can ruin the whole talk.

My advice is to pepper the speech with little tidbits of warm, gentle, good-natured humor. Not big gags, old jokes, or nightclub-comic routines. Just a few well-chosen, humorous comments that make the speaker seem a bit more human.

Never lead off with a prepared joke. Chances are, it will fall flat because the audience isn't expecting it. Worse, people will think you are there to clown and have nothing important to say.

5. Don't Try to Cover Too Much

Remember, a 20-minute speech has only 2,000 words—just eight pages of double-spaced manuscript. Add to this the fact that the spoken word is not as compact as written English, and you see that there's only so much information you can put in your talk.

Don't try to cover your whole subject. Just break off a little piece of it and tell your story with warmth, wit, humor, and authority. Delete trivial information and limit your talk to the important key points.

For example, "Your Career" is too broad a topic for a speech. "How to Break Into the Advertising Business" is a more manageable subject for an after-dinner talk.

Also, don't put too many numbers, statistics, or figures in your talk. Math doesn't make for a memorable speech.

6. Write in Conversational Tone

Speeches are to be heard, not read. A speech is one person talking—and it should *sound* like talking, not like an academic thesis or a corporate memorandum.

Write in a conversational tone. That means short words. Short sentences. Plenty of contractions. Even a colloquial expression every now and then.

The best test of a speech is to read it aloud. If it doesn't sound natural, rewrite it until it does.

Use bullets, headings, and numbers to divide the speech into sections. The speaker can catch his breath during the pauses between sections.

If the copy can't be broken up this way, then indicate places where the speaker can pause between paragraphs. These stops give nervous speakers a chance to slow down.

7. *Keep It Simple*

A speech is not the appropriate medium for delivering complex ideas and sophisticated theories.

For one thing, a speech is limited in the amount of information it can contain. For another, the listener can't stop to ponder a point or go back to information presented earlier (as he can when reading an article, ad, or brochure).

Ideally, your speech should be centered around one main point or theme. If a fact or observation doesn't tie in with this point, throw it out.

Give the listener easy-to-grasp tidbits of information and advice. Don't try to get the audience to follow a rigorous mathematical proof, a complex argument, or a complicated process. They won't.

8. *What About Visual Aids?*

When I worked in the corporate world in the 1970s, slides were the rage. No speaker would think of giving a presentation without a carousel full of brightly colored slides to back him up.

In some cases, slides can be useful. If you want to introduce the new corporate logo, you must show a slide or a chart; words alone can't adequately describe a graphic concept.

But slides often seem to hinder the speaker. Instead of acting relaxed and giving the talk at a natural pace, the speaker has to match his pace with that of the slide presentation.

Worse, in most 20-minute speeches, only two or three slides are really needed to communicate. So the rest of the carousel is filled with "word slides." The word slides use bulleted phrases that highlight key phrases from the speech and are completely unnecessary.

Another problem with visual aids is that they put the speaker completely at the mercy of mechanical devices— slides that get stuck in their trays; film projectors with bulbs that burn out; overhead transparencies that smudge in sweaty palms; unsteady flip-chart easels that collapse at the slightest touch. These mechanical disasters can ruin a speech. And they are not uncommon.

When I speak I do not use visual aids, and I advise my clients to do the same. Slides, flip-charts, and overheads hinder more than they help.

9. Handouts

Do not distribute your handouts until *after* the speech is over. If you distribute them beforehand, the audience will read the handouts and ignore the speaker.

A typed or typeset copy of your speech, cleanly reprinted on good-quality white paper, is the best handout you can give. If you don't have time to prepare copies of the speech, then distribute reprints of articles you've written on the same topic as the one covered in your talk.

10. Pick a Catchy Title for Your Speech

When you speak, you'll lead off with the first sentence, not the title.

But the title will be used in mailings, flyers, and other promotions aimed at attracting an audience for your talk. "The name of your speech can make the difference between an empty house and an attentive crowd," notes Ron

Huff, Executive Creative Director of Foote, Cone & Belding, New York.[7]

"Effective Management of Overseas Trade Show Exhibits" is a boring title. "How to Set Up a Booth at a Japanese Electronics Show—and Live to Tell About It" is much more enticing.

WRITING NEWSLETTERS

Many organizations publish newsletters that they distribute free to customers, clients, prospects, employees, journal editors, and decision makers in their industries.

The stories in these newsletters are similar in tone and content to the press releases and feature stories we've discussed. They are designed to promote, either directly or indirectly, the organization and its activities, services, or products.

The newsletter has less credibility than a story appearing in a trade magazine because readers know it is self-published by the firm.

On the other hand, a company can use the newsletter to say whatever it wants without fear of being censored, rewritten, or misquoted by an editor.

Newsletters do not tend to generate leads or sales. Rather, they build your image and reputation with a select group of prospects (those who receive the newsletter) over a period of time.

For this reason, the newsletter is usually the first item to be cut when a company's advertising program goes over budget.

Many clients start out with ambitious plans to publish the newsletter on a regular basis—every quarter, every other month, every month.

But when production costs run over budget for the new corporate brochure or product catalog, the ad manager will make up the difference by skipping an issue or two of his newsletter.

Companies try to lure freelancers and agencies to do their newsletters for a low price with the logic, "It's not as key as advertising or direct mail so we can't afford to spend a lot. But we'll make up the difference with volume, since it's a steady thing."

Writers and agencies should approach newsletters with caution. Often a promised assignment of six newsletters turns into two.

The typical newsletter is four pages long. Text is set in two or three columns, and there is little or no white space. There are three or four major feature stories (about 1,000 words each), a few short items (two to three paragraphs), and a number of photos with captions.

Most of the stories are not written especially for the newsletter but come from other sources: press releases, condensed feature articles, speeches, case histories, sales literature, ad campaigns. In this way, the newsletter gives additional exposure to messages you're communicating in other media.

Let's take a look at some examples.

My bank, Manufacturers Hanover Trust, publishes a newsletter called "As a Matter of Fact: A Consumer Newsletter With Money Facts for You." I pick it up from a rack whenever I'm standing on line to make a deposit.

The newsletter is filled with helpful information on personal finance. Recent articles include "The Mortgage Maze," "The 10% Factor . . . The Facts Behind Withholding Taxes On Interest," "Recovering from the Recession," and "The Pathway to Investing."

The relationship between a bank and its customers is based on trust. By providing investment counseling at no cost through their newsletter, Manufacturers Hanover is helping to cement that relationship.

My local supermarket, The Food Emporium, publishes a four-page newsletter on food; I pick it up at the checkout counter. It contains tips on nutrition, exercise, food shopping, and cooking. Each issue also features a number of recipes.

By helping me exercise and eat right, Food Emporium gains my good will. By giving me recipes, they get me to come into their store to buy more food.

American Express encloses its newsletter "For Members Only" with my monthly bill. The cover usually features an interview with a prominent figure who discusses an issue of the day or some other intriguing topic (recent issues featured Bill Moyers on creativity and Dr. Daniel Bell on the high-tech revolution). Inside are tips on traveling, dining out, and other leisure activities for which I pay with my American Express Card.

Gas Energy Inc., a division of Brooklyn Union Gas, publishes a newsletter, "Energy Decisions," which it sends to architects, engineers, building owners, and managers responsible for making energy decisions. Articles are a blend of tips (on how to cut building heating and cooling costs) and product stories (on the company's own energy-saving equipment).

These examples give you an idea of the types of stories published in promotional newsletters. The checklist below can serve as a source of ideas for putting together your own newsletter.

A Checklist of Newsletter Story Ideas

- News
- Explanatory articles ("how it works")
- Product stories
- Case histories
- Background information
- How to solve a problem
- Technical tips for using the product
- General how-to information and advice
- Do's and don'ts; checklists
- Industry updates

- Employee news
- Employee profiles
- Community relations news
- Financial news
- Roundup of recent sales activities
- Interviews and profiles
- Letters column
- Announcements or write-ups of conferences, seminars, trade shows, meetings
- Photos with captions
- Product selection guides

10

Writing Commercials

Writing television commercials is the most prestigious assignment in all of advertising. To a copywriter, getting a chance to write a commercial for a major prime-time advertiser is like a minor-league baseball player getting to pitch for the Yankees.

As a writer who has spent 95 percent of his career writing *print* advertising, I acknowledge this fact with a sigh. Personally, I believe print advertising has far more selling power than TV and that there is no greater challenge than writing a print ad that brings back checks, orders, or people to the store.

However, I recognize that you are eager to find out how to write good television as well as print. And so I have combined my limited TV experience with the thinking of colleagues, consultants, and other experts to come up with advice you may find useful.

Keep in mind, however, that television is not as dominant over print as you think. True, in 1981 nearly $13 billion was spent on television advertising versus only $3.5 billion for magazine advertising.

But $17.4 billion was spent on newspaper advertising. So print still beats TV by a healthy margin.

On the other hand, a lot more money goes into the production of a TV commercial than is spent on a print ad. Commercials today cost $40,000 to $125,000 and up to produce, while the average four-color magazine ad costs about $7,500.

THE CASE FOR MORE INFORMATION

Today, more commercials are competing for our attention than ever before. In 1983, advertisers ran 19,650 different TV commercials on prime-time network television.[1]

The challenge is to make your commercial stand out from the rest and attract the consumer's attention. But advertisers are unsure as to how to do this.

One school believes the "creative" approach is the solution to TV's clutter. Dramatic stories, fast-paced action, surreal fantasy landscapes, animation, computer graphics, the "new wave" look, and other techniques are used to give commercials distinct graphic appeal—often, in my opinion, at the expense of the sales pitch. These commercials do stand out, but they don't sell, because they tend to ignore the product and its appeal to the consumer.

A second school embraces old-fashioned values. They believe that simple commercials, with honest and straightforward presentations of the product and its benefits, are what convince consumers to write checks and open wallets. One recent example is MCI's commercials using Burt

Lancaster and Joan Rivers to deliver the pitch. No fancy computer graphics, no blue jeans turning into rocket-ships—just good old-fashioned selling that works.

Many advertising experts are rising to defend the straightforward approach to TV commercials. Faith Popcorn, President of BrainReserve Advertising in New York, predicts that the 1980s and 1990s will be an age of product intelligence, in which consumers will demand real information, "real sell."

Faith Popcorn and many others believe a new type of commercial—the "informmercial"—may change our approach to TV advertising. Thanks to the low cost of buying time on cable television stations, advertisers can now afford to run long, information-filled commercials that are five minutes in length or more.

At last, advertisers will be able to use television to give the complete information and sales pitch previously confined to print advertising. With new "interactive" technology, viewers might be able to choose which segments of an informmercial they wish to view, much as they flip through the pages of a catalog. And they will certainly be able to use their computer keyboards to order products or sales literature direct through their TV sets.

I predict that if the air time is affordable and the technology catches on, informmercials will become a popular advertising medium. And this popularity will prove that consumers are hungry for real information about products, not just hype and hoopla.

Today's commercials don't fill this need. According to one study, 85 percent of those surveyed said commercials are funny or clever. But 68 percent of these people said commercials don't give them any facts but just create an image.[2]

Not everyone in advertising believes commercials should be informative. On a recent Phil Donahue show, advertising executive Anne Tolstoi Wallach was asked why advertisers don't make commercials that are plain, blunt, and honest, with no frills.

Wallach replied that information alone is not remembered. She pointed out that teenagers have been exposed to a continuous stream of antidrug information, yet drug use is on the rise. "We don't take things in through information," said Wallach, "We take things in emotionally and in many other ways even we are not sure [of]." (Later in the broadcast, Donahue remarked, "Style and form get more attention than substance.")[3]

As an example, Wallach pointed to the Calvin Klein jeans commercials featuring Brooke Shields. She said the commercials were successful because of "one gorgeous girl and the world's greatest photographer."

It's true that certain ads and commercials achieve dramatic results by breaking the rules. But these successes are unpredictable. Only by knowing and using what works do copywriters achieve consistently high sales results.

And I disagree with the statement that people don't take in things through information. Browse the shelves of your local bookstore—you'll find that "how-to" and straight informational type books dominate the publishing industry. What's more, the authors of these books don't resort to trickery, grandstanding, or gimmicks; they tell their story through a straightforward presentation of the facts. They know that the real customer for their book is someone who wants and needs the information it contains.

And so it is with products. The *serious* prospect is an information seeker; she wants to be well informed before she spends her hard-earned dollars. Too many commercials waste their effort pitching to the *non*prospect— someone who is unlikely to turn into a paying customer.

Advertisers emulate the showmanship and production values of Hollywood feature films in their efforts to get these nonprospects to watch their commercials. They forget that the goal is not to get people to watch—it is to get people to buy or to prefer one brand to another. Long ago, David Ogilvy and other advertising pioneers proved there is no correlation between a person *liking* a commercial and being *sold* by it.

There are numerous examples of factual commercials outselling entertaining ones. Malcolm D. MacDougall, who produced commercials for Ronald Reagan's 1980 presidential campaign, tells how the campaign was built entirely on direct, factual, tough commercials that worked. According to MacDougall, research showed that hardhitting, informative commercials were far more effective in selling Reagan for president than a soft-sell image commercial they had run early in the campaign.[4]

"I have wondered often if 'creativity' doesn't sometimes get in the way of believability," writes *Advertising Age* columnist Sid Bernstein in a recent column on TV commercials. "I have a feeling that what we really need is more simplicity. More simple, honest selling. More dignity, more clarity. Less confusion . . . less emphasis on sensational entertainment and more emphasis on making a sensible buy."[5]

Some advertisers hope to make their campaigns stand out by spending large sums of money to produce lavish, dazzling commercials. But a big budget is no guarantee of success, nor does a small budget doom you to failure. TV's longest running commercial, the one offering the record set of "150 Music Masterpieces" by mail, was made in 1968 for $5,000. To date, it has sold $25 million worth of records.

THE 12 TYPES OF COMMERCIALS

I've always thought writing fiction was an original act, one that didn't fit into a formula.

But in a recent class on writing for the screen, the instructor surprised the class by saying, "I know you think what you've written is very special. But people who write and produce films have documented just 36 dramatic situations. All screenplays can be put in one of these categories." She listed some of the categories as *revolution*, *madness, crimes of love, ambition, remorse, disaster,* and *adultery.*

Although TV commercials seemingly offer infinite variety, there are less TV-commercial formats than there are screenplay situations. Twelve of these are described below.

1. Demonstrations

Demonstrations show how a product works. If you are selling a food processor, you show how quickly and easily it slices, dices, blends, and mixes.

Demonstrations are effective for comparing two products. On the left of the screen, you show how sticky and dull most car waxes are. On the right, you show how easy your wax goes on, how brightly it shines, and how it repels water like a duck.

Demonstrations can be quite dramatic. A commercial for HTH pool chlorinator showed a woman sitting by a pool as the voice-over told how crystal clear HTH makes pool water. Suddenly, the woman shoots up and swims up through the water. We find out she was actually *in* the pool and that the commercial was shot underwater, dramatically demonstrating the clarity of water treated with HTH.

Demonstrations are powerful sales boosters. Mail-order advertisers know the best way to motivate a viewer to pick up the phone and order a product is with a straightforward demonstration commercial.

2. Testimonials

Testimonials are used to add credibility to a claim. People more readily believe praise for a product when it comes from a customer or a third party rather than the manufacturer.

The most effective testimonials are those featuring real people who use and like the product. Real people are more believable than paid actors or "staged" interviews. To get genuine testimonials from real product users, commercial producers use hidden cameras to film reactions to product use and answers to questions.

Many advertisers pay celebrities to endorse their products, reasoning that celebrities draw attention and that people hang on their every word.

The jury is still out on celebrity advertising. Steve Wynn has had great success promoting his casino with celebrity-spokesman Frank Sinatra. Many other celebrity commercials—most recently Glenn Ford for Avis—have been failures.

Commercial makers do agree that a celebrity must be right for the product. Michael Jackson can generate excitement for Pepsi, but is less appropriate for investment-banking commercials.

3. Stand-up Presenter

Also known as a "talking head" or "pitchman." In this type of commercial, an actor stands before the camera and delivers a straightforward sales pitch on the virtues of the product.

The stand-up presenter can be especially effective when the sales pitch you have is so strong that it doesn't need to be gussied up. MCI uses stand-up presenter Burt Lancaster to deliver one single, powerful sales fact—that MCI long distance reaches all the places AT&T does but costs at least 30 percent less.

4. Slice-of-life

The slice of life is a miniature play centering around two or more people and a story involving the product. In one toothpaste commercial, a little boy in pajamas is teary eyed. He is sad because Mom scolded him for not brushing his teeth. Dad explains that Mom is not mad but concerned for his health; brushing will give him a mouth full of pearly white, cavity-free teeth. The little boy smiles and laughs; Mom loves him after all.

My condensed description makes the spot sound trite,

and many copywriters do indeed look down upon this type of commercial as hackneyed. But remember—there is no relationship between people liking a commercial and being sold by it. Slice-of-life may be a cliché but it is still an effective sales technique.

5. Life-style Advertising

A life-style commercial focuses on the user and how the product fits into his life-style. Miller Beer dedicates each of a series of commercials to blue-collar workers in different trades; the commercials are celebrations of the working man and woman and how a good cold Miller rewards them for their labor. The commercials do *not* center on price, methods of brewing, ingredients, taste, or other ways in which Miller differs from competing brands.

Another example of life-style advertising is the commercial for Grey Poupon mustard. We see that Grey Poupon is the mustard of the rich; they all carry it in the refrigerators in the back of their limo's. Grey Poupon is positioned as an *upper-class* mustard.

6. Animation

Animation—cartoons—is effective in selling to children. But animation generally fails to sell to adults.

7. Jingles

A jingle is an advertising slogan set to music. Famous jingles include McDonald's "You Deserve a Break Today," Pepsi's "Catch That Pepsi Spirit," and Diet Coke's "You're Gonna Drink It Just for the Taste of It." The best jingles implant slogans in people's minds by setting the slogans to catchy, memorable tunes that people just can't stop humming or singing.

8. Visual as Hero

Some advertisers treat commercial making as film-making, not as selling. They produce mini-feature films with color and visual quality that surpasses most television shows and motion pictures. An example of this is the recent auto commercial for the "Turbo Z." The action takes place in a steamy, dark "city of the future" reminiscent of the science-fiction film *Blade Runner*.

Unusual graphic treatments can glue viewers to the set. But do these far-out entertainments sell products? I haven't read any articles or case studies that say they do.

9. Humor

Funny commercials are in. Witness the popularity of Wendy's "Where's the beef?" and the fast-talking spots for Federal Express. We know for a fact that people like funny commercials. Whether they are sold by them is another story.

Very few copywriters are able to write humorous copy. And when a funny commercial falls flat, it becomes a sales *disaster*. Unless you are 99.9 percent sure that you are funny (and that your audience will think so, too), avoid the funny commercial. What is funny to one viewer is foolish to another.

10. Continuing Characters

The use of a continuing character—a fictional person who appears in a series of commercials and print ads—is extremely effective in building recognition of a brand. Successful fictional characters include Mr. Whipple, the Jolly Green Giant, Aunt Bluebell, Mr. Goodwrench, and the Pillsbury Doughboy. If you create a fictional character that captures the public's fancy, use him continuously and heavily until research or sales show that your customers are tiring of him.

11. Reason-why Copy

Reason-why copy lists the reasons why people should buy the product. A recent commercial for Hebrew National Franks shows people eating and enjoying hot dogs while voice-over narration lists the reasons why people like to eat the franks. Reason-why commercials can be effective, although reason-why copy seems to work better in print than on the air.

12. Emotion

Commercials that use nostalgia, charm, or sentimentality to tug at your heartstrings (and your wallet) can be both memorable and persuasive. In one of AT&T's famous "Reach Out and Touch Someone" commercials, a mother sheds tears of joy because her son calls long distance just to say he loves her. I remember being moved and thinking how nice it would be to call relatives I hadn't spoken to in a long time. The commercial worked—at least for me.

Like humor, genuine emotional copy is hard to write. If you can do it, more power to you. Most copywriters have a better shot sticking to demonstrations, pitchmen, testimonials, and other "straight-sell" formats.

TIPS ON WRITING EFFECTIVELY FOR TV

Here are some tips on writing TV commercials that are arresting, memorable, and persuasive:

- TV is primarily a medium of pictures, not words. Be sure your pictures deliver a selling message. If you can't figure out what is being sold when the sound is turned off, the commercial is a flop.
- However, sight and sound must work together. Words should explain what the pictures are showing.
- Viewers can take in a limited amount of sight and sound in 30 or 60 seconds. So, if your sales pitch requires a barrage of words, keep the pictures simple. On the other hand, if you use complex graphics, keep the words to a

minimum. Viewers can't handle a dazzling visual display and fast-talking announcer at the same time.

· Think about your customer—the guy or gal in front of the television. Is your commercial interesting and important enough to stop your customer from getting up and going to the refrigerator or the bathroom?

· Think and plan your commercial within existing budgetary limitations. Special effects, jingles, actors, animation, computer graphics, and shooting on location make the cost of commercials skyrocket. Only the stand-up presenter and straightforward, in-the-studio product demonstration are relatively inexpensive to produce.

· Go straight to the point. You have only 30 or 60 seconds—a maximum of 90 words—in which to make your pitch. A print ad, by comparison, can have more than 1,500 words. So the commercial must be simple, direct, and to the point. You can't afford to waste time with irrelevant lead-ins or warm-ups to your pitch. Go straight to it—and keeping selling every second you're on the air.

· And make sure the lead of your commercial is a real grabber. The first four seconds of a commercial are like the headline of a print ad—they decide whether the viewer will sit through your presentation or fix a snack. Open with something irresistible: snappy music, an arresting visual, a dramatic situation, a real-life problem.

· If you are selling a product that can be purchased off the supermarket shelf, show the label. Use close-ups to draw attention to the package. People will buy the product later if they remember the package from your commercial.

· Use motion. Film, unlike slide shows, is a medium of motion. Show cars driving, maple syrup pouring, airplanes flying, popcorn popping, club soda fizzing. Avoid stagnant commercials. Keep it moving.

- Also, don't forget that television offers sound as well as pictures. Let the viewer hear the car engine roaring, the pancakes frying, the airplane whooshing, the popcorn popping, the club soda fizzing, the ice cubes plopping into a cold, tall drink. Many people find the sound of sizzling bacon more appetizing than the look. (Smell may be even more appetizing, but television with smell is not yet a reality. Nor do I know of any manufacturers who are developing such a device.)

- Use "supers." These are titles, in white type, superimposed over the picture. The super reinforces a sales point made in the commercial or makes an additional point not covered in the spoken narration. If you are selling vitamins by mail, put up a super that says, "NOT AVAILABLE IN STORES." People will not buy from a mail-order commercial if they think they can get the product in a store.

- Repeat the product name and the main selling point at least twice. There are two reasons why you should do this. First, repetition aids the viewer in remembering the product. Second, many viewers may not have been paying attention during the beginning of your commercial, so you want to make sure they know who you are and what you are selling.

- Avoid hackneyed situations that bore viewers. Make your commercial fresh, memorable, a little bit different. Burger King's commercials with Emmanuel Lewis are essentially stand-up presenter spots. But they are made memorable by the use of Lewis—a cute, short 12 year old who could pass for 5.

- Don't neglect the product. Show people eating it, wearing it, riding it, using it, enjoying it. Demonstrate the product. Have people talk about how good the product is. Apply proven techniques of print advertising to television, and you will be delighted with the results.

- If you want viewers to call or write in to order a product or request more information, announce this at the beginning of the commercial ("Get paper and pencil ready to take advantage of this special TV offer . . ."). Few people keep a notepad handy while they watch TV.

- If you use a celebrity (either on camera or voice-over), identify the celebrity with a voice-over introduction or superimposed title ("Bill Cosby for Jello Pudding"). A large number of people will not recognize celebrities unless you identify them. And they will not be impressed or swayed by the celebrity unless they know who he is.

- In local retail commercials, give the address and clear directions to the store. If you have many locations, urge viewers to consult their phone books for the location nearest to them.

- The four basic commercial lengths are 10, 30, 60, and 120 seconds. Ten-second commercials are usually "ID" or identification spots. ID spots just drive home a product name and support the campaign's 30- or 60-second spots. However, some advertisers, such as C&C Cola, save money by delivering their entire pitch in 10-second spots. Commercials that build preference for a brand-name product are either 30 or 60 seconds long. Mail-order advertisers use two-minute campaigns because they need to deliver more complete information to convince people to respond.
  Ninety words is about the most you can cram into a 60-second commercial. Many contain much less.

- Because time is limited, a commercial should stick to one main thought or sales point—flame-broiling beats frying; Midas installs more mufflers than anyone else; MCI costs less than AT&T; IBM makes nice, friendly computers. Only in brochures, print ads, and direct mail do you have the space you need to cover all the facts. TV is more limiting.

TYPING YOUR SCRIPT

The manuscript format for TV commercials is simple: video (pictures) are typed on the left, audio (words and sound effects) are typed on the right.

What's important is writing a good commercial. Don't worry about the technical terms. You'll learn them when you need to, but they are not essential. All that counts is that your commercial is arresting, memorable, and persuasive.

Here are just a few of the basic terms to help get you started:

ANNCR—Announcer. The narrator of the commercial.

CU—Close-up. An extremely tight shot in which a single object, such as a package label, dominates the screen.

LS—Long shot. A shot of a distant subject.

MS—Medium shot. A shot of the subject in the foreground, showing a substantial amount of the scenery.

SFX—Sound effects. Background sound other than human voice or musical instruments.

TS—Tight shot. A shot leaving little or no space around the subject.

VO—Voice-over. The voice of an off-camera narrator.

The commercial below is typed in proper commercial manuscript format. It's also a good example of straightforward copy packed with product benefits.

```
                    Amy Bly
                    Product: Galantine Chicken
                    (30 seconds)
```

VIDEO:	AUDIO:
1. MS to CU: Golden brown Galantine chicken on platter.	1. ANNCR: (VO): You're looking at a plump, juicy Galan—

tine chicken. But
this is no ordinary
chicken. Because
we've taken out the
bones.

2. MS: Man slicing
chicken. One-quarter
to one-third of meat
is already sliced on
platter.

2. You can slice
right through
it . . .

3. CU: Array of
chicken dishes on
buffet table.

3. Prepare any num-
ber of delicious
chicken dishes, from
chicken marsala to
chicken salad,
quickly and easily,
without having to
cut around bones.

4. MS: Smiling fam-
ily eating chicken.

4. A Galantine
chicken costs more
than an ordinary
chicken.

5. CU: Fully sliced
chicken on platter.

5. But then there's
no waste. You get
100% meat.

6. CU: Packaged
chicken, showing
Galantine name and
logo.

6. So if you have a
bone to pick with
ordinary chicken,
try Galantine in-
stead. At your
butcher's and at
fine grocers every-
where.

There are a number of things I like about this commercial:

1. It's simple—easy to take in and inexpensive to produce.

2. The visuals show the product, a demonstration of the product (easy slicing of boneless chicken), people enjoying the product, and the package—all in 30 seconds.
3. The narration tells us the unique selling feature of the chicken (no bones), the benefits of this feature (slice right through it, no waste, quick and easy), and shows what you can do with the product (prepare any number of dishes).
4. The ending ("if you have a bone to pick with ordinary chicken") is a clever play on words that leaves a smile on your face. And it tells you where you can buy the product.

Here's another effective 30-second spot from the same writer (Amy Bly, my wife):

```
                    Amy Bly
                    Product: YOURS beer for women.
                    (30 seconds)
```

VIDEO:	AUDIO:
1. MS—well-dressed couple sitting in fancy restaurant. Man reaches for bottle of beer on table. Woman slaps his hand away playfully.	1. WOMAN: Hey, that's YOURS!
2. MS—man's face. He looks over at her, puzzled, grinning.	2. MAN: If it's mine, why can't I have it?
3. TS—woman's finger pointing at label on bottle.	3. WOMAN: Because *YOURS* is the beer that's made for women only.
4. MS—woman pouring beer.	4. SFX: Beer being poured into glass.

WOMAN: *YOURS* is bub-
bly, light, and has
fewer calories than
ordinary beer.

5. MS—Woman finishes
pouring beer and
picks up glass.

5. WOMAN: And, it
comes in convenient
ten—ounce bottles
that pour one per-
fect glass of beer
. . . enough to
quench your thirst—
without filling you
up.

6. MS—Man reaching
for glass of beer.

6. MAN: Why can't *I*
have YOURS?

7. MS—Woman pulls
glass away, smiling.

7. WOMAN: 'Cause
it's mine. . . .

8. TS—bottle of
YOURS against black
background.

8. ANNCR: (VO):
YOURS . . . the
first beer for women
only.

This is basically a life-style commercial combined with
a presentation of product benefits. YOURS is a beer for
women who eat in fancy restaurants, dress well, and have
attractive, personable dinner companions. You can picture Robert Wagner and Stefanie Powers playing the upscale duo.

Other things I like about the script:

1. It is fun, humorous, and playful. But all the play-
   fulness is relevant to the product!
2. The product has a strong position—"the first beer
   for women only."
3. The commercial highlights product features that
   would appeal to women: light, few calories, small
   servings per bottle.
4. The name is repeated five times and the label shown
   twice.

HOW TO WRITE FOR RADIO

Radio is different from TV and print. And the difference is: no pictures.

The radio copywriter works with words and sounds. His words and sounds must create a picture of the product in the reader's mind.

A radio commercial for "Aunt Lucy's Luscious Blueberry Pie" can't show the family eating and enjoying the pie. So you must use *sound* to paint the picture—the sound of pie being sliced, of a fork cutting into crust, of chewing, of people "mmm"-ing in delight and praising their hostess.

Suppose the blueberry pies are sold in local supermarkets in a distinctive blue foil wrapper. You can't show the package on radio. You must have the announcer say, "Look for the homemade pie in the blue foil wrapper at your local supermarket and bake shop."

A mini-industry has developed around independent radio production houses that write and produce radio commercials for ad agencies and their clients. Many ad agency writers and creative directors look down their noses at radio (perhaps because the money involved is insignificant compared with television) and are happy to pass on radio commercials to outsiders.

There are trends and stars in radio advertising. For years, Stan Freiberg was the rage with humorous radio commercials for Chung King and others. Then, Dick Orkin and Bert Berdis were the reigning kings. More recently, John Cleese of Monty Python fame has become a hit with his spots for Callard & Bowser candies and Kronenborg beer.

In a recent article published in *Writer's Digest*,[6] copywriter David Campiti offered these tips to radio novices.

1. *Lock onto a salesperson's "keys."* This is "inside information" a company's salespeople get from talking with customers.

Feedback from customers can reveal key selling points. For instance, a copywriter interviewed farmers to find out why his radio commercial was not selling rat poison by mail. He discovered that farmers with rat problems were embarrassed about it and didn't want the postman or neighbors to see them receive rat poison packages in the mail. The copywriter added a line to the commercial about how the poison was mailed in a plain brown wrapper, and sales soared.

2. *Talk about benefits. Tell the audience what the client's goods will do for them.*

3. *Be concise.* Use short sentences.

4. *Repeat key information.* Minimum: list store names twice; addresses once toward the end, or twice if confusing. Include phone numbers at least twice, more in a 60-second commercial.

5. *Know what you're writing about.* Research the product.

6. *Know what resources are available to the producers of radio commercials.* Learn to use production facilities. Know the extent of their music and sound effects libraries, the quality and capability of recording equipment, and the abilities of actors who will read your copy over the air.

TWO COMMERCIALS I LIKE

Here are two commercials I like and the reasons why. First, a 60-second spot from the Masonry Institute of St. Louis:

MAN: Uh, today we're speaking with the Three Little Pigs, is that? . . .

PIGS: Yes. That's right. You got it, buddy.

MAN: Yeah, well tell me, ever since you guys opted to build with brick, have you had any further difficulties with uh . . .

PIG #1: Big, bad, and breathless?

MAN: Right.

PIG #2: No, he never comes around any more.

MAN: That's good.

PIG #3: He knows better than to try and blow this pad down, boy!

MAN: Yes, well besides solving your security problems, there must have been other reasons for your choosing brick.

PIG #1: Listen, when you're spending 80 big ones on a house these days you want something that'll last, right guys?

PIG #2: Oh yeah.

PIG #3: You said it.

MAN: Well, brick certainly does that, all right.

PIG #1: With little or no maintenance.

MAN: Right.

PIG #2: Not only keeps the wolf from the door but withstands fire, hail . . .

PIG #3: . . . aluminum-siding salesmen.

MAN: Yes, well I notice you also have a solid brick fireplace as well.

PIG #1: Yes we do.

MAN: Very attractive.

PIG #2: We think it adds a nice little touch.

PIG #3: Especially when the girls come over.

MAN: Safe too, I'll bet.

PIG #1: It is—they aren't.

(man and pigs laugh)

MAN: Is there anything else we should know about building with brick?

PIG #1: If there is, don't ask us.

MAN: Oh?

PIG #2: Ask the folks at the Masonry Institute.

MAN: The Masonry Institute?

PIG #3: They'll be happy to send you complete information.

MAN: On brick.

PIG #1: No, on paper.

MAN: What?!

PIG #1: They couldn't get a brick in the envelope . . .

(music)

ANNCR: If you'd like to know more about building with brick, call the Masonry Institute of St. Louis at 645-5888. That's 645-5888.[7]

The commercial caught and kept my attention because it is both fast paced and genuinely funny. The banter between the three pigs and the interviewer keeps things lively. Yet, this clever little dialogue manages to pack a great deal of product information into 60 seconds. We learn that:

1. Brick stands up to the environment—hail, wind, storms.
2. Brick lasts a long time and requires little or no maintenance.
3. It is fireproof.
4. If your house is made of brick you won't need aluminum siding.
5. You can use brick to build a safe, attractive fireplace.

6. The Masonry Institute will send free information
   on building with brick to anyone who asks for it.

The second spot that caught my ear is this 60-second
commercial for the California Milk Advisory Board. The
commercial was produced and performed by Dick Orkin
and Bert Berdis.

MILK EXECUTIVE: Hello.

SIDNEY: California Milk Advisory Board?

EXECUTIVE: Yes.

SIDNEY: May I make a small suggestion about
your jingle?

EXECUTIVE: ''Any time is the right time for
milk''?

SIDNEY: Yes, it's real catchy, but maybe you
ought to change it to, ''Any time is the
right time for milk except at a bull
fight.''

EXECUTIVE (laughs): Sounded almost like you
said, ''Any time is the right time for milk
except at a bull fight.''

SIDNEY: That's what I said.

EXECUTIVE: What? . . .

SIDNEY: Allow me to introduce myself. I'm
Sidney Feltzer, freelance matador.

EXECUTIVE: Uh—huh.

SIDNEY: I love your milk . . .

EXECUTIVE: Uh—huh.

SIDNEY: Drink it all the time. It's cold and
refreshing . . .

EXECUTIVE: Go on, Sidney.

SIDNEY: But trying to drink milk with one
hand and wave my cape with the other is just
so . . .

EXECUTIVE: Sidney, you didn't try to, uh. . . .?

SIDNEY: Just today I went through six cartons.

EXECUTIVE: Of milk?

SIDNEY: Pants.

EXECUTIVE: Pants?

SIDNEY: See, when you turn and run, the bull is right there . . .

EXECUTIVE: Sidney, why not have your milk afterward?

SIDNEY: In the hospital?

EXECUTIVE: No, no, I meant after you exercise, milk is terrific, or with snacks, or just sitting down watching television.

SIDNEY: Oh, I can't do that.

EXECUTIVE: Watch television?

SIDNEY: No, sit.

EXECUTIVE: Oh.

SIDNEY: See, when you turn and run, the bull is right there.

EXECUTIVE: I see, I get it, all right Sidney.

JINGLE: Yeah! Any time at all . . . is the time for milk!

SIDNEY: Except during a bull fight.

EXECUTIVE: Hang it up, Sidney.

SIDNEY: My cape?

EXECUTIVE: The phone.

SIDNEY: Oh, right.

(music fades)

ANNCR: This phone call brought to you by the California Milk Advisory Board.[8]

Again, a fast-paced, humorous commercial with a persuasive message. Note the use of very short (one and two word) sentences to set the pace.

NONBROADCAST AV

Radio and TV commercials are the most visible part of the copywriter's work, because we hear them every day.

But each year, there are thousands of scripts written and produced that we never get to hear or see.

This area of copywriting is known as *nonbroadcast AV*.

These are audiovisual presentations created by a company and used to reach select, small audiences. Instead of being aired over radio or TV, these presentations are shown at meetings, trade shows, seminars, presentations, and in one-on-one sales pitches where the salesman is sitting down with a customer.

Many different media are available for nonbroadcast AV. These include:

- Single-projector slide show
- Dual-projector slide show
- Filmstrip
- Videotape
- Film
- Multimedia (combination film and slides with multiple projectors)
- Videotext
- Software

And these presentations are used in many different applications:

- Employee communications
- Trade show exhibits

- Seminars and conferences
- Recruitment
- Community relations
- Public relations
- Sales support
- Advertising inquiry fulfillment (tapes or films sent to select prospects who respond to your ads)
- Presentations to top management
- Training
- Product introduction
- Product demonstration
- Case histories
- Meetings
- Sales aids for company salespeople and sales reps
- Point-of-purchase display in retail locations
- Executive summaries of annual reports, sales presentations, and other printed literature
- To record historic events

The script format for slide shows and films is the same as for TV commercials: Visuals on the left, audio on the right.

But nonbroadcast AV is not limited to 30 or 60 seconds. You can make it as long or as short as you like.

Eight to ten minutes is the best length for a slide show or film. Twenty minutes is the maximum. Beyond that, your audience will begin to fade.

Nonbroadcast AV is much less expensive to produce than TV commercials. A one-minute commercial could cost $40,000 or more. A ten-minute nonbroadcast videotape can be produced for $5,000 or less.

John Baldoni, a freelance scriptwriter, offers these tips for writing nonbroadcast AV: [9]

1. Write for words for the ear, not for the eye. A script is not simply words on a page, but words that are spoken aloud.

2. The spoken words should be precise, coherent, and full of vivid images.

3. Be crystal clear. The listener doesn't have the luxury of referring back to the text. Your writing must be readily understood the first time it is heard.

4. Research. Find out all you can about the topic, the product, the purpose, the audience.

5. The script should repeat the key selling points several times.

6. The beginning is critical and must "hook" the audience, locking their attention.

7. Be lively, catching, precise. Use active verbs, colorful words and phrases.

8. Spoon-feed the audience. Don't assault them with fact after fact. Be selective about the facts you choose. An AV presentation doesn't tell the whole story but should leave the viewer hungry for more information.

9. Use words to paint pictures that complement the actual visuals on the screen.

10. Be as concise and direct as possible. Avoid complicated sentences.

PART III

THE COPYWRITING BUSINESS

How to Succeed as a Freelance Copywriter
How to Get a Great Job as an Ad Agency Copywriter
How to Hire and Work With Copywriters
What Every Copywriter Should Know About Graphic
Design

11

How to Succeed as a Freelance Copywriter

WHY FREELANCE COPYWRITERS?

"I can't imagine how you make a living as a freelance copywriter," a friend told me recently. "Companies can hire ad agencies to write their copy. And the ad agencies have writers on staff. Why would anyone ever need a freelance copywriter?"

Maybe you, too, wondering if copywriting was something you could do on your own, have asked the same question. The good news is that there are thousands of firms—ad agencies, public relations firms, manufacturers, retailers, wholesalers, service businesses, graphic design studios—that hire freelancers to write copy for them.

There are four basic reasons why these firms turn to freelancers for copywriting services.

1. The Company has No Staff Writer or Ad Agency

Many companies don't produce enough advertising to justify the cost of hiring staff writers or a full-service ad agency. So they turn to freelancers for the occasional ad, brochure, mailer, or newsletter. There are even numerous small advertising agencies that keep the overhead low by farming out most of their copy to freelancers.

2. The Company Can't Do the Job Themselves

Or, they can't do it as well as you can. For example, an ad agency with consumer accounts may take on a high-tech client. Their staff copywriters don't have the expertise to write about microchips and modems (they're more at home with beer and wine), so they hire a freelancer specializing in technical copy.

3. The Company (or Agency) Doesn't Have Time to Do the Job

A company's ad agency may be too busy trying to meet print-ad deadlines to give much attention to a product brochure. So they hire a freelancer who can devote a week of his time to handling the job.

4. The Freelancer Can Do It Cheaper

Let's say a company wants to write and place an article with a trade magazine. Most public relations firms charge hefty monthly retainers and don't want to take on one-shot projects. The company can hire a freelancer to ghostwrite the article for them at a reasonable price.

To summarize: Companies hire freelancers to do it better, faster, or cheaper.

IS FREELANCING FOR YOU?

I don't like it when freelancers boast that "freelancing is better than working at an ad agency" or agency writers make the put-down that "Freelancing is for people who can't get jobs with a good agency." A staff job isn't *better* than freelancing; it's just different. Whether to be staff or freelance is something only you can decide, based on the way you like to live your life.

To help you make the choice, I've put together a list of the pros and cons of freelance copywriting.

Some of the advantages of freelance life include:

- *Freedom to set your own hours.* No nine-to-five routine. You can take the afternoon off to read a paperback on a park bench, then work from dusk till midnight, if that's the way you like it.

- *Freedom to work at home.* Eliminates commuting and office politics; allows you to dress as you please. (Also, working in comfortable surroundings can add to your income; a recent study by the Buffalo Organization for Social and Technical Innovation showed that a comfortable office environment creates an extra $1,600 of productivity annually for professionals and managers.)

- *Independence.* You work by yourself and don't have to worry about whether others have done their part of the job.

- *Autonomy.* You are your own boss. You can make decisions faster on your own than you can working for someone else.

- *Creative freedom.* You can submit to the client the copy you feel is best. No need to have others approve your work before you show it.

- *Pride of authorship.* This comes from creative freedom. You know—and your client knows—that the work you produce is yours and yours alone. At an ad agency, the agency's product is produced by committee. The free-lancer's work is produced by an individual.

- *Money.* If you want to write, and not supervise others, you'll probably make more money than you would working at an agency.

- *More variety.* As a freelancer, you work for many different clients, not just two or three accounts. And you can take on a new client whenever you like.

- *Control of workload.* Unlike the agency business, where people are rumored to work from dawn till dusk, the freelancer is only as busy as he wants to be. If you want to work less, you turn away business. If you want to work more, you take on new clients. Although there is the occasional rush project, most freelancers lead a peaceful, stress-free existence compared with their ad agency counterparts.

- *Freedom to walk away.* If an ad agency copywriter doesn't like his boss, his art director, or the client, he pretty much has to live with it or look for another job. And that's a major move. But if a freelancer isn't happy with a client, the freelancer can simply finish the job, send the bill, and be done with it. Although repeat business is the bread-and-butter of freelancing, there's more freedom to pick and choose clients. There's also less formal commitment to an account than in an ad agency/client relationship.

- *Respect.* Most clients treat their freelancers better than their staff writers. As an outside consultant, the freelancer is brought in to be a hero, to solve problems others could not. Also, people respect what they pay for, and when the freelancer enters the room, the meter's running. With a staff writer, you can waste his time with the knowledge that you won't see a bill for it.

Now, some of the drawbacks of freelance life:

- *Cash flow is uneven.* You can go six weeks without seeing a dollar, then open up the mailbox one morning and pull out $10,000 worth of checks. Freelancers have to learn to live without the steady paycheck.

- *Work flow is uneven.* Many freelancers become uneasy and depressed when the phone stops ringing and no new business comes through the door. As your reputation grows, you'll have the opposite problem—the pressure of being asked to take on more work than you can handle. Until you're secure enough in your trade to call your own shots, you have to learn to live with this crisis-lull-crisis rhythm.

- *Clients don't pay their bills on time.* Even when your invoice says "net 30 days," you may not see a check for 60, 90, 120 days or more. Paying outside vendors seems to be last on every company's list, and freelancers are no exception. Even worse, there is the occasional deadbeat who doesn't pay at all and forces you to go through the trouble and agony of collecting your bill through a series of phone calls, dunning letters, collection agencies, and, as a last resort, lawyers and courts.

- *Prospects will gladly waste your time,* if you let them. They will keep you waiting in the reception area for hours on end. They'll ask you to send your samples and other goodies to them in the mail and then never return your phone call. And they won't be in when you show up for an appointment. This is why you should keep free consultations and meetings to a minimum—people won't respect your time unless they know they're paying for it.

- *Some prospects will go to great lengths to get something for nothing.* They'll call you up and expect you to spend hours on the phone giving free advice—even if they have no intention of becoming your client. When you meet, they'll pull out their ads (which aren't working) and say, "Well, what headline would *you* use?" They'll ask for free copies of your books, articles, speeches. Now, there's nothing wrong with giving away a little free advice to prove your savvy. But watch out for the client who tries to wangle unlimited free service out of you.

- *Sleazes.* Freelancers, consultants, and even agencies are frequently called up by fly-by-night operators who want free advertising services in exchange for "a piece of the pie" or some other nebulous promise of future rewards if the venture grows. Don't do business with clients who say, "Work with me now, and we'll grow together." The best clients pay up front.

- *No comrades.* Freelancing can be a lonely business. The ad agency copywriter has other writers, art directors, account executives, and a whole peer group of fun, creative people to bounce ideas off of and pal around with. The freelancer sits alone in a room and writes. I like it this way, but you may not. If you're a people-person, freelancing may be too solitary for you.

- *You're not part of the big picture.* An advertising manager or agency copywriter sees the whole process, from strategy and planning to copy and design to printing and execution. A freelancer writes the copy, mails it out, and that's the end of his involvement in the campaign—except for writing more copy.

- *It's harder to build a portfolio of published work when you're a freelancer.* Clients rarely send you copies of your brochures or tear sheets of the ads you've written. But staff writers can usually get their hands on as many reprints as they want.

I wrote the above checklist of pros and cons to give you a way of weighing the benefits and drawbacks of freelance life.

But I can only describe the nature of freelance writing. I can't tell you whether you'd enjoy it. That depends on you—your personality, work habits, likes, and dislikes.

For example: As I write this on a rainy Monday morning, I look out the window and see people in three-piece suits scrambling for the York Avenue bus. (I'm sure some of them are copywriters headed down to their agencies on Madison Avenue.)

As I watch them from the comfort of my study (my office is in the spare bedroom of our New York apartment), I think, "I'm sure glad I'm not out there." I prefer the quiet solitude of working at home, unencumbered by a jacket and tie, a two-hour commute, or an office full of people, morning meetings, ringing telephones, and other distractions.

I'll spend most of today working on this book, because I like working on one project for a day-long stretch. Tomorrow, I'll work on one of the other four or five projects sitting on my desk: a brochure for a banking client, a sales letter for a producer of corporate audiovisual shows, an article I'm ghostwriting for a business executive, a couple of ads for an industrial firm.

I get up late—about a quarter of nine—but, because I don't have to travel or dress for work, I'm at my desk and ready to work by nine. I spend most of the day writing on my word processor, thinking of headlines and copy ideas, or studying background material for client projects. And I do it in the clothes I find comfortable—jeans, an old gray sweater, and my favorite pair of slippers.

Some freelance copywriters team up with graphic artists, marketing consultants, or A/V producers. I prefer to work alone. I detest the ad agency tradition of "brainstorming" and "group creativity." I agree with political advertising consultant David Garth, who said: "When you have 15 of the greatest minds working, you come up with zero."[1]

I work where I want, on what I want, pretty much when I want to.

You may be able to think of a better life than that.

I can't.

QUALIFICATIONS FOR THE FREELANCE COPYWRITER

Two skills are vital to success as a freelance copywriter.

One, obviously, is the ability to write good copy.

You don't have to be an advertising genius. You don't have to have a portfolio full of ads and commercials for "glamour" accounts. You don't have to write trendy, stylish copy or win an armload of creative awards for your work. But you must write good, clean, competent copy—solid work that is persuasive, accurate, crisp, and hard-selling.

The second skill is one you may not have thought of: To succeed as a freelancer, you have to be able to *sell* yourself.

Ad agency writers have their assignments handed to them by account executives. But freelancers must go out, find potential clients, and sell their copywriting services to these clients.

How do you gain these two different skills?

Copywriting skill comes from experience. You can get this experience in a number of ways: By working as an ad agency writer, as a staff writer for an advertiser, as an advertising manager, or by moonlighting while you hold a full-time job in another area. If you work for an agency or advertiser in an area other than copywriting, see if you can move, or at least if you can take on some copywriting in addition to your regular duties.

I started as a staff writer for Westinghouse, writing sales brochures, films, and slide presentations on electronic defense systems. My next job was as advertising manager for Koch Engineering, a manufacturer of equipment used in chemical plants and oil refineries. After a year at Westinghouse and a year and a half at Koch, I went freelance.

While you build your skills, you should also build a portfolio of your published work. Each time an ad, brochure, or catalog you've written is published, get as many copies as you can. When you are freelance, you will send copies of your work to prospective clients to demonstrate your ability and the fact that your work has been published.

Also, try to write copy for more than one company. If you're an ad agency writer, work on several accounts. If you work for a company, moonlight, or write copy for different divisions, branches, subsidiaries, and product lines of your corporation. A diverse, impressive client list is one of the freelancer's most powerful sales tools.

Building skill in selling your services is a little harder. Most writers don't have an opportunity to do any selling on the job. You'll learn the selling skills you need by trial and error when you leave your job and go out on your own.

Yes, you'll make mistakes and lose business as a result. But don't worry. Making mistakes is the only way you learn. After six months, you'll be confident and successful in selling yourself. And, assuming you're good at what you do, clients will flock to you by word of mouth, you'll have more business than you can handle, and you won't have to sell as hard because you can afford to turn down work.

WHAT IT TAKES

Let's say you have the skill and desire to be a freelance copywriter. What else do you need to get started? The list presented below covers the basics:

An Office

You need a place to work. Most freelancers I know work at home. They enjoy the comfortable surroundings, convenience, and increased productivity. When you work at home, you save money by not having to rent an office. And you can even deduct a portion of your mortgage or apartment rental as a business expense.

If you feel a strong need to separate home from work life, you might consider setting up shop in an outside office. But if you're thinking that renting a fancy office will bring in more business, forget it: It's extremely rare for a client to visit the copywriter. And your portfolio is a lot more important than your address.

A Typewriter

I recommend the IBM Selectric or a comparable electric machine. As a professional writer, words are your product, and they must look sharp.

Even better would be a personal computer with a word-processing program. You can get several good machines for under $2,500. The computer will pay for itself within a few months by increasing your productivity as a writer. I personally recommend the Kaypro II or IV and WordStar (which is included when you buy the machine).

A Telephone

A desirable feature is "call waiting," which lets an ordinary home phone handle two incoming calls simultaneously. You also need either an answering service or phone machine to cover calls when you step away from the office. I prefer answering machines: They cost less, and unlike some live operators, they can't be rude or misplace messages.

Other Equipment

You need file cabinets, a desk, a strong lamp, bookshelves. A copier is a nice luxury but not necessary if there's a copy center near your office.

Stationery

You must have envelopes, letterhead, business cards, mailing labels. Your stationery should look clean, crisp, professional. A fine paper stock always makes a positive impression. Don't buy cheap-looking "ready made" letterhead designs from the printer. Hire a professional graphic artist to handle the job. Design and mechanicals of business stationery should cost between $150 and $400.

Sales Literature

As a freelancer, you're in business, and like any business, you need sales literature. You simply can't visit everyone who calls up and expresses interest in your service. You need printed material you can mail to prospects to tell them all about your services.

My own literature package is more comprehensive than most. It includes:

- A brief, personally typed cover letter thanking the prospect for his interest and calling his attention to the material enclosed.
- A four-page form letter explaining, in detail, my copywriting services—my background, my specialties, how I work with clients, what I charge, how long it takes for me to complete assignments, my policy on revisions, and how the prospect can order copy from me.
- A one-page fact sheet giving a more detailed description of my background.
- A two-page list of my clients and other experience (teaching experience, lectures, books, magazine articles).
- Letters from past clients expressing satisfaction with my services.
- Reprints of articles I've written on advertising and copywriting.
- Samples of my work (ads, brochures, sales letters).
- A detailed schedule of estimated fees giving prices for various projects as well as an explanation of terms and guarantees.

- An order form the reader can complete and mail back to me to order his copy.

Some copywriters send much, much less. But, since I do most of my business by mail, my package has to be complete. Your own package can be as complex as mine or as simple as a résumé and a business card. The choice depends on your background, your personality, and your way of doing business.

Money

There may be some lean times in freelancing, especially at the beginning, so be sure you have money in the bank before you quit your job—enough to carry you through six months of hard times (twelve months if you have a family, own a house or a yacht, or have other large, regular expenses).

THE ADVANTAGES OF SPECIALIZATION

A word about specialization: You'll probably handle the types of accounts that interest you. And that's the way it should be. Don't force yourself into an area you're not enthusiastic about simply because you think it's lucrative. Happy, successful people rarely work for money alone.

But, if you haven't settled on an area of copywriting, think about this: In freelancing, specialists are more in demand than generalists. Specialists generally earn more money and have no trouble getting all the business they can handle.

A generalist is someone who works on a broad range of accounts without concentrating in any one area. You'd think generalists would get more work because they are so flexible. But the problem is, clients want specialists. If I'm a specialist with a portfolio full of financial ads, and you're a generalist, we may both be able to write a good banking ad. But, all else being equal, the banking client will choose me over you every time—because I've got the portfolio and the client list that says I'm in tune with their type of advertising.

Copywriters specialize by the type of accounts they handle or by the medium they work in. Some popular areas of specialization include:

- Direct mail and mail order
- Medical/pharmaceutical/health care
- Financial
- High-tech
- Industrial
- Package goods
- Automotive
- Retail
- Radio advertising
- Corporate communications

My own specialty is industrial and high-tech advertising. I handle clients in computers, telecommunications, chemicals, industrial equipment, pollution control, electronics, software, publishing, and related areas.

When a client calls on me, he doesn't have to worry about whether I'll be able to understand his product or his marketing problem. He *knows* he's getting a writer with expertise in his industry. And, because I've dealt in his area of business before, I can do more than write copy: I can give him advice, alert him to a flaw in his advertising or sales strategy, and offer new ideas he may not have thought of before.

Specialization is also beneficial to the writer. As a specialist, I can charge more than a generalist, because my type of service is harder to come by. Also, by working in a limited number of fields, I become an expert in these industries. So, when I take on a new job in an area I know, I don't have to spend time learning a whole new field. This way, I make more money for each hour spent on the client's project.

Of course, I frequently *do* take on assignments in new areas. I enjoy the challenge and the opportunity to learn something new. But, it is repeat business from old clients that keeps the roof over my head.

Many successful writers have two, three, or even four areas of specialization. I know one copywriter who spends half his time writing speeches and in public relations and the other half writing direct mail. Another writer produces TV commercials by day and suspense novels by night. So specialization doesn't limit you. It *does* allow you to build from strength.

GETTING SALES LEADS

You've set up your office, designed your letterhead, and quit your job. Now what?

If you're lucky, your former colleagues, vendors, and business associates are pounding down your door, begging to give you dozens of lucrative assignments.

But, more likely, an awful silence fills the air around you. The phone isn't ringing. Your appointment book is blank. The mailbox contains nothing but junk mail.

Things aren't happening. But that's part of the freelance game. As an entrepreneur, you can't wait for things to happen. You've got to *make* them happen. For the beginning freelance copywriter, this means going out and getting people to hire you to write copy for them.

The first step is to generate *sales leads*.

A sales lead is a potential customer—a prospect who says, "Yes, I might have use of your service or product. Tell me more about it." The best sales leads are inquiries from those people who have the money and authority to buy your services, and who have an immediate project in mind. Second best are inquiries from people who don't have an immediate need but frequently use copywriters and are interested in getting to know you for possible use on future projects.

In the beginning, you'll probably follow up just about every lead. After a while, you'll develop a sense that tells you which leads are serious and which are just wasting your time.

But the first step is simply to generate the leads. (You can't follow up on leads you don't have.) And a question other copywriters frequently ask me is, "What's the best way to get new business leads?"

I can't give a definitive answer. But I can tell you what has worked for me—and what hasn't.

When I started, I used direct mail to launch my copywriting business. Coming from an ad manager's job with a fairly obscure company, I had never been a part of the mainstream of advertising and had relatively few leads or contacts to speak of.

I couldn't afford a display ad in the advertising magazines. And I was really aiming at a narrow audience—ad agency creative directors and corporate ad managers in the New York/New Jersey area. So I created a simple direct-mail package, got a mailing list, and mailed 500 letters to these folks (I'll tell where to find lists of potential clients a little later on in the chapter).

I ran downstairs to look for reply cards in the mail about five times a day. Each trip to an empty mailbox sent me back to the Pepto-Bismol bottle for another dose of quick relief.

Then, one day—eureka! A reply! And within weeks, more replies followed—35 in all. My mailing, which consisted of a one-page sales letter and a return postcard, had generated a 7 percent response. Within six months, leads from the mailing had turned into nine clients and a total of $15,000 in assignments. I was in business!

Here's the text of the sales letter that worked so well for me:

HOW AN ENGINEER AND FORMER AD MANAGER
CAN HELP YOU WRITE
BETTER ADS AND BROCHURES.

For many ad agency people, industrial advertising is a difficult chore. It's detailed
work, and highly technical. To write the
copy, you need someone with the technical
know-how of an engineer and the communications skills of a copywriter.

That's where I can help.

As a freelance industrial copywriter who is
also a graduate engineer, I know how to
write clear, jargon-free, technically sound
copy. You'll like my writing samples—ads,
brochures, catalogs, direct mail, PR, and
AV. And you'll like having a writer on call
who works only when you need him—by the
hour, by the day, or by the project.

Here are my qualifications:

I have an engineering background (BS, chemical engineering, University of Rochester). I
started out writing brochures and AV scripts
for the Westinghouse Defense Center. After I
left Westinghouse, I became advertising manager for Koch Engineering, a manufacturer of
chemical process equipment.

In my freelance work, I've handled projects
in a wide variety of industries including
computers, construction, chemical equipment,
electronics, telecommunications, and many
other areas.

Recently, I wrote a book on writing for industry. It's called Technical Writing:
Structure, Standards, and Style, and it will
be published this year by McGraw-Hill.

```
Now, I'd like to help you create ads, bro-
chures, and other promotions. Call me when
your creative team is overloaded, or when
the project is highly technical.

If it sounds like I can be of service,
please complete and mail the enclosed post-
card.

Sincerely,


Bob Bly
```

One or two more mass mailings of this letter, at about 300 a mailing, helped bring in more leads and business. Nowadays, I don't need to do mass mailings because I have leads coming in from referrals, word-of-mouth, speaking engagements, and other sources.

But I still keep a stack of these letters handy. If I read an article about a new company, a new ad campaign, or an agency that just gained an account in my area, I can look up the company or agency in one of the industry directories (more about these later), type an envelope, stuff a form letter and reply card into the envelope, and mail it. Instead of spending half an hour or more writing an individual letter, I can bait my hook and go lead-fishing in about two minutes. So, even if you don't do bulk mailings, a mass-produced direct-mail package is a quick, efficient way of dropping prospects a line and letting them know you're out there.

My sales technique was to do the mailing, then follow up with a phone call. If the prospect was genuinely interested in my services, I'd send my literature package. Then I'd follow up again, and if he had an immediate project in mind, we'd have a meeting to discuss it in detail.

Some freelancers do the reverse: They make "cold calls" to lists of prospects, explaining who they are and what they do. If the prospect says "no thanks," they end the call and save themselves the price of a mailing. Only when the prospect says "send some information" do they put a letter, résumé, or package in the mail.

You can try it both ways and see what works best for you—call first and then mail, or mail and follow up by phone. But I've found that advertising people, because they're so busy, don't want to be bothered by a call out of the blue. They're also wary of responding to a cold call because they get many calls from people who, unlike you, are rank amateurs. So I suggest you mail first. That way, when you do call, the prospect knows who you are and why you are calling.

Although I don't do large mailings anymore, I regularly run small (one-inch) classified or display ads in several advertising magazines—*Adweek, Advertising Age,* and *Business Marketing.* Small ads are so inexpensive (a month in the eastern edition of *Adweek* costs me less than $80) that it's easy to experiment, to try ads in various publications and see which ones work.

I get my best response from *Adweek*—perhaps because the ad runs in a special advertising section offering freelance copy, art, printing, consultation, and other outside services.

Second best for me is *Business Marketing,* a magazine covering business-to-business advertising and marketing. It works for me because I specialize in this field.

Experiment with your ads—the copy, the size, and where you place them.

Don't ignore small publications: regional advertising magazines, program notes, newsletters of local advertising clubs. A 12-dollar ad I placed in the *IABC Employment Letter,* a local newsletter, generated a response from a client who paid me $5,000 to write an annual report. This client later recommended half a dozen of his friends to me, resulting in an additional $4,000 in business.

Some freelancers experiment with ads in journals in the specific industries in which they specialize (a financial copywriter, for example, might try an ad in *The Wall Street*

Journal). These ads usually do poorly, and you are better off advertising in advertising magazines rather than in industry-specific journals.

So far, I've only run with the one-inch ads. Large display advertising is usually beyond the finances of most freelancers. I've created a third-of-a-page ad that will run in one of the major magazines soon, and the cost of the space is $1,000. But I have reason to believe the copy will get results because it's an expanded version of my successful one-inch ad.

I recommend you test your ad copy in small versions. When you find the headline that pulls the best results, you can be pretty sure (though never certain) that the concept will get more attention and leads in a larger size.

(I give the same advice to some of the smaller companies I write ads for. I've seen too many businesses blow their whole promotional budget in a large ad that cost thousands of dollars and produced only a handful of responses.)

When I started, I wrote a press release on my new copywriting business and mailed it to all the advertising magazines. It was largely ignored. One or two newsletters mentioned my name, but I got no calls or business as a result.

I don't think the press release is an effective promotional tool for the freelancer. In the first place, editors are interested in the doings of big agencies and their multi-million dollar campaigns; the fact that Bob Bly is now a freelance writer doesn't hold much interest for them.

Secondly, press releases take too long to see their way into print. It may be three months from the time a release is mailed to its publication in a magazine. Freelancers need more immediate results—the kind you get with direct mail or print advertising.

Press releases didn't work for me, but I do get a lot of publicity from writing articles for trade publications and giving talks before groups of advertising professionals. Articles and speeches do generate some leads that turn into immediate business. But their real value is building your reputation over the long run.

Nothing will establish you as an expert in your field as solidly and as quickly as writing and publishing articles on copywriting. "The reverence people have for the printed word is amazing," observes publisher Edward Uhlan in his autobiography, *The Rogue of Publishers' Row* (Exposition Press). "Simply because a man appears in print, the public assumes that he has something authoritative to say."

I hate to say it, but writing articles about writing ads can do more to build a copywriter's reputation than the actual writing of ads can. But the truth is, an experienced writer can give much valuable advice, tips, and techniques to his peers in advertising, and the best way to do this is to write articles for the trade press. I regularly contribute to *Business Marketing* and have also been published in *Direct Marketing, Communicator's Journal, Writer's Digest, Audio-Visual Directions,* and half a dozen other trade journals.

This activity pays off in three ways. First, it's educational: I always come away from an article thinking I've learned at least as much about the subject as the person who's going to read it.

Second, reprints of the article make a welcome addition to my package of self-promotional literature. Article reprints are an inexpensive way for any advertiser—a copywriter or his clients—to supplement their own self-published sales materials.

Third, the articles get my name around. Many potential clients have told me, "I've seen your name in *Business Marketing,*" or "I just photocopied your latest article and sent it around my agency!" In addition to being flattering, this recognition makes it easier to close the sale.

On top of all this, articles let you give back to the industry some of what it has given to you—by educating others in your craft. And some trade magazines may even pay you a small amount for your articles, although the majority do not, figuring you're getting valuable exposure in exchange for your editorial contribution.

Most of the above advantages also apply to giving speeches. Lecturing is educational; it gives you publicity, and copies of speeches make good supplementary sales literature. Speeches reach smaller audiences than articles (I've spoken in front of groups ranging from five to eighty-five), but the presentation is more personal: You can answer questions on the spot and chat with your listeners before and after the talk to make contacts for new business.

However, preparing and giving a speech is more time-consuming than preparing an article for publication. And the speech reaches perhaps a tenth of a percent of the people that your article does. So you should limit your speaking activities to those groups with the largest number of high-level members. I give only half a dozen talks a year and rarely travel more than 50 miles to an engagement. Otherwise, the time commitment would be too great in proportion to the return.

Of course, you can attend meetings without being a speaker. Ask around, and you'll discover at least two or three advertising clubs or associations in your area. Joining and attending meetings can be a great way for a freelancer to make contacts and get new business leads.

But I must confess: I don't do this myself. The reason has to do with my own personality: I'm a solitary sort and don't enjoy large groups or engagements that mix socializing and business. I find it hard to "mix" in groups, and so I don't go to meetings (although I am a dues-paying member of the Business/Professional Advertising Association).

Based on firsthand observation and chats with other writers, I suspect that less new-business prospecting is done at these luncheons and dinners than is widely reported. Most people go for the food, drink, and company of their peers and are not receptive to a freelancer's sales pitch, no matter how soft the sell. For my money, I think mailings, ads, and article writing are more effective methods of freelance self-promotion.

When you first get started, you'll need good solid leads—and fast. A combination of direct mail and small ads is probably the best way of generating these leads.

After you've been in business for a year or so, you'll get a lot of business through referrals and "word of mouth." Turning prospects into clients, not generating initial interest, will become your major challenge. You'll concentrate on your literature package, articles, speeches, maybe even a book on advertising. And you may want to keep running small ads in the journals so people can find you when they need you.

Another way to build your reputation is to teach a course in copywriting or advertising at a local college or university. For several years, I've taught writing at the New York University School of Continuing Education.

I can't say I've gotten any business out of this. But teaching at NYU impresses people when I mention it. And preparing for the course has sharpened my own thinking about the copywriting process.

A LOOK AT THE MARKETS

At the beginning of the chapter, I touched upon the types of companies that use freelance copywriting services.

Now let's take a look at the nature of these markets and how you can reach them.

Advertising Agencies

There are two major markets for freelance copywriting services: ad agencies and advertisers. The advertiser market is more diverse, ranging from accounting firms and art galleries to manufacturers and mail-order markets to theaters and typing services. The ad agency market is uniform, with all prospects being in the same business: the advertising business.

Just about every major advertising agency is listed in *The Standard Directory of Advertising Agencies* (also known as "The Agency Red Book"), published by the National Register Publishing Company, 3004 Glenview Road, Wilmette, Illinois 60091, (312) 256–6067. The Red Book is published three times a year and can be ordered direct from the publisher. Most libraries also have a copy in their reference room.

The Agency Red Book lists some 4,400 ad agencies in alphabetical order and is indexed by state. For each agency, it gives the address, phone number, branch offices, key personnel, major accounts, number of employees, year founded, annual billings (gross sales), and a breakdown of billings by media (newspaper, magazine, TV, radio, direct mail, collateral).

There are also thousands of smaller agencies not listed with the Red Book. You'll find local agencies listed in the Yellow Pages under "advertising agency."

The person you want to reach in the agency probably has the title of "creative director." In a larger agency, this person may be called a "creative group head," "creative supervisor," or "copy chief." In a very small agency (ten people or less), you might deal directly with the agency president or owner.

Your best prospects are agencies in your area that handle the type of business you specialize in. Size is not a key factor—you can get as much business from a small agency as you can from one of the giants.

Advertisers

Almost every advertiser needs help in copywriting. Even the ones with full-service ad agencies have many tasks—newsletters, product bulletins, annual reports—that they'd rather farm out to freelancers.

National Register also publishes a *Standard Directory of Advertisers,* which lists 17,000 companies that spend $30,000 a year or more on advertising. This "Advertiser Red Book" lists each company's ad budget, products manufactured, and key company personnel. In larger firms, the person you want to reach is the advertising manager (sometimes called "manager of marketing communications"). In smaller companies, where the advertising program is not large enough to justify hiring a full-time advertising person, the marketing manager, sales manager, product manager, or even the company president may handle the advertising.

As you specialize, you'll find that every industry has its own directory. In cable television, there's the *Cable Contacts Yearbook*, published by Larimi Communications Associates. In chemical processing, *Chemical Engineering Equipment Buyer's Guide* and *Chemical Equipment Catalog* are the two "bibles" of the industry. In some instances, you'll receive this type of directory free with your subscription to the leading industry trade journal. These directories can be invaluable as mailing lists and sources of new business leads for the freelance copywriter.

Public Relations Agencies

Many PR firms depend on freelancers to get their news releases, feature stories, and press kits out on time. *O'-Dwyer's Directory of Public Relations Firms* (published by J. R. O'Dwyer and Co., Inc., 271 Madison Avenue, New York, NY 10016, 212-679-2471) lists more than 1,200 PR companies including their addresses, phone numbers, top executives, number of employees, and areas of specialization.

Audiovisual Producers

Many A/V firms use freelancers to write scripts for slide shows, films, videotapes, and multimedia presentations. *Audio-Visual Directions* magazine publishes an annual directory of A/V production companies and suppliers. (Both the directory and the magazine are published by Montage Publishing, Inc., 5173 Overland Avenue, Culver City, CA 90230, 213-204-3313.)

Graphic Design Firms

Graphic design firms produce brochures, annual reports, invitations, folders, and other printed graphic material for their corporate clients. When the corporate client asks for copy as well as layout, the design firm obliges by hiring a freelance copywriter to handle the editorial portion of the job.

Local graphic design firms can be found in the Yellow Pages under "graphic arts studios," "design," or "art studios." Two nationwide directories that include design studios are *The Creative Black Book* (published by Friendly Publications, Inc., 401 Park Avenue South, New York, NY 10016, 212-228-9750) and *Adweek/Art Directors' Index* (co-published by *Adweek* magazine, 820 Second Avenue, New York, NY 10017, 212-661-8080).

When I started out, I went after the ad agency side of the business because I thought they'd be easier to reach. (I live in New York City, so there are about a thousand agencies within a ten-minute cab ride of my front door.) As things progressed, more and more advertisers asked me to write for them directly.

Right now, 70 percent of my clients are ad agencies and 30 percent are advertisers. But I welcome both types of clients.

I don't prefer one over the other—advertiser or agency. But there are some differences I can tell you about.

Ad agencies use your copy in ads, commercials, and other promotions they sell to their clients. They are buying your service, putting a markup on it, and then reselling it to the client.

What does this mean to you?

For one thing, your copy has to go through more levels of approval. You may have to do one rewrite to satisfy the agency, then another when the client makes changes.

On the other hand, many agencies handle minor revisions in-house once the copy is submitted by the freelancer, so you may not be asked to do anything more after you hand in your original manuscript. It all depends on the particular agency.

To maintain a good cash flow, the agency may not pay the freelancer until it receives payment from its client, the advertiser. This practice is unfair, because the terms the freelancer sets for payment have nothing to do with when (or whether) the ad agency's client pays its bills. But unfair or not, it's done all the time. So you may have to wait longer than you'd like—sometimes two months or more—before you see your money. If this is unacceptable to you, you can always demand some of the money up front.

A word of caution: The smallest ad agencies (less than five people) have a reputation for not paying freelancer's bills promptly—and sometimes not paying them at all.

In reality, nine out of ten small agencies are honest and will honor their contract with you. But be cautious when dealing with tiny ad agencies. Make sure you can trust them. If in doubt, get the cash up front.

The nice thing about doing business with ad agencies is that you know you're dealing with professionals who are knowledgeable in the field. In a subjective business, such as writing, there's a danger in working with amateurs—people who don't understand what you're doing or how it works.

The danger is that they won't "stand back" and let you do your job. They'll reject work based on aesthetics rather than on the standards of effective advertising.

Working with amateurs is a problem you might face when you work with advertisers directly. It isn't a problem when your client is a large company, because large companies hire professional advertising and marketing people who know what they're doing. The danger is working with smaller firms, where the person supervising the advertising is not an advertising professional but a manager or technician from another area who got "stuck" taking care of the ads.

This person spells trouble for the freelance writer. He

doesn't know what he wants, doesn't know what to expect from you, doesn't know how to work with you, and won't recognize a good ad when you write it. He'll pester you on the phone, drag you in for half a dozen meetings on the smallest project, and threaten not to pay your bill if you don't obey his every command.

You'll learn to spot this type after a few months in business. If you decide to do business with such a person, make sure you set ground rules in advance. The relationship will work only if the client respects you and is willing to trust your superior knowledge of advertising just as he trusts his lawyer in legal matters and his accountant at tax time.

If the small business can acknowledge your expertise in your trade, you can build a profitable relationship—one that can last for years.

As a rule, however, I'd say a larger corporation makes a better client than a small one. One reason, as I've said, is that you're dealing with professionals. Another is that they have the money to pay you what you're worth. And a third is that a large company does more advertising than a small company, so there is more repeat business for the copywriter.

In my own work, I serve a blend of large agencies, small agencies, and large, small, and medium-size advertisers. I enjoy working with them all, because they are all good clients. If I take on a job for a new client and do not enjoy working with them, I complete the job and don't work for that company again. As the saying goes, life's too short . . .

SETTING YOUR FEES

"How much do you charge?"

There's a question designed to stir up the butterflies in a beginning freelancer's stomach. Most novice freelance copywriters have *no idea* of what the going rates are, let alone what they should charge.

It took me a year of trial and error before I came up with a price schedule that made sense. Let me save you that year by giving you this price schedule now.

First, recognize that there are three ways you can charge your clients: by the hour, by the day, or by the project.

When I started, I offered all three. Now, on 99 percent of all jobs, I charge by the project. There are a number of advantages to this method—for me and my clients.

With a fixed project price and a contract in hand, I know what I'm earning when I take on the job. And the client is assured of getting the copy he needs at a price he can afford.

Some writers prefer to charge by the hour—so much for the first draft, more for a revision, and more for additional polishing. There's no way they can tell, in advance, what they'll make on a job, hence no way of determining if the job is worth taking.

Worse, an hourly arrangement leaves you open to objections when you present your bill. The client can claim that you didn't keep him informed as to how much time you had accumulated on the job, or that he didn't agree to pay such a large amount. But when you set a fee in advance, you can get a purchase order or contract in writing. That way, there's no question as to how much the client agreed to pay.

The only time I charge by the day is for editorial work that can't be priced by the project, such as a computer manual or catalog of unknown length or a "top secret" project the client can't tell me much about. I also have a flat day rate for in-person consultation with clients who want advice and information rather than copy.

Okay. You're charging by the project. But how much for an ad, letter, commercial, brochure?

In talking with freelance copywriters, I've found that there really are no standards. Fees range from the dirt cheap to the unbelievably expensive. For example, I know one experienced Chicago-based copywriter who charges

$250 for a sales letter, while his peer in New Jersey charges nearly $3,000 for a letter of similar length. So fees are, as freelancer Sig Rosenblum puts it, "all over the lot."

Still, I've managed to compile rough pricing guidelines based on typical copywriter's fees. These guidelines, presented below, will give you a some logical basis for setting your own fees.

If you're a beginner, you might charge toward the bottom range of these fees; if you're an old pro, you might charge much more than what is listed below. It all depends on your skills, your aggressiveness, and the demand for your services.

TYPICAL FEES FOR FREELANCE COPY

Type of Assignment	*Fee Range*
Full-page ad (7″ × 10″)	$250–$1000
Two-page ad	$500–$1000 and up
Brochure	$200–$750 per page
Sales letter	$250–$750 per page
Catalog copy	$200–$500 per page (or $40–$100 per item)
Newsletter	$250–$400 per page
Press release	$100–$300
Feature article	$1,000–$3,000
Film, slide presentation, or other audiovisual show	$100 per minute
Instruction manual	$25–$65 an hour
Speech (20-minute)	$1,000–$3,000
Annual report	$5,000–$10,000
Radio commercial	$300–$600
TV commercial	$600–$1,000
Consulting services	$250–$1,000 a day and up

I send all my prospects a sheet listing these projects and the fees I charge for writing them. But my schedule of fees is not inflexible; it's a rough guideline only. If there's a lot of extra work involved, or if the project is part of a major ad campaign for a large corporation, I charge more. If the project is simple, or if the client has a limited budget, I may charge a little less.

Whatever you decide to charge, you should get the client's approval of your fee, in writing, before you begin the project. Insist on a purchase order or at least a letter of authorization written on the client's letterhead. This is the professional way of doing business, and it ensures a mutual understanding between writer and client before the service is performed.

Many copywriters require payment of all or part of the fee up front. (I get half up front from all new clients.) This is just an additional form of protection against the occasional deadbeat.

My fee includes all revisions and rewrites, provided revisions are assigned within 60 days of delivery of the copy *and* provided the revision is not based on a change in the assignment made after the copy is submitted.

I wrote the 60-day clause into my fee schedule when a one-shot client called me two years after I'd written an ad for him and expected me to do a rewrite free of charge (after he'd run the original ad and paid my bill, no less!).

Free revisions cover all reasonable copy changes. But if the client decides on a brand-new strategy (for example, he decides to change the focus of his campaign from the consumer to the distributor), then the nature of the assignment has changed and the copywriter should charge for a new series of ads according to his fee schedule.

BUILDING A SUCCESSFUL FREELANCE COPYWRITING PRACTICE

When I studied direct-marketing copy with veteran copywriter Milt Pierce, Milt gave the class a short lecture on "23 Tips for Building a Freelance Copywriting Practice." Ten of Milt's tips are reprinted below (and the other 13 are covered within the text of my chapter).

- Never tell anyone that you're not successful. Always say you are.
- It's better to work for a little money than not to work at all.
- Write thank-you notes . . . even for the smallest reasons.
- Offer old clients new ideas.
- Don't let your fears get in the way.
- If it's a choice between missing a deadline or handing in shoddy work, miss the deadline—but let the client know in advance.
- Don't allow yourself to be exploited.
- Always get your bills paid. The client who owes you money will never give you another job.
- Charge for outside consultations. But don't charge if they come to your office.
- Use outside services. Don't become a typing and messenger service.

To Milt's tips I add a few of my own:

- Don't miss deadlines. Use Express Mail, Federal Express, or a messenger service if you have to, but make sure the copy is on the client's desk by the deadline date—or sooner.
- Make it look good. The copy should be neatly and perfectly typed—no cross-outs, white-outs, typos, or inser-

tions. If you don't want to waste half your life retyping copy, invest in a computer with a word processing program. Or hire a part-time secretary.

- Be yourself. Don't put on a false front when going after new business. If you get hired because of this false front, the client will dump you when your true self is revealed in the course of your working relationship.

- Keep your cool. Never get defensive when clients criticize your copy—even if they're wrong or rude in the way they do it. Be professional. If the client is a rotten S.O.B., don't fight with him—dump him.

- Don't be afraid to ask questions. If the client asks whether you understand something, and you don't understand, don't pretend that you do. Instead, ask the client to explain it to you. Remember, it's the client's job to know his business inside and out. Your job is to learn enough about the business to write effective copy. There's no shame in not knowing a technical fact or term.

- If the client asks you a question, and you don't know the answer, don't fudge it. Instead, say "I don't know—but I'll find out." American business would be in much better shape if its consultants said "I don't know" more often.

- Be flexible. If a business opportunity out of the ordinary comes along, be cautious, but take a look. It may lead to profitable ventures you never thought of before.

12

How to Get a Great Job as an Ad Agency Copywriter

Advertising executive Fairfax Cone once remarked, "The inventory of an advertising agency goes down in the elevator every night." [1]

In other words, people are an agency's most valuable resource. And the copywriter ranks as one of the more important "people resources" in the ad agency business.

Copywriters write the words we read and hear in ads and commercials. Aside from the art director, no advertising professional's work has as much visibility as the copywriter's.

Many other people make equally significant contributions to the advertising campaign. Account executives help plan the advertising strategy. Market researchers delve into the mind of the consumer and come up with the real reasons why they buy your product. Media buyers buy the best space at the best price.

But this is all invisible to everyone save the client and the agency. The only thing the general public sees is the finished product: the ads and commercials.

This fact is to the copywriter's advantage in job-hunting. The copywriter can present a book of ad clippings or a film reel of TV commercials and say, "This is mine. I wrote it." The contributions of media planners, account executives, market researchers, print production managers, traffic managers, and other agency people are harder to pinpoint.

Writers who work at advertising agencies are more in the "mainstream" of advertising than freelancers. Staff copywriters write print ads for major consumer publications. They also write most of the television commercials.

Freelancers handle the leftovers—direct mail, radio commercials, trade ads, brochures. Freelancers almost never get to write TV commercials (and many people feel television is the most glamorous and prestigious advertising medium to work in).

As an ad agency writer, you have a wealth of resources at your fingertips. There are artists to sketch out your concepts. Creative directors to give you assignments and guidance in your work. Other writers to read your copy and to bounce ideas off of. Account executives to handle client meetings and provide whatever background information you need.

Plus, there are all the resources of any large office—a nice desk, a fancy typewriter, a photocopy machine, free paper and pencils and white-out, maybe even a secretary and a plush private office.

The freelancer has no one but himself to depend on. Worse, he has to buy his own paper and pencils.

Agency copywriters get nice, steady paychecks. The freelancer can go months without seeing a dime.

Speaking of paychecks: Copywriters earn respectable salaries.

Beginning salaries range from the low teens to the low twenties—maybe a little more if you're specializing in a high-demand area such as high-tech or direct marketing.

According to the *1983 Adweek Salary Survey,* the median salary for all copywriters is $25,200. Copywriters in the top 10 percent income bracket earn an average of $44,300.

Experienced writers at big agencies can make $60,000, $70,000, even $80,000 a year. And a handful of superstars make more. But you generally have to become a creative director to see a six-figure income.

The creative director is the person responsible for the production and coordination of all creative work in the agency—copy, art, print, and broadcast production.

Adweek reports the median salary of creative directors as $61,000. The top 10 percent earn an average of $168,700.

For many copywriters, the position of creative director is the next step up the corporate ladder. But, if you make the move, you'll spend more time supervising others and less time writing.

Agency writers are usually assigned to one or two accounts, and they stick with these accounts for a long time. Agency writers work on continuous ad *campaigns,* rather than one-shot projects, as freelancers do.

If you want to write "prestige" copy—major campaigns for large national consumer accounts such as Burger King, Pepsi, Ford, or AT&T—you can do it only by getting a job with the large agency that handles the account. This type of work is handled by agency staff writers 99.9 percent of the time; freelancers rarely get an opportunity to handle big campaigns for "blue chip" accounts.

Finally, if you want to be part of the advertising industry's "in" crowd, your best bet of making it is to work for a big-name agency handling a big-name account. For the most part, writers who work freelance, in the advertising departments of manufacturers, or for small, unknown agencies are outsiders in the business.

WHERE THE JOBS ARE

Hundreds of job openings are advertised each week in the "help wanted" sections of dozens of national and regional advertising journals. Two excellent sources for job hunters are the help-wanted classifieds in *Adweek* and *Advertising Age.* (A list of advertising magazines appears at the end of this book.)

Another source of job opportunities is the help-wanted section of your local paper. The help-wanted classified section of the Sunday *New York Times,* for example, lists dozens of ad agency openings in the New York/New Jersey area.

Help-wanted ads are a good place to start your job hunt. After all, when you respond to a help-wanted ad, you know for a fact that the company has a job opening they want to fill.

Job seekers reading help-wanted ads spend a great deal of time agonizing over whether they're qualified for the position being offered. They wonder, "Is the agency rigid about the job's qualifications? Or will they take a look at you even if you don't have the experience and background they ask for in the ad?"

The answer lies somewhere between these two extremes. The agency realizes that the "ideal" candidate is a rare breed and will interview people even if they lack some of the qualifications. On the other hand, an agency advertising for a top-level creative director is not going to hire a college graduate fresh out of Advertising 101.

Here are a few recent help-wanted ads, along with my analysis of what the agency is really looking for:

HOW TO GET YOUR BEST ADS OUT OF THE AGENCY.

Send them to us.

Right now we're looking for terrific writers and art directors. For starters, we'd like to see copies of your five best samples (product or spec). If it's what we're looking for, not only will your best work get out of your agency in one piece, so will you.

Comment: The key here is "product or spec." A "spec" ad is an ad you write on your own to demonstrate your copywriting skill. It's not an assignment from a real client.

By accepting spec work, the agency is in effect saying, "What's most important is that you're good and can prove it. We don't care whether you've had a lot of experience." This ad tells me the agency will hire a talented beginner. But, if you respond to the ad with spec work, it had better be great.

COPY CHIEF, DIRECT MARKETING/PROMOTION.

_____is looking for a Writer/Supervisor for package goods direct marketing accounts. A thorough knowledge of direct mail, promotion, and consumer writing is required. Min. 5 years experience. If you can handle a fast pace, lots of responsibility, and want to grow, send résumé, salary requirement, and photocopy of your favorite sample.

Comment: They're looking for someone with experience in a highly specific field. To get the job you'd have to be a direct-marketing copy specialist with a portfolio full of projects done for major package-goods account. They're not going to settle for someone who has done mostly trade ads, product brochures, or business and industrial copy.

WRITER

Expanding Connecticut Advertising/P.R. Agency with blue chip national accounts needs an experienced Writer or Writer/Creative Director. Print, collateral, some broadcast, audio visual, P.R. Business-to-business experience essential; consumer background a plus.

Comment: By calling for a "Writer or Writer/Creative Director" the agency is saying, "We are looking for people who are solid writers, but we might also be interested in hiring someone who's a little more heavyweight, someone who can take on more supervisory responsibility."

They sound flexible about most of the requirements. For example, "some broadcast" means they'll probably overlook the fact that you haven't written TV commercials if you've done some other form of audiovisual work. I'd guess that a good writer with two to five years of experience could qualify for this job, yet someone with ten years experience could also be in the running.

> COPYWRITER WHO SHARES OUR CONCEPT OF CONCEPT.
>
> You're an advertising copywriter who already understands that concept is what it's all about. Sparkling, fresh, bold, daring, intrusive concepts.
>
> Concepts that not only break through the clutter, but also get results by being on-target in terms of advertising and marketing objectives.
>
> That means you use the wealth of computerized research and other data available to you, but you don't get bogged down with it. Because your striving for exciting creative product won't let you.
>
> If that's your concept of concept, send samples of your work (spec or produced) that demonstrate that you're more than a writer. You're our new advertising copywriter. Salary commensurate with experience, employment commensurate on creativity.

Comment: The style of this copy and the emphasis on vague notions of "concept" and "creativity" have me worried. Instead of listing specific qualifications, the ad talks in glowing but general terms. It sounds like they really don't know what they want—or if they do, they aren't telling you about it. As a hard-sell, straightforward copywriter, I'm not moved by this ad. But other writers may be excited and enthusiastic about it.

These critiques were designed to help you interpret help-wanted ads and get a feel for whether a position is right for you (and whether you're qualified for the job). When in doubt, write the letter and send the résumé. It never hurts to ask, and you're only gambling a 20-cent stamp.

Keep in mind, though, that the majority of job openings are never advertised. They are filled through contacts, through executive search firms, and through job seekers getting in touch with the right person at the right time.

Look through a copy of *The Standard Directory of Advertising Agencies*. See which agencies handle the types of accounts and specific clients you'd like to write for.

Write letters to the creative directors of these agencies. Tell them you'd like to write copy for them and give them reasons why they should take a look at your portfolio and give you an interview. (I'll give you some tips on how to write letters and résumés a little later on in the chapter.)

WHAT TYPE OF AGENCY IS BEST FOR YOU?

Agencies come in many different varieties. The two basic types are large and small.

You'll have to decide which type is right for you.

Big agencies have many advantages: They have the most opportunity for advancement. They handle the most prestigious accounts. They have different jobs, departments, and clients to choose from. And a few big agencies even have special training programs for entry-level copywriters.

What's more, big agencies pay better salaries than small agencies. According to the *1983 Adweek Salary Survey*, copywriters at the country's biggest agencies earn about 46 percent more than writers at small (under $1 million in billings) agencies.

Big agencies let you concentrate on one account. If you land a job with IBM's agency and work on the IBM account, you may spend all your time planning and writing print ads for IBM personal computers.

At a small agency, you will probably work on many different accounts. And they'll be smaller in scope: everything from local auto dealers and restaurants to software firms and industrial manufacturers.

Big agencies tend to concentrate on print ads and commercials. Small agencies attract clients by promising to do other tasks as well: direct mail, sales literature, technical publications, manuals, catalogs . . . even public relations work.

Big agency copywriters are somewhat insulated from clients, outside vendors, and other departments in the agency. The writers write and leave other tasks to specialists.

At a small agency, you become less of a specialist, more of a generalist, because the small agency can't afford to hire a separate person for every task. For instance, a copywriter at a small agency may also act as the account executive. (Such a copywriter is called a "copy/contact person" because, in addition to writing copy, he is the agency's contact with the client.) The copywriter might also be responsible for producing radio and TV commercials or working with outside artists and printers to produce ads and brochures.

Another choice is whether to work for a "creative shop" or a "marketing shop."

"Shop" is advertising slang for "ad agency." A creative shop is an agency whose strength lies in the ads and commercials it produces, rather than in the planning and strategy stage. Doyle Dane Bernbach is known as a creative shop because of the advertising it produced for Volkswagen, Polaroid, and other accounts. Ally & Gargano is one of the hottest creative shops around today because of its commercials for Federal Express and MCI Long Distance.

A marketing shop is an agency known for its marketing savvy—skill in market research, advertising strategy, business planning, media selection. Ted Bates is well-known as a marketing shop.

At creative shops, the creative department—copywriters, art directors, producers—reign supreme. At marketing shops, the account executives have more clout.

The ideal agency is probably a blend of both. It encourages fresh, original creative work but uses this creative talent to achieve the client's sales and marketing objectives. (Beware of agencies that care more about advertising's aesthetic qualities than the sales results it produces.) Choose an agency whose work environment you feel most comfortable with. Make sure their idea of what makes for good advertising is in sync with your own.

Finally, there's the choice of whether to go with a "general" agency—one that produces print ads and commercials for a broad range of consumer accounts—or to work for an agency that specializes in an area such as financial, retail, direct marketing, high-tech, industrial, or medical advertising.

The advantage of specialization is that specialists can command greater salaries when they switch agencies, because other agencies need their industry-specific experience to handle accounts in these areas.

The danger is that, once you become established in a speciality (such as automotive copy or package goods), you'll become tagged as an "automotive writer," "soap writer," "food writer," or whatever.

The longer you stay in a particular specialty, the harder it becomes to break out and work in new areas. One writer complained to me, "When I started in this business 35 years ago, I never thought about being a specialist or generalist. Now, after 35 years on hardware accounts, no one will hire me to do anything else."

Many writers avoid specializing because they like the variety of working on many new products and accounts. They don't want to be limited or stuck in one area.

Writers who want to be generalists would do best to go with a general agency. At a general agency, you can get experience on a wide variety of accounts without getting pigeonholed as a product specialist.

Copywriters planning an eventual move to freelance life would be better off working for a specialty agency. The reason is that in freelancing, specialists are more in demand and command higher fees than generalists. And the quickest way of becoming a specialist is to do it writing copy for an ad agency with accounts in the specialty you are interested in.

This brief overview can only give you a general idea of what to look for in an ad agency. But remember: Each agency is unique. Each has its own character, its own personality, its own special environment.

When you go in for a job interview, you should check out the agency as thoroughly as they check you out. You want to be sure the job is right for you before you accept an offer. And so . . .

Start by looking over the agency's client list published in The Agency Red Book. Does the agency handle accounts that interest you?

Next, take a look at the ads they've produced for these accounts. You'll probably find framed reprints of these ads plastered all over the walls of the agency's lobby and hallway.

When you look over this work, do you see ads you admire? Or do you get the feeling that you and the agency have a different conception of what good advertising should be? You want to work at an agency whose "philosophy" and style is in tune with your own.

Get the creative director to give you a tour of the agency. Do the people look happy, energetic, productive, enthusiastic? Do they look like they are having fun? Are they people you would enjoy working with? They'd better be, because you're going to spend at least the next year or two of your life with them.

Here are some questions I'd ask of an agency I was considering working for:

- What type of assignments do your copywriters work on? What's the mix between print ads, TV and radio commercials, direct mail, brochures, public relations? What, specifically, will I be doing all day?

- What accounts will I be assigned to? What do these companies manufacture? Which products will I be working on? How do the billings (gross income) produced by these accounts rank with other accounts handled by the agency? (This tells you whether you're working on important accounts or minor business.)

- How many other people are assigned to the account? Am I the only writer or part of a team? Do I work with an account executive or handle client contact myself?

- What is the career path for copywriters in this agency? Can copywriters get promoted and still write copy? Or are senior copywriters, copy chiefs, and creative directors mainly supervisors?

- Which accounts did the agency gain in the last two years? Which did it lose?

- What will the agency's billings be this year? What were they last year and the year before?

- Will I be working in an open area? A partially enclosed "modular office"? Or will I have a real office with a door I can close? (Depending on how you like to work, this may be important to you.)

TIPS ON RÉSUMÉS AND COVER LETTERS

"Advertising is a creative business," thinks the aspiring copywriter, "and so my best bet of getting an interview is to write the most far-out résumé possible. It will stand out from the crowd and prove how creative I am."

Wrong.

Advertising isn't just creativity for creativity's sake. It's the application of creative ideas to the selling and marketing of a product or service. Advertising is a serious business, and the executive who hires you wants a hardworking, talented professional—not a far-out whacko. Your résumé should sell your experience, skill, and professionalism in a straightforward, persuasive manner.

"Don't submit a 'creative' résumé," warns Hugh Farrell, president of Hammond Farrell, Inc., a New York advertising agency. "We don't read résumés to be entertained. The résumé should be brief and simply state the facts. The cover letter should make it clear you know the nature of the agency you're applying to and, in brief form, why you think you're right for that company.[2]

Unusual mailings may get attention but rarely result in an interview. Hal Riney, a senior vice president of Ogilvy & Mather, recalls receiving such "creative" packages as a poem, a cartoon, and a box containing a set of teeth and a note that said, "I'd give my eye teeth to work for you."[3]

Other than being brief (preferably one page, no longer than two) and neatly typed, there's really no standard format for résumés. Some people list their background in chronological order; others do it by the types of jobs or experiences they've had or by their skills in different areas.

What's important is that the résumé gives the reader a quick and complete overview of who you are and what you do. The key to writing a successful résumé, says Paula Green, head of her own ad agency, is "putting your résumé together so that it reflects your accomplishments and skills, not just your height, weight, date of birth, etc."[4]

Let's say you've held two positions in which you did some copywriting on the job. In listing these jobs on your résumé, you should tell the name of the company you worked for, what business they were in, and the type of copy you wrote (product sheets, catalog listings, sales letters, trade ads).

Other items of interest to readers of your résumé include:

- A statement of your objectives or your profession (e.g., "Objective: to write copy for major package goods accounts"). This statement should appear at the top of your résumé.
- Experience in selling, marketing, other facets of business
- Freelance copywriting experience. Even one or two assignments count for something.
- Other writing experience—journalism, feature writing, books, public relations, proofreading, copy editing
- Other responsibilities related to advertising, such as overseeing the production and printing of sales literature or coordinating trade show exhibits and seminars
- Creative awards your copy has won, sales results your copy has produced.

You've already seen how, in a direct-mail package, "the letter sells, the brochure tells." And so it is with cover letters and résumés. The letter makes the sales pitch. It tells the reader, "You should give me a job. Here are the reasons why." The résumé elaborates on these sales points and includes complete background too detailed to cover in a letter. The résumé *tells* the reader all about you. The letter *sells* him on giving you an interview.

A tip: Do not waste the reader's time telling him how interested and enthusiastic you are about the advertising field, or how you came to be that way. It's already assumed that you like advertising—otherwise, why would you be asking for a job with an ad agency?

Let's take a look at a cover letter that was effective in getting interviews.

A few years ago, I considered getting a job with an ad agency. The problem was, a lot of the help-wanted ads I saw insisted that the writer have ad-agency experience, which I did not.

I decided to write a letter that would turn my lack of credentials into a plus for me and get me the interview.

Here's what I wrote:

```
Mr. John Wilson
Box ABCD
New York, NY


Dear Mr. Wilson:

   Your ADWEEK help-wanted ad says you're
looking for a copywriter with agency experi-
ence.
   Why?
   I'm a writer on the client side. The
product managers I worked for aren't inter-
ested in slick, pretty ads that win creative
awards. They demand (and I give them) copy
and concepts that generate leads, create
awareness, and increase sales.
   Rather than build a portfolio of splashy
four-color advertisements, I've built cam-
paigns that achieve marketing objectives
within set budgets.
   Now, the average agency copywriter may
write more ads than I do. But my book will
show you that I do first-rate work. And if
that's not enough, I challenge you to try me
out on a few assignments and see if I don't
top every agency-experienced writer that ap-
plies for this job.


Sincerely,


Bob Bly
```

I'm not saying this is a perfect letter or that there isn't a better way to write it. But, of three ads I responded to, all three agencies gave me an interview.

My letter was written in response to an ad. Here's a letter written to an agency that was not advertising for copywriters at the time:

Dear Mr. Carriello:

What do you look for in a copywriter?

Is it skill in persuasive writing? The enclosed ''spec'' samples will give you a good idea of my ability to write hard-selling, attention-getting print ads.

Is it experience in writing? I've been a newspaper reporter, a proofreader, and a marketing communications writer for General Electric. The enclosed résumé will give you the full story.

Is it experience working for an ad agency? That I don't have. And that's why I'm writing to you.

I'd like a job writing copy for your agency.

Salary and title are unimportant right now. I just want to get in the door, to prove myself to you. Once you see me perform I won't have to ask for more responsibility. You'll want to give me all I can handle (and that's an armful!).

You know I can write. But can I sell? I'm going to call you next week. Give me five minutes on the phone, and I'll do my best to sell you on giving me a half hour of your time in an interview. You'll see me. And, you'll see a book full of first-rate spec copy.

Then, I'll know how well I can write. And sell.

Thanks for your consideration. Talk to you next week.

Sincerely,

Brad Frankel

HOW TO PUT YOUR BOOK TOGETHER

A "book" is a portfolio—a collection of ads and other promotions you've written.

You must have a book to get a job in advertising. Everybody who interviews you will ask to see it. They will judge you as much by the work in your book as by the cover letter, résumé, and how you handle yourself in the interview.

The actual portfolio is a plastic or leather case with pages similar to those in a photo album. The pages are heavy paper or cardboard covered with clear plastic. Reprints of your ads are pasted down on the cardboard and protected by the plastic covers.

The outside of the portfolio is usually plastic, vinyl, leather, or imitation leather. Most are black, some brown. Portfolios can be zipped shut and come with a handle for easy carrying.

You can buy a portfolio case at an art supply store. Many stores that specialize in leather products such as briefcases, handbags, and luggage also carry portfolios.

Portfolios come in many sizes. Choose one that is small enough to be carried conveniently, but with pages large enough to display your simple ads. For magazine ads, a 7-by-10-inch or 8½-by-11-inch page is big enough. But for newspaper ads, oversize brochures, or direct-mail packages with many pieces, you may need a larger size to display the material adequately.

The simplest way to display your ads is to paste them up in a portfolio, one ad per page. Some copywriters also paste a descriptive label or index card beneath the ad. The label tells which agency produced the ad, where it ran, the sales results it produced, and the awards it won, if any.

You can organize your portfolio by type of assignment, putting all ads in one section, all brochures in another, all sales letters in a third.

You can organize your portfolio by campaign. Each section contains the ads, commercial scripts, and collateral for a different ad campaign.

Or, you can organize your portfolio by product area—package goods, consumer electronics, medical products, office equipment.

There's no "right size" for a portfolio. Two samples is probably too few. A hundred is probably too many. Somewhere between six and sixteen samples seem about right.

Experienced copywriters may have more. Novices will have fewer.

Portfolios can contain both "published" and "on spec" work. Published ads are those that are actual assignments from real clients and have been published in magazines or newspapers. Spec ads, as you've seen, are assignments you make up on your own to demonstrate your copywriting skill.

Published ads are more impressive. There's something about a book filled with typewritten sheets of spec copy that says "amateur," just as a book filled with sharp-looking magazine tear sheets says "professional."

However, the real test is not whether the work is published or spec, but whether it's good, brilliant, or mediocre. Brilliant spec copy can make a creative director sit up and take notice of a novice writer. And a seasoned pro with a book of bland, unexciting, unoriginal work is not going to get a job with a top agency no matter how long he's been in business.

If you are just starting out, you have no published work to show, and so you will have to go about writing a portfolio of spec ads.

A good way to get started is to go through magazines and clip half a dozen or so ads you think you can improve on. Rewrite these ads. Then, in your book, put the original ads on left-hand pages with the rewrites facing them on the right-hand pages. This before-and-after technique can make a dramatic presentation of your copywriting skills.

Portfolios can—and should—be tailored for specific interviews. If you're interviewing with a direct-mail agency, begin your portfolio with some hard-selling sales letters. If you're going after a job with an agency known for its creative approach, make sure your ad copy reflects their level of creativity.

Put together a spare portfolio. That way, you can go on interviews even if a creative director asks to hold on to your original portfolio for a few days.

MAKING THE MOST OF THE INTERVIEW

How you look, act, and talk during an interview can decide whether you get the job. A great interview can, in part, make up for a so-so book. And a poor interview can eliminate a great copywriter from the running.

Here are some pointers for doing your best in the interview:

1. Be Sharp

Surviving a job interview takes a great deal of concentration, so you should be at your best. This means getting a good night's sleep the night before. And, if a big meal makes you groggy, don't eat or drink until after the interview.

2. Be On Time

Few things are as important in advertising as meeting deadlines. Make sure you show up for your interview on time; if you aren't on time for your interview, how will you meet your deadlines on the job?

Leave your house to go to the interview with plenty of time to spare. If you get there early, sit in the reception room or walk around the block until it's time. If you have to rush to get there on time, you'll be disheveled, sweaty, and flustered, and you won't be at your best for the interview.

3. Look Professional

Dress in business clothes: three-piece suits for men, conservative skirt and blazer for women. Be well-groomed, clean, neat. Short, clean hair is more appealing than long, unkempt, stringy hair. Like it or not, appearance makes a strong first impression, and you can blow your chance by dressing too casually or too "mod."

4. Bring Samples of Your Work

Always bring your portfolio. Also carry a file folder with other materials you might need: additional samples of your work, extra copies of your résumé, reprints of articles you've written, letters of recommendation from clients and colleagues. You want to have these items handy in case the interviewer asks to see them.

5. Listen

Don't go into the interview with a memorized sales pitch. Let the interviewer ask questions. Listen. And give the best answers you can.

Keep your answers friendly but brief and to the point. If you start blabbing, you're bound to say the wrong thing and hang yourself with it. Which brings us to our next tip . . .

6. Let the Interviewer Do Most of the Talking

When the interviewer is doing most of the talking, it's a sure sign that the interview is going well. It means the interviewer is comfortable with you, doesn't need to be sold on your qualifications anymore, and is in fact trying to sell you on the agency and why you should work there.

One way to get the interviewer to do the talking is to ask a lot of questions—about the agency, the clients, the

work environment, the job, and even about the interviewer himself.

7. Be Aggressive

Don't be bashful about promoting yourself; no one else
is going to do it for you.

You don't want to lie or put up a false front. But you
should apply "the 10 percent rule"—advertise yourself as
10 percent better than you really are.

For example, if you've written two or three press releases for a couple of clients, you can say, "Yes, I've handled public relations projects for a number of different
firms." Don't be "redder than the rose" and volunteer the
fact that the number is only two.

8. Don't Let Yourself Be Put on the Spot

Some interviewers may ask you to perform for them.
They might ask you to write some copy on the spot, or
critique some ads and come up with better headlines, or
solve a hypothetical marketing problem.

If you can come up with the answers right then and
there—great! Show them your stuff.

But, if you don't feel comfortable being put on the spot,
don't submit. Say, "I'll be glad to take these problems back
to my office and come up with the ads in a day or two for
you. But frankly, I don't write copy or come up with
strategy without going off and carefully studying the
problem. That's how I work best, and I know you wouldn't
want less than my best." Don't submit to the test and blow
your chances if you think you can't do well in a "quickie"
quiz.

9. Don't Apologize

Every interviewer will ask you if you have background
or experience in something that you don't. Most writers,
being humble and insecure, will bow their heads, apologize for their shortcomings, and beg forgiveness and a
chance to get the job anyway.

Don't beg, don't apologize. Instead, turn strength to weakness.

For example, the interviewer says, "I see you don't have any experience in insurance. We handle a lot of insurance accounts. How do you expect to be able to jump in and take on the work?"

You reply, "Well, it's true that I don't have a *lot* of experience in the area. But I've done plenty of work in related areas—banking, personal finance, real estate. And I didn't mention it on my résumé, but years ago I edited an in-house newsletter for Prudential Insurance. So I do know quite a bit about the industry and their products."

Or, suppose the interviewer says, "You're a medical copywriter. But we handle a lot of computer accounts, which are highly technical. You don't have any computer experience or training. How are you going to be able to learn it?"

You say, "You're right—I haven't worked on computers before. But I'm not a doctor, and I became a first-rate medical copywriter, and medical products are also highly technical. So you see, I have an aptitude for technical copy. It doesn't matter what the product is. With research and background material, I can quickly study and learn enough to write effective copy on any subject—including drugs *and* computers."

ON THE JOB

With a great background, portfolio, résumé, cover letter, and interview technique, you are bound to get a job in copywriting—sooner or later.

Advertising is a highly competitive industry, so finding a job may take some time. I know one copywriter with seven years experience who looked for three months before she was hired. I know another writer who is a beginner; it took her a year to get an offer.

When you show up for work, you'll be assigned a desk,

an art director, a creative director, an account executive, and one or more accounts.

The art director is your creative partner. The two of you will spend much time working together, dreaming up concepts for ads and commercials.

You'll write the copy. The art director will design the layout.

Sometimes, you'll think of a better way to design the ad and the art director will use your idea. Sometimes, the headline for the ad will come from the art director, not the writer.

The creative director is your boss. He or she runs the creative department. The creative director supervises and works with the agency's writers, artists, TV producers, and print production department. The creative director's job is essentially quality control of print and broadcast advertising.

When a new campaign is launched, the creative director may work with the artist and writer to establish an overall direction for the campaign. Then the artist and copywriter go off to produce the ads and commercials.

The account executive is the marketing expert of the team. He works with the client to plan advertising and marketing strategies. Then he goes back to the agency and explains the strategy to the writer and artist so they can create ads that achieve the objectives of the plan.

In addition to being a business expert and planner, the account executive is the liaison between client and agency. The account executive gives the writer the background information he needs to write accurate, effective copy. If the background information is wrong, the copy will be wrong, no matter how skilled the writer is.

The "account" is the client. The client is the one who approves, disapproves, or asks for changes in the copy you've written.

If the client turns down work you feel strongly about, you will try to convince the account executive that you are right and that the work should run as is. If the account executive can be persuaded to see your point of view, he may go back to the client to defend your work and try to get approval for it.

However, the client is paying the bill and has final say over what is published and what is rejected.

Studies have been done to determine how much of an ad agency employee's time is spent doing billable work.[5] "Billable work" is work that can be billed to the client. A copywriter's billable work includes time spent on writing, editing, thinking, working with the art director, and meeting with the account executive, creative director, or client to discuss the client's campaign.

The results of the study may interest you:

62.5% of the copywriter's time is spent on billable work

11.5% is spent on days off—vacation, personal, sick days, holidays

10% is spent in internal agency meetings

7% is spent on miscellaneous breaks (coffee, bathroom, staring out the window)

7% is spent working on presentations and speculative work to attract new business

2% is spent promoting the agency

WORKING ON THE CLIENT SIDE: THE AGENCY ALTERNATIVE

Not all advertising writers work at agencies.

Many work for the advertisers—the companies that manufacture products or offer services. This side of the business is called "the client side."

Because of its glamorous image, most people would prefer to work on the agency side. As a result, the client side is less competitive, and it's easier to get a writing job on the in-house staff of a corporation than it is at an agency.

Working on the client side is excellent training for an agency career. Not only will you build a portfolio of published copy, but you'll gain an intimate knowledge of the client's business and of how people on the client side think and feel. Most copywriters without client-side experience have very little idea of what goes on inside the client's mind or how the agency's work is really reviewed and approved.

After a year or two with a client, you're ready to make the move to an agency. Don't wait too much longer than that. Older writers who have been on the client side their whole careers are viewed as second-rate talents by many big-agency creative directors.

Snobbery? Yes. But that's the way it is. So, if you plan an agency career, use your client job as a training period and a stepping stone.

However, you may find that you enjoy the client side. Many people do, and they spend enjoyable, profitable, rewarding careers working for manufacturers, service firms, and retailers.

The following points of comparison between clients and agencies will help you decide which is right for you:

Agency Life Is More Hectic

Agency writers have more projects and tighter deadlines. It's an unfortunate fact of agency life that clients often don't give the agency a reasonable amount of time to complete their work. And the agencies take this abuse because they're afraid of losing the account.

Writers on the client side generally have fewer projects and more leisurely deadlines. They have a more secure relationship with the people they write for because they're all in the same office (or at least in the same company). So it's easier for a client-side writer to get a deadline extension or to set a deadline that gives him plenty of breathing room.

All the agency writers I know complain of putting in several 10- or 12-hour days every week. When I was a writer on the client side, I rarely worked past 5:00 P.M. And when I did, it was by choice—not because I had to.

Agency Writers Have More Variety

They work on many different accounts and many different products. The writer employed by an advertiser lives with the company's one product or product line day after day. And that can be boring, especially when you consider that client-side writers tend to change jobs less frequently than agency writers.

The Client-Side Writer Becomes a Product Expert

Because they work for the company that makes the product they write about, client-side writers gain a far greater and more intimate knowledge of their product than any agency or freelance writer can. They have much more opportunity to chat with engineers and designers, tour the labs and the plant, visit conventions, hobnob with top-level marketing and product managers. They get to go into the field to see the product in operation and to accompany salespeople when they call on their customers. The client-side writer has the luxury of becoming a product expert—an enjoyable position for a writer to be in.

Client-Side Writers See the "Big Picture"

Client-side writers work side-by-side with the people who design, manufacture, and sell the product as well as with the people who plan its marketing and advertising strategy. Also, client-side writers are frequently responsible for the *total* communications campaign, which may include trade show exhibits, seminars, sales presentations, technical literature, instruction manuals, product labels, dealer promotions, and sales meetings in addition to advertising and publicity. Agency writers, on the other hand, usually write the major print ads and TV commercials only.

They don't get to dig into the complete campaign the way in-house writers do.

Team Spirit

The in-house writer is part of the team, the corporate family. He's an insider, working in the office next door to the product manager or brand manager. The writer and his product manager attend the same company picnics, shoot the breeze by the same water fountain, ride in the same carpool. They might drop by each other's office five or six times a day to discuss a project or have a friendly chat.

The agency writer is viewed as an outsider. He's a hired gun—not part of the team. Some clients resent their agencies and would prefer to handle the advertising in-house. And even though most clients are on a friendly basis with their agency writer, there is rarely the close relationship that develops with the company's own writing staff.

CLIENT SIDE: WHERE THE JOBS ARE

Corporations have many different departments that hire staff writers. These include:

Advertising Department

The advertising manager in charge of this department works with his outside agency to develop major ad campaigns. The agency buys space and places ads according to a media plan approved by the ad manager. The ad manager also hires and supervises staff writers who produce trade ads, brochures, catalogs, trade show displays, and product data sheets. They might also write the company magazine and the annual report.

The In-house Agency

The in-house agency is an advertising department that functions as a full-service advertising agency. The in-house agency buys space, places ads, and receives commissions from the media, just like a regular advertising agency. The in-house agency offers the advertiser a broader range of services than the advertising department (these include media planning and buying and television production). Some in-house agencies even take on outside clients whose businesses don't conflict with the corporation's.

Marketing Communications

The marketing communications department produces communications that support a company's marketing efforts. They write industrial films, slide shows, sales brochures, easel presentations, and point-of-purchase displays. Marketing communications writers spend all of their time writing advertising support material; they rarely write the ads themselves.

Public Relations

Many advertisers have a separate department that handles public relations. Writers in these departments turn out news releases, feature stories, and other publicity-related material, such as newsletters and fact sheets.

Employee Communications

The writers in the employee communications department help top management communicate with the employees. As an employee communications writer, you may be asked to write a slide show used for recruiting new engineers and MBAs from universities, a film that gives plant workers an overview of the company, a series of booklets explaining the benefits programs, or the weekly employee newsletter.

Audiovisual Communications

The A/V department produces videotapes, films, and slide shows used by such departments as corporate, employee relations, marketing, sales, advertising, and training. Many A/V departments hire full-time writers to write scripts for these films and presentations.

Corporate Communications

Corporate communications is a service department that helps corporate management communicate. Corporate communications writers ghostwrite speeches and articles for busy executives. They may also be in charge of the annual report, the corporate ad campaign, and other communications aimed at stockholders, investors, and the general public.

Technical Publications

The technical publications department is a team of technical writers, editors, and artists who produce reports, proposals, manuals, and other technical documents. They may also get involved in data sheets and product brochures.

13

How to Hire and Work With Copywriters

"The advertising business is neatly split down the middle between people who make and create things and the people who approve and disapprove things," writes *Adweek* columnist Ed Buxton. "There are the doers and the undoers, the builders and the destroyers, the white hats and the black hats." [1]

This chapter is written to help these two warring factions—advertising professionals and their clients—work together more efficiently and more profitably and in relative peace and harmony.

If you are a client—someone with the power to approve or disapprove advertising—you will learn how to hire the best copywriters and how to work with them to get the best copy and ideas for your money.

If you are a copywriter (agency or freelance), you will learn how to get your copy reviewed and approved and how to avoid misunderstandings, arguments, and bad feelings between you and your clients.

WHY SOME CLIENTS DON'T RESPECT THEIR COPYWRITERS

The copywriting business is full of horror stories about abominable clients who bully and insult their writers.

One writer tells of a client who, displeased with a sales letter, sat the copywriter down at a typewriter and called in the entire office staff to stand over the writer as he rewrote the letter. Each time he typed in a new word, the office staff members would give their opinions on whether the word was acceptable and what should come next.

Another writer was hired to write a brochure for a pharmaceutical company. After submitting his copy, the writer never heard from the client again, even after repeated calls and letters to the company. Disgusted, he sent an invoice for his services. The firm sent back a note that said, "We decided to rewrite the copy ourselves. Enclosed is payment for your invoice minus our cost for rewriting your manuscript." Attached to the note was a check for only a small fraction of the agreed-upon amount.

Few murder suspects would tell their lawyers how to conduct their defense. And most sick people have faith in their physician's diagnosis. But almost every advertiser thinks he can write copy better than his agency, and most don't hesitate to take their editor's blue pencil to the copywriter's work.

Why don't copywriters "get no respect"? I can think of two reasons.

First, writing is more subjective than most other fields.

An accountant can point to a ledger and prove that the books balance. A lawyer can back up his case with legal precedents and logical arguments.

Writing copy is not so cut and dried. There may be dozens of ways of writing an ad, each with merit. The copywriter can *say* he thinks his way is best. But he can't *prove* his ideas are superior. The client has to take it on faith—and few do.

Of course, there are guidelines for effective copy (my versions of them are presented in the first two sections of this book). Unfortunately, many clients and writers are not aware of these rules. And without a clear idea of what makes good copy, how can the copywriter defend his work and say that it *is* good?

The second reason clients don't respect writers is that, way down deep, many clients fancy themselves better writers than their copywriters.

Doctors, lawyers, accountants, plumbers, mechanics, and TV repairmen deal in areas so technical and complex that their clients don't know enough to interfere. But everybody can write. (Even parrots and mockingbirds use language!) So there is less mystery to the copywriter's work, and clients are more confident that they could write the ad or letter "if only I had the time."

What can you do to improve the situation? Here's a three-step recommendation:

1. Hire the right copywriter for the job—someone who fits in with the product and your company.
2. Work with the writer on a *professional* basis. Treat the writer with the same respect you would your lawyer, accountant, or doctor. Stand back, and let the writer do his job. Don't interfere.
3. Establish logical guidelines for reviewing copy. Base your review on these concrete standards, not on subjective or aesthetic judgments. And above all, be *specific* in your criticism.

Let's look at each step of the plan in more detail.

HIRING THE RIGHT WRITER FOR YOUR BUSINESS

How do you go about finding freelance copywriters? And how do you know which writer is right for your business?

Here are ten tips for finding and selecting the best copywriter for the job at hand.

1. Ask Around

Need to find a writer? The best way to find one is through referrals. Ask your friends, colleagues, and acquaintances to recommend writers they have used in the past.

The people most likely to know the name of a good copywriter include:

* Local advertising agencies and PR firms
* Magazine space reps and editors
* Printers, typesetters, photographers, graphic artists, design studios, and other outside vendors
* Communications managers of nearby manufacturing and service firms

Some copywriters advertise their services in advertising journals. *Adweek*, for example, publishes a weekly "Creative Services Guide" that contains a number of ads offering freelance copywriting services.

Adweek also publishes an annual *Adweek/Art Directors' Index USA*. The book contains a section listing freelance copywriters.

Many copywriters advertise in the Yellow Pages under "copywriter," "writer," or "advertising agency."

2. Choose a Writer with Experience in Your Industry

There are three advantages to using a writer who knows your business. First, you'll spend less time briefing him and bringing him up to speed in your technology and your markets.

Second, because the writer already speaks the jargon of your industry, your employees will accept him more readily than they would an "outsider" who didn't speak their language. This may be important if you want your managers and engineers to work closely with the writer.

Third, the writer may be able to criticize your strategy or suggest new ideas based on his experience working with clients whose products are similar to your own.

Clients have asked me, "Do you have to be a computer programmer to write copy on a computer account?" You don't, and many great computer ads have been written by writers who didn't know a minicomputer from a microcomputer when they started. On the other hand, a writer with programming experience does have a head start over the writer who has never touched a computer keyboard.

The writer you hire doesn't have to be an expert in your particular product. (He won't ever know as much about your business as you do.) But he should have a feel for your industry and a knack for writing the type of copy you need.

For example: If you need a writer to write a brochure on your new Caribbean cruise package, don't insist that the writer have a portfolio full of brochures on Caribbean cruises. Chances are you won't be able to find such an individual. But you should look for a copywriter specializing in travel rather than one who is more at home with subscription mailings, annual reports, or fashion advertising.

In other words, *don't* insist that the writer have specific experience in your product line. *Do* look for a writer who specializes in your general *type* of advertising, be it travel, high-tech, home furnishings, or pharmaceuticals.

3. Hire Someone in Your League

Not all copywriting assignments require the same level of skill. Writing a bulletin-board notice to sell your 1978

Chevrolet doesn't take the same level of copywriting sophistication that writing a corporate ad campaign for Exxon does.

Copywriters also operate on different levels. There are high-paid specialists. Middle-level generalists. And beginners to handle the easy stuff. These writers charge according to their level of skill, and you can save money by not over-hiring for the job.

An advertising manager at a small industrial firm needed a cover letter to accompany a new brochure he was mailing to customers, sales reps, and regional offices. When he called a direct-mail specialist, the copywriter said, "I'd be glad to do the job, but my specialty is doing large mass mailings for big-name publishers and direct marketers. Because my letters are successful for these firms, I charge accordingly—$1,000 minimum for a short letter. I'm saying this not to brag, but to suggest that the job you have in mind doesn't require an experienced—and costly—top direct-mail writer. Hiring me to do this letter is like nuking a house to kill a mouse."

The direct-mail writer recommended an industrial writer who was willing to do the letter for only $350. The ad manager hired the industrial writer and was pleased with the copy he received.

4. Pick a Writer Whose Style is in Sync With Your Own

The conservative company, thinking that it's time to improve their image, hires the most creative agency in town.

The first ads come in. They're what you'd expect from a creative agency—creative. "A little too far out for us, though," says the conservative client. "Can you come up with something a little more dignified. We're just not sure about the dancing chemical drums . . ."

"You're stifling our creativity!" screams the agency. They pick up their presentation, stamp out of the conference room, send a bill, and refuse to work with the barbaric client anymore.

Moral of the story: An ad agency or freelancer is unlikely to convince the client to make a radical change in his way of doing business. So clients would do well to select copywriters whose approach and style are in tune with their own.

If you like hard-sell ads—ads with coupons, with benefits in the headlines, with price and where-to-buy information, with straightforward body copy that sells the features and benefits of the product—you probably won't like the ads you get from a copywriter trained on splashy "image" campaigns for national brands. After all, this writer probably believes an ad should have a "clever" headline, a glossy color visual, and that people "don't read long copy."

Well, he's not going to convert you to his point of view. And you're not going to waste your hard-earned ad dollars so he can win creative awards. The best bet is to stay away from each other in the first place. Hire a writer whose portfolio is full of your type of fact-filled ads. Let a company who wants "showplace" ads hire the creative guy.

Do you like long-copy ads or short-copy ads? Fancy color photos or plain-jane graphics? Informational copy or emotional copy? Plain language or purple prose? Choose a copywriter whose style and "advertising philosophy" fits in with your own. You'll both be happier with the working relationship—and with the copy it produces.

5. *The First Step*

Let's say you have the name of a copywriter you want to hire. The first step is to phone or write him and ask to see background material on his copywriting services.

At the very least, you want to see samples of his work, a résumé or capsule biography, and a list of his clients. Experienced copywriters already have a standard package prepared that contains all this and more. Novices have to be told what to send you.

Here are the things to look for when evaluating the freelancer's package:

- *Is it well written?* If the freelancer can't promote himself effectively, how can he write copy for services and products with which he's *not* intimately familiar?

- *Do you like the sample work?* The samples represent what he considers to be his best ads. If you don't think they show promise, keep looking. This isn't the right writer for you, and asking to see more samples isn't going to change anything.

- *Look at the client list.* Make sure the copywriter has experience in your industry or in related fields. Don't hire a straight technical writer to write your new perfume ad. Find a writer who likes doing perfume ads and is good at it.

- *Did the copywriter include information on his fee rate and structure?* A true professional will give you his rates up front. He doesn't want to waste your time—or his—if you can't afford to pay him.

- *What related writing and communications experience does the copywriter have?* A well-rounded copywriter does more than write copy. What else has your copywriter written? Any books? Articles? Papers? Speeches? Seminars? Teaching experience?

- *What overall feeling do you get from the whole thing?* You've looked over the writer's material and chatted with him over the phone. Do his package and presentation say "professional" or "amateur?" Do you feel comfortable with the writer and confident that he can handle the job? Gut feelings are important. Go with your instincts.

6. Don't Expect Something for Nothing

An amazing number of smaller companies will call me up and say, "We're a small manufacturer in South Jersey. We don't do much advertising, but we saw your ad and may need a one-page press release to announce our president's retirement next month. We'd like to meet with you to check you over. Can you come over this afternoon? Get a pencil and I'll give you directions . . ."

I have news for you. Unless you're a major advertiser or ad agency with a large project in hand or the promise of a *lot* of business for me, you are not going to see me. Ever. And why not? Because if I jumped in that car and spent the better part of the day visiting every small business that wanted a $150 press release, I'd have no time to write copy for my dozens of paying clients.

My point is: The copywriter, like a lawyer or doctor, is a professional. If you want his time, you must be willing to pay for it. Few copywriters give free house calls these days.

You may object, "But I want to hire you! Isn't a meeting the next step?"

It doesn't have to be. We can handle the assignment by mail and phone.

"But I *want* to meet you!"

Fine. Come to my office and there is no charge. If I have to leave the house, though, I have to charge you for my time—if it's just an exploratory meeting. If you have an assignment for me, I'll include the meeting as part of my fee, provided we've already agreed that I'm going to handle the project for you.

As I've said, I may make an exception if you're a big advertiser or agency or if you're dangling an attractive project in front of my nose. But it's unreasonable for most clients—smaller companies with infrequent copywriting assignments—to expect the copywriter to come running without compensation. The few projects they have to offer don't justify the time spent in travel and meetings.

Most copywriters wll be glad to chat with you at length over the phone or in their office. But don't expect the copywriter to make an out-of-office trip to your plant unless you're willing to pay for a consultation. A writer who earns $400 or $600 or $800 a day isn't going to spend half a day chasing down a $200 assignment.

7. Discuss Fees Up Front

There's no point in talking if you can't afford the writer's rates. Save yourself a lot of time and find out fees up front.

Most writers can give you rough estimates of what they charge for different jobs—so much for an ad, so much for a sales letter, more for a brochure. Ask to see the copywriter's fee schedule, if he has one.

These estimates are "ballpark" figures only. The exact fee depends on the specific assignment. But the ballpark figures give you a good idea of what you'll pay for the copy you need.

If the copywriter charges by time instead of project, find out his rate for a week, day, half-day, or hour. Ask how long he thinks your project will take. Multiply the number of days by the day rate to get the total cost estimate.

Also discuss deadlines up front. The top copywriters are often booked weeks in advance and cannot always handle rush jobs. Some prospects are shocked to learn that I can't write their ad overnight. They don't realize that I already have six jobs on my desk, all due in a week or so.

Find out how much time the writer normally takes to do small projects (ads, letters) and large ones (brochures, catalogs). If your deadlines are short, say so, and ask the writer if he can meet them.

Copy revisions should also be discussed up front. Are they included in the copywriter's initial fee or do they cost extra? How many drafts are included in the basic project price? How quickly can the writer make revisions? What happens if there is a change in the nature of the assignment—are revisions still included? Is there a time limit in which revisions must be assigned?

Make sure you understand the writer's policy toward revisions. Otherwise, it can become a problem area later on.

8. Provide Complete Background Information on the Project

Send the writer all the background information you can. With this material in hand, the writer can give the most accurate estimate as to what the job will cost. Without it, he is "flying blind" because he doesn't know how much research is involved—and his high estimate will reflect this degree of uncertainty.

You'll get the best price by giving the writer whatever information he needs to make an informed, accurate estimate of what the copy will cost.

9. Get It in Writing

Put the fee, terms, deadlines, and a description of the assignment in a purchase order or letter of agreement and send it to the copywriter.

A written agreement eliminates confusion and spells out what the client is buying and what the writer is selling. Too many buyers and sellers in all fields of business have gone to court because they made their deals orally.

Don't you make the same mistake. A written agreement protects the client *and* the writer. So don't just shake hands on it. *Put it in writing.*

10. Stand Back

Once you've hired the writer and give him the background material, stand back and let him do his job. Don't interfere, don't ask to "take a look at a the first few pages," don't badger the writer with constant "how's it going?" phone calls.

You've hired a professional. Now let the professional do his job.

You'll get your copy by the deadline date—or sooner. And it will be copy that pleases you and is effective in selling your product.

If you need changes, the writer will make them—fast. After all, that's what you're paying for.

A FEW TIPS ON WORKING WITH COPYWRITERS

The best way to work with your writer is to leave him alone during the first-draft stage of the project. He knows what he's doing, and you trust him. Otherwise, you wouldn't have hired him in the first place.

But, even though the copywriter is working at a distance, it's important that the two of you start off with a comfortable, mutually agreeable working relationship. Copywriting is a partnership: You provide the information and direction, the copywriter provides the persuasive writing, and together you sell more of a product or service.

If one or both partners isn't happy, someone won't be doing his job with enthusiasm. And a job done without enthusiasm is a job done poorly.

Here are some suggestions for maintaining a good working relationship between client and copywriter.

1. Pay Fairly

Pay fair rates for copywriting services performed. Remember: An underpaid worker is an unhappy and unproductive worker. Writers writing for slave wages rarely produce exciting prose.

Everything in life is negotiable, but only so far. A good writer with a steady business may take 10 or 20 percent off his price if your assignment is interesting to him. But he can't afford to—and won't—go much below that.

A writer who needs the work may come very cheaply. But, even if you sense you can get it for less, pay a fair wage. If you force the writer down to the bargain-basement price, he's not going to feel very good about your project.

And you want your writer to be *enthusiastic*—not apathetic.

2. Pay On Time

There are few things as unpleasant in business life as trying to collect an unpaid invoice. Unfortunately, it's not unusual for clients to be four, six, even eight weeks or more behind in their payments to their freelancers.

Pay on time—in 30 days—and the freelancer will get a warm glow inside whenever you call. Better still, get a check out in ten days or less, and the freelancer will try to perform miracles for you on your next ad or campaign.

Agencies feel pretty much the same way, and although the agency writer doesn't get paid by you directly, accounts that pay their bills on time get special attention and love.

3. Cooperate

Provide complete background information on the product, your audience, and your objectives. Be available to answer questions or give direction. Review outlines and rough drafts in a timely fashion.

One person from the client organization should be the contact between the company and the copywriter. It is inefficient for the copywriter to have to track down executives from half a dozen different departments of your firm.

4. Don't Waste Time

Avoid unnecessary meetings. Maybe a meeting or two will be needed, but most of the writing and revision can be handled by mail and phone.

Don't feed information or revisions to the writer one piece at a time. Give him the background information or the instructions for the rewrite in one shot.

It is good manners not to keep people waiting when

they have an appointment with you. This applies to copywriters, too.

To the copywriter and the ad agency, time is money. If you do not waste their time, your account will be profitable to them, and they will gladly devote themselves to giving you the best advertising possible.

On the other hand, the more you waste the writer's time, the less profitable the project becomes. The writer will either devote less time to writing your copy. Or, he will drop your account.

In general, writing copy should not require a great deal of contact between client and copywriter. The fewer number of contacts, the better. Meetings should never be more than two hours and should follow a tight agenda. Phone conferences should be brief and to the point.

Not only will the writer save time (and possibly charge you less as a result), but you will save time, too.

5. Let Them Hear From You

The copywriter mails his copy and never hears from the client until the next project. His insides are twisted with worry: Did the client hate the copy or did they love it? Probably they loved it—no news is good news—but the writer doesn't know.

A kind word from a client—a quick phone call, a brief, one-line note of praise—can do wonders for the copywriter's ego. Writers seldom receive feedback on their work, even when the reaction is favorable.

A thank-you note will be much appreciated by the writer starved for praise and ego gratification. Sincere flattery can quickly put you at the top of the writer's "favorite clients" list. And the benefits of this—better service, better copy—are far in excess of the effort involved.

6. Critique Copy Rationally

"I don't like it" is a meaningless critique and a frustrating response for the copywriter to deal with.

The key to reviewing copy is to give specific, objective criticisms. Subjective and vague comments don't give the writer any guidelines for revision and often lead to hurt feelings, defensiveness, and a gradual collapse of the client/copywriter relationship.

Below are nine rules for reviewing and approving copy. They will eliminate bad feelings and misunderstandings and give the copywriter the guidelines he needs to re-write the copy so that it will be acceptable and effective.

HOW TO REVIEW AND APPROVE COPY

1. Be Specific

Make your critique of the copy factual and specific. Show the copywriter where he went wrong—and how you want him to fix it.

Some examples of nonspecific vs. specific criticisms:

Nonspecific:	*Specific:*
"Not enough pizzazz."	"Our product is the only one that offers these features. The copy should stress its uniqueness more strongly."
"The copy doesn't 'position' the product."	"Our process is 20% more efficient than the competition's. That should be in the headline."
"The ad is dull and boring."	"Put in less about the technical features and more about what the product can do for *people*."

"It doesn't tell the story we want to tell."	"Here are the four consumer benefits the copy should cover. . . ."
"I don't like it."	"This is a good start. But there are some changes I'd like to see. Let me tell you what I have in mind. . . ."

The copywriter is not a mind reader. It is not enough to say you want changes in the copy; you must specify what those changes are.

This does not mean that you do the copywriter's job and rewrite the copy yourself. It does require that you write down specific, factual changes and corrections you want made and give them to the copywriter so he can rewrite your copy to incorporate these changes. And be sure to give these instructions *in writing,* not orally (unless they are very brief and very minor). The act of writing out your comments forces you to be more specific.

2. *The Fewer Levels of Approval, the Better*

Who should have approval authority? The marketing expert—usually a product manager. A technical expert—usually an engineer or scientist. The advertising manager. And the company president. But certainly no more than that.

Everybody has a different opinion of what should appear in an ad. By trying to please a committee, you end up with an ad that is too spread out, one that is weak, watered down, with no strong selling message or point of view.

Four reviewers or less is ideal. Six should be the maximum. Any more, and you are writing ads by committee—and committees cannot write effective ads.

When I write for small companies, my copy is usually

approved by one person: the company owner or president. Some of my best copy has been published this way.

If others in your organization want to see the copy before it is published, put them on a "c.c." list of people who receive informational copies. These people can give you their opinion if they want to, but they have no right of approval or disapproval. Only a handful of high-level managers should have say over what the final content of the ad will be.

Clients and prospects frequently ask me, "Do you find that your copy is improved once it has gone through the approval process?"

Occasionally, a revision will sharpen and improve the copy. But honesty compels me to admit that 99 out of 100 times the original version is better than the copy that is published after that ad has gone through the numerous layers of corporate approval.

The fewer revisions made, the better.

3. *Attach an Approval Form to the Copy*

When you route the copy for approval, attach a standard approval form to it.

The form lists the reviewers in the order in which they are to review the copy. The reviewer of least authority sees the copy first, the person with final say sees it last.

List each person's name along with the date by which they should sign off on the copy and send it to the next reviewer. Ask each reviewer to initial the approval sheet and to date their initials (this will speed the approval process).

Any discrepancies in reviewers' comments should be reconciled by the advertising manager before the copy is returned to the writer for revision.

4. *What About Legal?*

Lawyers can ruin good copy.

Don't allow the legal department to rewrite copy. If

there's a legal problem with the copy, the lawyers should point it out so the copywriter can make the necessary revisions. But lawyers don't understand the nature of salesmanship in print, and they can ruin a good piece of copy by changing strong, sharp language into weak, vague, lawyerlike prose.

One advertiser experienced a 56 percent drop in response to their mailings after the legal department changed the order form. The change was minor—the words "annual subscription" were replaced with "12-month lease"—but the editing had a devastating impact on sales. As consultant Shell Alpert explains, "The monumental difference lies not in the meaning of the words, but in their connotation. The *perceived risk* that the word 'lease' almost viscerally evokes is far more intimidating than 'subscription.' "[2]

On the other hand, there are some situations in which it can be dangerous *not* to show the copy to your lawyer. In 1982, the FDA ruled that Pfizer's new campaign for Procardia, a heart medication, was "false and misleading." They ordered Pfizer to revise its promotional materials, send letters to all physicians who might have received the original literature, and run "remedial ads" in two issues of each medical magazine that carried the original ads. My guess is that this cost Pfizer hundreds of thousands of dollars.

Not every ad has to be run by legal. But you should show copy to the lawyers when:

- You're advertising a highly regulated product such as ethical drugs or financial services (an "ethical drug" is one that can only be purchased with a prescription from a medical doctor)
- The promotion involves a sweepstakes or contest
- You're running comparative advertising that names the competition

- There is a question as to whether you might be violating a trademark or copyright
- You are making product claims that are difficult to prove
- The market is highly competitive, and there's a chance a competitor might take legal action to stop your ads from running.

5. Be Civil

Some clients love to tear apart a writer's work. Others are merely insensitive. They don't realize that writing is a highly personal act, and writers take criticism on a personal level.

Amil Gargano says that some people "take delight in browbeating creative people. These are people who have a very fragile ego and a difficult time handling rejection. You should comment on their work in a way that is thoughtful, considerate and articulate."[3]

You don't have to baby writers. Just remember they're people. And, like your own employees, they are quick to respond to praise and to insult.

Be tactful when you have to tell a writer that his work doesn't meet your standards. Don't say, "The copy isn't very good, and we need a total rewrite."

Rather, start with praise, then get to the defects. Say, "Overall you've done a good job in putting this together. Let me show you our reactions and the changes we'd like you to make."

Companies spend a great deal of money motivating employees. Outside vendors also respond to the motivators of praise, kindness, courtesy, and decency. Treat your copywriter well, and he'll give you his best.

6. Let Writers Write

"Good clients don't write copy," says Malcolm MacDougall, president of SSC&B. "Good clients know in their hearts that nobody from Harvard Business School ever wrote a great ad campaign. That is why they have an agency."[4]

Let your writers do their job. Don't write or rewrite copy. If you want changes made, write out what these changes are. But don't make them yourself. Give them to the copywriter and let him redo the words.

Don't play schoolteacher or amateur grammarian. The copywriter is the expert on how to use language as a selling tool.

If you think the ad doesn't reflect your strategy and objective, say so. If there's a wrong fact, point it out. But don't change commas to semicolons or dot i's and cross t's. Leave writing to the writer.

7. *Don't Take Opinion Polls*

One of my clients had me come up with two versions of a brochure cover. He made his selection by asking his mother, his father, his wife, his wife's parents, his grandfather, and several friends which they liked best. Cover "B" got more votes and that's the one he went with.

Don't make the same mistake as my client. Ad copy should be judged by professional business people—not by friends, relatives, and neighbors.

When viewing an ad layout or reading a piece of copy, amateurs judge the ad by aesthetics. Not by whether it would move them to buy the product. They'll pick the pretty layout, the flowery, poetic-sounding copy every time. So—nice as these folks may be—their opinion of your ad shouldn't play a part in your approval process.

8. *Read Copy as a Customer, not as an Advertiser or an Editor*

I worry when the client reads copy with pen or pencil in hand. It tells me he's reading the ad as an editor—and not as a buyer.

Instead, read the copy from the customer's point of view. Ask, "If I were my customer, would this ad get my attention? Does it hold my interest strongly enough to get me to read or at least skim the body copy? Would I remember the ad, want to buy the product, or be moved to clip the coupon and respond?"

Don't worry if the ad doesn't show a picture of the company president or talk about the new conveyor belts in the Kentucky factory. If the customer doesn't care, then you shouldn't either.

9. Develop and Publish Guidelines for Copy Review

As I said, the copywriter can't read your mind. He can't know your corporate guidelines, your company's likes and dislikes, unless you tell him what they are.

Develop a set of rules and guidelines for your writers to follow. These rules should contain both mandatory stylistic requirements (for example: "The company name is to be set in all caps and followed by a registered trademark symbol") and suggested guidelines.

The suggested guidelines clue copywriters in on the way you're used to doing things. (For example, you might prefer long, informative subheads in brochures rather than short, snappy ones.) However, the copywriter should consider these guidelines as suggestions only. Rules can be bent and broken to make the copy more effective.

You can enlist the aid of your freelance copywriter, advertising consultant, or ad agency in developing these rules and guidelines. Together you may decide to add new rules or delete those guidelines that serve no real purpose.

Of course, the wisest thing you can do is to forget about your prejudices and tastes and give the copywriter total freedom to write the best copy he can.

14

What Every Copywriter Should Know About Graphic Design

This is going to be the shortest chapter in the book.

The reason is that it deals with a simple question.

The question is: "What does the copywriter need to know about designing an ad layout?"

And the answer is: "Not much."

This is a relief to those of you who can't draw. But it may puzzle readers who do ads in which the words are strongly tied to a visual concept.

Let's see how involved the copywriter gets with the design side of advertising.

DRAWING VERSUS VISUALIZING

The copywriter is not a graphic artist. It's not his job to design ad layouts, select photographs, specify type style and size, or select paper stock. These tasks are handled by art directors.

The copywriter's job is to come up with *selling ideas.*

Most of the copywriter's ideas can be expressed primarily with words. The layout serves only as a framework to contain the words. The visual supports, enhances, and explains the ideas in the copy, but the copy doesn't *depend* on the visual and can stand on its own.

Some concepts, however, can be expressed only by a strong combination of words *and* pictures. A classic Volkswagen ad showed a cartoon of a man holding a gas pump to his head as if he were shooting himself with it. The headline underneath the cartoon read, "Or buy a Volkswagen." Obviously, this idea depends on a combination of words and images to get its point across. The copywriter who dreamed it up could not have presented it to the client without a rough sketch of the layout.

There are times when you, as a copywriter, need more than copy to get your ideas across. You may need to describe your visual in words, or sketches, or in a mock-up of the final version.

However, these need not be elaborate or well drawn. Stick figures, scribbles, and crudely drawn lines, boxes, and lettering will do. No one expects the copywriter to be an artist; clients understand that your drawing is a *rough* sketch only.

In fact, the term *copywriter's rough* is used to describe ad layouts and brochure dummies drawn by copywriters (a "dummy" is a paper mock-up of the brochure as it will be printed in its final form).

Some prospective clients ask, "Do you do the artwork also?" I reply, "I don't do mechanicals or comps. If my concept depends on a visual, I'll either write a description of the visual in the copy or provide a copywriter's rough."

Although I'm a writer, I know something about graphic art and its jargon. Here are a few basic terms you should be aware of:

Art. A drawing or photograph used in advertising.

Comp. Short for "comprehensive." A comp is an artist's drawing of a layout. It is used for review purposes and as a guide for the printer.

Dummy. Mock-up of a brochure, catalog, or other piece of printed literature. The dummy is used to indicate the layout, look, weight, and feel of the finished piece.

Four color. Printed material reproduced in full color.

Layout. The positioning of the elements of a printed piece. These elements include the headline, subheads, body copy, coupon, logo, photos, and illustrations.

Mechanical. A paste-up of the type and visual elements of the layout. The mechanical is used by the printer to make reproductions of the ad or brochure.

Rough. An artist's crude sketch of the layout, used for showing the basic idea. If the rough is approved, the next step is a comp, then a mechanical.

Thumbnail. Small sketch (about the dimensions of a wallet-size photo) used to give a quick impression of a layout or visual idea.

Two color. Ad or printed promotion reproduced in two colors, usually black and a second color such as blue, red, or yellow.

White space. Blank area on a page.

A freelance copywriter submits a copywriter's rough to his client, whether the client is an ad agency or an advertiser.

An agency writer turns his copy and copywriter's rough over to the art director for polishing. A good art director enhances the writer's visual concept by adding his own ideas and creativity to it.

The art director may do a series of thumbnail sketches. These sketches can present a number of different visual concepts in rough form.

The writer, art director, and account executive review the thumbnails and choose the ones they want to develop into full-size artist's roughs. These roughs, along with the copy, are submitted to the client for approval.

Some agencies submit two or three versions of the layout so the client can select the one he likes best. To me, this is like having my lawyer say, "Which defense do you think I ought to use?" I believe the *agency* should select the version it thinks is best and submit this to the client. After all, the client is paying the agency to make judgments in the creative area.

Once the rough is approved, the agency may submit a more polished drawing—the comp—before photos are taken and type is set.

Why do agencies go through the process of submitting roughs? Because of the cost of revisions. It is relatively inexpensive to make changes to a rough. It is costlier to redo mechanicals, set new type, or retouch or reshoot a photo if the client requests changes in the later stages of ad production.

ART DIRECTION FOR THE INDEPENDENT COPYWRITER

Agency copywriters know they have staff artists who can put their layout ideas in polished form.

Freelancers don't. They can either hire a graphic artist, or draw their own crude copywriter's roughs.

There is *no need* for the freelancer to hire an artist; just let your clients know that you will be providing copywriter's roughs, not finished comps. If the client demands comps, and if you are willing to provide this service, you can hire an artist.

In return for supervising the artwork, you add an extra charge for artwork to your bill. This charge can be based on a percentage of the cost of hiring the artist. Or it can be whatever fee you think is reasonable.

If all this talk of drawing and art has you, as a "pure" writer, a bit worried—stop worrying.

On nine out of ten projects I do *not* do a copywriter's rough or any other type of sketch. It's not necessary: either my concept doesn't depend on a visual, or if it does, the visual can easily be described, in words, in the manuscript I submit.

Only one out of ten of my ads is so visually complex or dependent upon a visual that I need to sketch it out. And doing the crude sketch never takes more than ten minutes!

Here are a few of my recent projects and how I handled the visual element:

Four-page Brochure for a Bank

The client told me, "We'll have the headline on the cover, the logo and address on the back cover, and the copy in the inside two-page spread. Our design studio will come up with the appropriate graphics." Since my description of the bank's service did not need to be illustrated visually, I submitted a typed manuscript of copy only, with no rough layout or descriptions of visuals.

Brochure for a Software Firm

The firm needed a folded pamphlet to fit in a number-ten business envelope. Such a brochure can be folded in several different ways, and the manner of folding affects the order in which the reader sees the sections of copy.

To make sure my copy would be read in sequence, I submitted a dummy of the brochure that indicated the manner of folding and which sections of copy would be printed on each panel of the brochure. I wrote in headlines and subheads and used squiggly lines to indicate body copy.

Again, the brochure contained no photos or drawings.

Annual Report

A graphic design studio hired me to write an annual report for one of its clients. Since the studio would do the actual design and the text was not tied to specific visuals, I did not submit a dummy or rough.

I did include a list of suggested visuals—charts, graphs, tables, and photos that I knew would enhance the message of the copy. The design studio, not being as familiar with the company's story as I was, needed this guidance to come up with the *subject matter* for appropriate visuals. However, the style and execution was all theirs.

Eight-page Brochure for a Radar System

I attached a detailed list of suggested visuals and photo captions. After all, there are a lot of things to show in a brochure on a radar—transmitters, receivers, control panels, the antenna, the scope, interior circuitry, results of test flights, the manufacture of the components.

One-page Sales Letter for a Producer of Corporate Slide Shows and Films

No need for any layout—I typed the manuscript for the letter single-space, exactly as it would be printed on the client's stationery in its final version.

Series of Full-page Ads on Industrial Products

An ad agency hired me to write three ads, each on a different piece of industrial equipment. The agency had already come up with layouts and rough headlines, so there was no need for me to do a sketch or come up with a visual.

Full-page ad for a Software Firm

Although the ad contained no visual (it was an all-copy ad), I did a rough sketch to indicate the positions of the headline, logo, and the coupon. (The company had not used coupons in its ads before, and mishandling the design of the coupon—making it too small or placing it in a position other than the bottom right-hand corner—can drastically reduce reader response.)

Feature Article for a Corporate Executive

I submitted a typed manuscript only. Most articles don't require visuals. If yours does, you can just attach a list of suggested photos at the end of the manuscript.

DESIGN TIPS FOR COPYWRITERS

The writer doesn't design the ad or brochure. But he should know what works in design—and what doesn't.

Ad agencies, graphic design studios, and large corporations have their own resources for producing print material. Smaller companies may not have a graphics expert to guide them. They look to the copywriter for advice on how to put together print promotions.

Here is a miscellany of graphic-arts tips, rules, and techniques that every copywriter should know:

- First, there's the magic of the "Basic A" ad layout. This is the simplest, most standard layout: Large picture at the top, headline underneath, body copy in two or three columns under the headline, logo and address in the bottom right-hand corner.

  Basic A is not spectacular, and some art directors consider it "old hat." But it's sensible, it draws the reader into the copy, and it's easy to read.

  You may want something different. Fine. But at least

consider Basic A before going on to a more "creative" design.

- A layout should have a single "focal point" where the eye goes to first. This is usually the visual; it can also be the headline.

- A layout should pull the eye from headline and visual through the body copy in logical sequence to the signature and logo. Subheads and bullets can help accomplish this.

- Setting the headline in big, bold type helps draw attention to it. A powerfully written headline, splashed across the page in large letters, can be a real stopper in an ad.

- If you want the reader to respond to your ad, use a coupon. The coupon should appear in the lower right-hand corner of the ad; the ad should be run against the outer edge of the right-hand page. If a coupon borders the "gutter"—the fold running down the middle of a magazine or newspaper—people will not tear it out.

- If you want people to respond to your ad by phoning, set the phone number in large type at the end of the body copy. A toll-free number gets more calls than a pay number—even if you invite the reader to call on your pay number "collect."

- Photos make better visuals than drawings. They are more real, more believable, than illustrations.

- Full-color gets more attention and gives a better impression than black and white. But full-color is much more expensive to produce and to run.

- In the hands of a skilled graphic artist, a second color can add to a brochure or ad's effectiveness. In the hands of an amateur, it can look chintzy and cheap. Be careful when using a second color in your layout.

- The simpler the layout, the better. Ads with too many elements—small pictures, graphs, tables, charts, sidebars—have a complex look that discourages people from reading the copy. It takes a highly skilled graphic designer to produce a multi-element ad that doesn't look cluttered and ponderous.

- The most important factor in selecting type is its readability. Type should be clear, easy on the eye, friendly, and inviting. Style is important—the choice of typeface is one of many elements that contributes to the image conveyed by the ad—but readability comes first. Always.

- Photos should be sharp, clear, and simple. If you have to choose between using a photo of poor quality or no photo, don't use a photo. Professional photography is expensive but necessary in advertising. Few amateur shutterbugs are capable of producing ad-quality photographs, although they may think otherwise.

- The best photos demonstrate a product benefit or make you think, "That looks interesting. I wonder what is going on here?" The latter type of photo has story appeal but doesn't tell the whole story; it leaves something to the imagination and arouses curiosity so that you will read the body copy to find out what the photo is about.
An example of this type of story-telling photo is one used in an ad for Paco Rabanne cologne. The photo shows a handsome young man lying in bed in his artist's studio. He is talking on the phone and, although covered by sheets, has obviously been sleeping in the nude. Who is he talking to? What happened in that room last night? You want to read the copy to find out.

- Never do anything to make the copy difficult to read. Type should be set in black against a clear white background—not a tint, not white on black, not in color. I just saw an ad in which the copy was printed on a tablecloth and shot as a photo! Naturally, it was quite difficult to read.

PARTING THOUGHTS

Here are a few opinions I've developed on copywriters, art, and art directors:

1. Some copywriters try to add to their value in the marketplace by taking on a second skill. There are copywriter-photographers, copywriter-art directors, copywriter-narrators, and copywriter-television producers.

   The logic makes sense. By hiring the dual-function copywriter, the client gets two services for the price of one.

   In reality, the best copywriters are those that write copy exclusively. People who do two jobs are usually not very good at either one.

   For example, all the copywriter-photographers I know are mediocre writers and mediocre photographers. The reason may be that a skilled writer is so in demand that he has no time for picture taking, just as a skilled photographer commands such high fees that there is no need for him to develop a secondary talent.

   But whatever the reason, I've never met a "combination copywriter" that was truly a first-rate writer.

2. Successful copywriters—at least, the ones I know—are good at visualizing their ideas, but their visual concepts and layouts are always simple in design. The reason may be that copywriters don't have the drawing skills needed to express complex visual concepts on paper. So they stick to layouts they can illustrate with stick figures and squiggly lines.

   Art directors, on the other hand, have the ability to do elaborate sketches, and so their layouts tend to be more sophisticated and complex.

   A good art director can take a writer's simple concept and add graphic elements that enhance its selling power.

A clear-thinking copywriter can look at an art director's layout and see ways to make it cleaner, simpler, easier to read, and easier to respond to.

3. Designing ads is not the complex, mysterious task some people make it out to be.

Laypeople believe—and artists encourage this belief—that there is some arcane formula of color combinations, type styles, photography, illustration, graphic elements, and positioning that creates ads with magical selling power.

The truth is, design has a minor effect on sales compared with the nature of the product (its appearance, function, features, and benefits), the consumer's needs, the price, the availability of the product (how it is distributed), the seller's reputation, and the sales pitch made in the copy of the ad.

So, much of the fuss and bother clients and art directors make over the ad's graphic design doesn't make much difference one way or the other.

4. Simple layouts are the best layouts. They are easier to conceive and cost much less to produce. Yet, they are often the most effective.

A copywriter friend of mine wrote a small (6½ - by-4⅞-inch) black-and-white ad selling a home-study foreign language course. The ad's layout is very undistinguished—all copy except for a small line drawing of the study kit in the bottom right-hand corner. Yet, this plain-jane ad has produced sales of more than $5 million!

5. Some freelance writers team up with freelance artists and offer a single source for copy and art. As a client, you'll pay more for freelance ads produced this way because, in addition to time spent writing and designing, the copywriter and artist have to bill you for the time they spend coordinating your project and meeting with one another.

I've worked this way in the past, and it isn't efficient. If the two freelancers don't work in the same office, they can make five or six trips just to complete a simple ad or flyer. And this extra time will find its way into the client's bill somehow.

6. Words, not pictures, are the most important way of communicating great ideas. The *Bible* contains many thousands of words and not a single picture.

A Glossary of
Advertising Terms

Account—An advertising agency's client.

Account executive—An advertising agency employee who serves as the liaison between the agency and the client.

Advertisement—A paid message in which the sponsor is identified.

Advertising manager—A professional employed by an advertiser to coordinate and manage the company's advertising program.

Art—A photograph or illustration used in an advertisment.

Art director—An ad agency employee responsible for designing and producing the artwork and layout for advertisements.

Audiovisual presentation—A presentation involving both pic-

331

tures and spoken words. TV commercials, slide shows, videotapes, and films are all audiovisual presentations.

A/V—Audiovisual.

B&W—Black and white.

Billings—The fees an ad agency charges its clients.

Bleed—An illustration that goes to the edge of the page. Bleed artwork has no borders or margins.

Blue chip—A highly profitable company or product.

Boilerplate—Standard copy used because of legal requirements or company policy.

Book—See *portfolio.*

Bounceback—Second mailing sent to a prospective customer who responded to an ad. Bouncebacks are designed to increase response to the initial mailing of product information.

Brand—The label by which a product is identified.

Brand manager—A manager employed by an advertiser to take charge of the marketing and advertising of a brand.

Broadside—A one-page promotional flyer folded for mailing.

Brochure—A booklet promoting a product or service.

Budget—The amount of money the advertiser plans to spend on advertising.

Bulk mailing—The mailing of a large number of identical pieces of third-class mail at a reduced rate.

Bullet—A heavy dot used to separate lines or paragraphs of copy.

Buried ad—An ad surrounded by other ads.

Business-to-business advertising—Advertising of products and services sold by a business to other businesses.

Campaign—A coordinated program of advertising and promotion.

Client—A company that uses the services of advertising professionals.

Clios—Advertising-industry awards given for the best television commercials of the year.

Collateral—Printed product information such as brochures, fliers, catalogs, and direct mail.

Considered purchase—A purchase made after careful evaluation of the product.

Consumer—One who buys or uses products and services.

Consumer advertising—Advertising of products sold to the general public.

Consumer products—Goods sold to individuals rather than to business or industry.

Contest—Sales promotion in which the consumer uses his skill to try and win a prize. Some contests require proof of purchase.

Copy—The text of an ad, commercial, or promotion.

Copy/Contact—An ad-agency copywriter who works directly with the client instead of through an account executive.

Copywriter—A person who writes copy.

Creative—Describes activities directly related to the creation of advertising. These include copywriting, photography, illustration, and design.

Creative director—Ad-agency employee responsible for supervising the work of copywriters, art directors, and others who produce advertising.

Demographics—Statistics describing the characteristics of a segment of the population. These characteristics include age, sex, income, religion, and race.

Direct mail—Unsolicited advertising material delivered by mail.

Direct response—Advertising that seeks to get orders or leads directly and immediately rather than build an image or awareness over a period of time.

Downscale—Consumers on the low end of the social scale in terms of income, education, and status.

Editorial—Those portions of a magazine's or newspaper's reading matter that are *not* advertisements—articles, news briefs, fillers, and other material produced by the publication's editors and writers.

Farm out—To assign work to an outside vendor rather than handle it in-house.

Feature story—A full-length magazine article.

Fee—The charge made by an agency or advertising professional to the client for services performed.

Four A's—American Association of Advertising Agencies, an industry trade association.

Four color—Artwork reproduced in full color.

Fractional ad—An ad that takes less than a full page in a magazine or newspaper.

Freelance—A self-employed copywriter, photographer, artist, media buyer, or other advertising professional.

Full-service agency—An ad agency that offers its clients a full range of advertising services including creative services, media buying, planning, marketing, and research.

General advertising—Advertising that seeks to instill a preference for the product in the consumer's mind to promote the future sale of the product at a retail outlet or through a distributor or agent. This is the opposite of *direct response* advertising.

House organ—A company-published newsletter or magazine.

Image—The public's perception of a firm or product.

Impulse buy—A purchase motivated by chance rather than by plan.

Industrial advertising—Advertising of industrial products and services.

In-house—Anything done internally within a company.

Inquiry—A request for information made by a potential customer responding to an ad or promotion.

Inquiry fulfillment package—Product literature sent in response to an inquiry.

Jingle—Music and lyrics used in a commercial.

Layout—A drawing used to get a rough idea of how a finished ad, poster, or brochure will look.

Lead—See *sales lead.*

Lettershop—A firm that reproduces sales letters and other advertising literature.

Lift letter—A second letter included in a direct-mail package; the lift letter is designed to increase response to the mailing. Also known as a *publisher's letter* because it is primarily used in mailings that solicit magazine subscriptions.

List broker—A person who rents mailing lists.

Logo—The name of a company set in specially designed lettering.

Lottery—In a lottery, winners are chosen by chance and must make a purchase to enter.

Madison Avenue—The mainstream of the New York City advertising community. Madison Avenue is a street that runs along the East Side of Manhattan, but used in the advertising sense, the term "Madison Avenue" refers to agencies located in the heart of midtown Manhattan.

Market—A portion of the population representing potential and current customers for a product or service.

Marketing—The activities companies perform to produce, distribute, promote, and sell products and services to their customers.

Marketing communications—Communications used in marketing a product or service. "Marketing communications" includes advertising, public relations, and sales promotion.

Mass advertising—Advertising aimed at the general public.

Mechanical—Type and artwork pasted up on a board for reproduction by the printer.

Media—Any method of communication that brings information, entertainment, and advertising to the public or the business community.

Merchandising—Activities designed to promote retail sales.

On speculation—Work that the client will pay for only if he likes it and uses it.

Package goods—Products wrapped or packaged by the manufacturer. Package goods are low in cost and typically sold on store shelves.

Per diem—Fees charged by the day.

PI—Per inquiry advertising. Advertising for which the publisher or broadcast station is paid according to the number of inquiries produced by the ad or commercial.

Portfolio—A presentation folder containing samples of your work. Shown to prospective employers when you are interviewing for a job.

Premium—Gift offered to potential customers as motivation for buying a product.

Press release—Written news information mailed to the press.

Product manager—A manager employed by an advertiser to supervise the marketing and advertising of a product or product line.

Promotion—Activities other than advertising that are used to encourage the purchase of a product or service.

Prospect—A person with the money, authority, and desire to buy a product or service; a potential customer.

Psychographics—Statistics relating to the personalities, attitudes, and life-styles of various groups of people.

Pub-set—Ads designed and typeset by the publication in which they will appear.

Public relations—The activity of influencing the press so that they print (and broadcast) stories that promote a favorable image of a company and its products.

Publisher's letter—See *lift letter*.

Puffery—Exaggerated product claims made by an advertiser.

Pull—The response generated by an advertisement.

Red Book—Refers to both *The Standard Directory of Advertising Agencies* and *The Standard Directory of Advertisers*.

Reel—A reel of film or videotape containing sample commercials written by the copywriter.

Research—Surveys, interviews, and studies designed to show an advertiser how the public perceives his product and company or how they react to the advertiser's ads and commercials.

Reply card—A self-addressed postcard sent with advertising material to encourage the prospect to respond.

Sales lead—An inquiry from a qualified prospect.

Sales promotion—A temporary marketing effort designed to generate short-term interest in the purchase of a product. Coupons, sales, discounts, premiums, sweepstakes, and contests are all examples of sales promotion.

Space—The portion of a magazine or newspaper devoted to advertisements.

Split run test—Two versions of an ad are run in different copies of a publication to test the effectiveness of one version against the other.

Storyboard—Rough series of illustrations showing what a finished TV commercial will look like.

Sweepstakes—A sales promotion in which prizes are awarded by chance and the consumer does not have to make a purchase to enter.

Teaser—Copy printed on the outside envelope of a direct-mail package.

Trade advertising—Advertising aimed at wholesalers, distributors, sales reps, agents, and retailers rather than consumers.

Two color—An ad or sales brochure printed in two colors—usually black and a second color such as blue, red, or yellow.

Type—Text set in lettering that can be reproduced by a printer.

Universe—The total number of people who are prospects for your product.

Upscale—Prospects at the upper end of the social scale in terms of income, education, and status.

Vertical publication—Magazine intended for a narrow group of special-interest readers.

14 Magazines Every Copywriter Should Know About

Like any business professional, the copywriter should keep up-to-date by reading magazines in his field.

There are dozens of excellent publications covering various areas of advertising, sales, and marketing. Here, I list thirteen I've found useful. Some I subscribe to; others I read on a hit or miss basis. But all will help you learn more about copywriting in particular and advertising in general.

Ad Day/U.S.A.
400 East 54th Street
New York, NY 10022
(212) 421–3713

Ad Day is a weekly newsletter on what's happening in the advertising business. It reports on account changes, new ad campaigns, and who's moving where. Useful for its late-breaking news.

Ad Forum
18 East 53rd Street
New York, NY 10022
(212) 751–2670

This magazine is aimed at the marketing manager who works for a consumer company. Much of the editorial content focuses on creating, managing, and measuring print and broadcast advertising campaigns aimed at a mass audience. Published monthly.

Advertising Age
740 N. Rush Street
Chicago, IL 60611
(312) 649-5000

This twice-weekly news magazine is one of the two top industry publications (the other being *Adweek*). *Advertising Age* contains in-depth coverage of newsworthy events in advertising; the midweek edition features a special "magazine section" that focuses on a specific area of advertising. Recent magazine sections have profiled computer, retail, direct response, grocery, and fashion advertising.

Adweek
820 Second Avenue
New York, NY 10017
(212) 661-8080

Adweek is *Advertising Age*'s main competitor. *Adweek* is smaller, slimmer, more compact than *Ad Age*. And, it comes out only once a week. (To make up for this, *Adweek* recently purchased *Ad Day*, which it publishes on Thursdays to compete with *Ad Age's* Thursday edition.) *Adweek* offers readers a blend of news, features, how-to articles, and lively columns. I subscribe to both magazines, but prefer *Adweek* for its concise format that lets me get the news in less time.

Business Marketing
220 East 42nd Street
New York, NY 10017
(212) 210-0100

Business Marketing covers advertising, sales, and marketing of products and services sold to business and industry. It's a "must-read" for industrial, high-tech, medical, and financial copywriters. *Business Marketing*'s editorial content is heavy on long feature articles—both "how-to" articles and analytical pieces. Published monthly.

Direct Marketing
224 Seventh Street
Garden City, NY 11530
(516) 746-6700

Direct Marketing is for readers involved in direct-response marketing—direct mail, mail order, telemarketing. Every issue is loaded with "how-to" articles on various facets of copywriting. I subscribe to *Direct Marketing* and recommend it even if you're not involved in direct mail or mail order. Published monthly.

DM News
156 East 52nd Street
New York, NY 10022
(212) 741-2095

A newspaper-style tabloid. Coverage is similar to *Direct Marketing*, but articles are briefer and more oriented toward late-breaking news rather than general information. But *DM News* also publishes several helpful how-to articles in each issue. Published twice a month.

High-Tech Marketing
163 Main Street
Westport, CT 06880
(203) 222–0935

High-Tech Marketing reaches a senior level of marketing management within high-technology firms. Articles discuss advertising, publicity, distribution, and many other facets of marketing. Published monthly.

Madison Avenue
369 Lexington Avenue
New York, NY 10017
(212) 972-0600

As the name implies, *Madison Avenue* is for people involved in the world of big-agency, big-account advertising. It's a well-written, attractively designed magazine with many useful articles on advertising and the ad agency business. Published monthly.

Magazine Age
225 Park Avenue
New York, NY 10017
(212) 986-7366

Magazine Age covers all aspects of magazine publishing, including advertising. It's a helpful publication for copywriters who write print ads for consumer and business magazines. Published monthly.

Marketing Communications
475 Park Avenue South
New York, NY 10016
(212) 725-2300

A down-to-earth, informative publication, primarily for advertising professionals involved in retail advertising. Published monthly.

Public Relations Journal
845 Third Avenue
New York, NY 10022
(212) 826-1757

This is the official monthly magazine of the Public Relations Society of America, a society of public relations professionals. Copywriters just getting into public relations can learn a lot from this magazine on how to write material that editors will read and publish.

Sales and Marketing Management
633 Third Avenue
New York, NY 10017
(212) 986-4800

A monthly magazine for sales managers and marketing managers. *Sales and Marketing Management* runs informative articles on all facets of marketing—including advertising. Most of the articles are brief and instructive.

Zip Magazine
545 Madison Avenue
New York, NY 10022
(212) 371-7800

Zip deals primarily with the mailing-list aspect of direct marketing. It will give copywriters a good overview of direct marketing as well as specific tips on creative direct mail that works. Published monthly.

Notes

chapter 1   *An Introduction to Copywriting*

1. Luther Brock, "Put the Spotlight on Benefits, Not Gimmicks," *Direct Marketing*, May, 1983, p. 108.
2. Hank Seiden, "The Delivery Doesn't Fly," *Advertising Age*, October 31, 1983, p. MM–66. Reprinted with permission from the October 31, 1983 issue of *Advertising Age*. Copyright 1983 by Crain Communications Inc.
3. Alvin Eicoff, *Or Your Money Back* (New York: Crown Publishers, Inc., 1982), pp. 1–3.
4. Keith V. Monk, "Consumers Care Little for Creativity," *Advertising Age*, August 1, 1983, pp. 3–4. Reprinted with permission from the August 1, 1983 issue of *Advertising Age*. Copyright 1983 by Crain Communications Inc.
5. Howard G. Sawyer, *Business-to-Business Advertising* (Chicago: Crain Books, 1978), p. 266.
6. Lewis Kornfeld, *To Catch a Mouse, Make a Noise Like a Cheese* (Engle-

wood Cliffs, NJ: Prentice-Hall, Inc., 1983), pp. 56–58.

7. Robert M. Snodell, "Why TV Spots Fail," *Advertising Age*, July 2, 1984, p. 18. Reprinted with permission from the July 2, 1984 issue of *Advertising Age*. Copyright 1984 by Crain Communications Inc.

chapter 4   *Writing to Sell*

1. Andrew J. Byrne, "Long Copy Increases Chances of Making Sale," *Direct Marketing.*

2. Russell H. Colley, *Defining Advertising Goals for Measured Advertising Results* (New York: Association of National Advertisers, 1961), p. 39.

3. Malcolm D. MacDougall, "How to Sell Parity Products," *Adweek*, February 13, 1984, p. 30.

4. Donald J. Moine, "To Trust, Perchance to Buy," *Psychology Today*, August, 1982, p. 52.

5. Andrew J. Byrne, "Long Copy Increases Chances of Making Sale," *Direct Marketing.*

6. Jack Trout and Al Ries, "The Positioning Era" (reprinted from *Advertising Age,* April 24, May 1, and May 8, 1972).

chapter 5   *Getting Ready to Write*

1. Betsy Sharkey, "Krone's Back Home," *Adweek*, August 29, 1983, p. 24.

2. Dorothy Hinshaw Patent, "Interviewing the Experts," *The Writer*, May, 1983, p. 20.

3. Don Hauptman, "The Art of Creative Capitalism: Eleven Ways to Dream Up Profitable Business Ideas," *Success Unlimited*, May and June, 1978.

4. John Caples, *How to Make Your Advertising Make Money* (Englewood Cliffs, NJ: Prentice-Hall, Inc., 1983), pp. 25–37.

chapter 6   *Writing Print Advertisements*

1. Robert F. Lauterborn, "Never Underestimate the Power of the Printed Word," speech presented at the February 2, 1984, meeting of the New York Chapter of the Business/Professional Advertising Association.

2. "Go, Gargano!", an ad for *The Wall Street Journal,* published in *Business Marketing* (April 1984). Copyright Dow Jones & Company, Inc., 1984, all rights reserved.

chapter 7 **Writing Direct Mail**

1. "From the Test Tube: To Tease or Not to Tease," *Test Patterns* (Newsletter published by Bloom & Gelb, Inc.), Vol. II, No. I. Spring 1984.
2. Sources for these tips include: *Direct Marketing: Strategy, Planning, and Execution* by Ed Nash (McGraw-Hill, 1982); "How to Create and Produce Successful Direct Mail" (Cahners Publishing); "The How Not to Mail Booklet" (Hayden Direct Marketing Services); "444 Begged, Borrowed, Stolen & Even a Few Original! Direct Response Marketing Ideas!" (Rockingham/Jutkins Marketing); "Direct Mail Editor's Checklist" (*Adweek*, December 13, 1982, p. 32).

chapter 8 **Writing Brochures, Catalogs, and Other Sales Literature**

1. Howard G. Sawyer, *Business-to-Business Advertising* (Chicago: Crain Books, 1978), p. 139.

chapter 9 **Writing Public Relations Material**

1. Alan Caruba, "Public Relations: What Is It?", *New Jersey Business*, November, 1982, p. 70.
2. Carol Rose Carey, "A New Image for an Old Product," *INC.*, June 1982, p. 93.
3. "Lawpoll: Big Firms Favor P.R.; Little Firms Like Ads," *American Bar Association Journal*, 1983, p. 892.
4. Len Kirsch, "Press Releases: Format, Content . . . Do's and Don'ts," Kirsch Communications.
5. Pamela Clark, "Running in Place," *Popular Computing*, July 1984, p. 6.
6. Nancy Edmonds Hanson, *How You Can Make $20,000 a Year Writing (No Matter Where You Live)*, (Cincinnati, Ohio: Writer's Digest Books, 1980), pp. 186–187.
7. Ron Huff, "That Speaking Invitation: It Sounds Flattering, But—", *Advertising Age*, September 4, 1978, p. 40.

chapter 10 **Writing Commercials**

1. Ed McMahon, "TV's Greatest Censored Commercial Bloopers," Channel 4, NBC, Monday, November 7, 1983, 8:00 A.M.
2. Richard Morgan, "Public to 4A's: We Still Don't Like Advertising," *Adweek*, May 16, 1983, p. 2.

3. Donahue transcript #09032, copyright 1982, Multimedia Program Productions, Inc., Cincinnati, Ohio.
4. Malcolm D. MacDougall, "No Big Mistake," *Adweek*, June 4, 1984, p. 14.
5. Sid Bernstein, "Maybe We Are Too Creative," *Advertising Age*, June 18, 1984, p. 16.
6. David Campiti, "Writing Radio Commercials," *Writer's Digest*, November 1983, pp. 30–33.
7. Reprinted with permission of The Masonry Institute of St. Louis.
8. Copyright 1978, The DOCSI Corporation.
9. John Baldoni, "The Vision Translated into Words: An Overview of Script Writing," *Audio-Visual Directions*, October 1982, pp. 36–41.

chapter 11   *How to Succeed As a Freelance Copywriter*

1. "Political Arithmetic," *Adweek*, April 30, 1984, p. 94.

chapter 12   *How to Get a Great Job As An Ad-Agency Copywriter*

1. Barrington Boardman, "Ad Agencies' Biggest Neglect: Their People," *Adweek*, December 6, 1982, p. 28.
2. Robert W. Bly and Gary Blake, *Dream Jobs: A Guide to Tomorrow's Top Careers* (New York: John Wiley & Sons, Inc., 1983), pp. 8–9.
3. "Tips on Top Job Hunting Tactics," *Advertising Age*, February 23, 1981, p. S–15.
4. *Ibid.*, p. S–4.
5. George Tibball, "An Agency's Message to Clients," *Business Marketing*, September 1983, p. 95.

chapter 13   *How to Hire and Work With Copywriters*

1. Ed Buxton, "Doers vs. Undoers on Ad Row," *Adweek*, January 16, 1984, p. 24.
2. Shell R. Alpert, "In Direct Marketing Testing, Details Can Be Everything," *Business Marketing*, February 1984, p. 84.
3. Dr. Adweek and Betsy Sharkey, "How to Manage Creative People," *Adweek*, February 1984, p. C.R. 28.
4. Malcolm MacDougall, "Just Deserts: Why Clients Get the Advertising They Deserve," *Adweek*, April 1984, p. B.W.C. 4.

Index

ABOUT THE AUTHOR

Robert W. Bly is an independent copywriter and consultant specializing in industrial and high-tech advertising. He has written copy for more than three dozen advertising agencies and corporations including Brooklyn Union Gas, Chemical Bank, J. Walter Thompson, Westinghouse, and Prentice-Hall.

Mr. Bly is the author of nine books including *How to Promote Your Own Business* (New American Library) and *A Dictionary of Computer Words* (Dell/Banbury). He has been published in such magazines as *Writer's Digest*, *Cosmo*, *Amtrak Express*, *The Communicator's Journal*, *Business Marketing*, and *Direct Marketing*.

Bob Bly currently teaches copywriting and technical writing at the New York University School of Continuing Education. Before becoming a freelance copywriter, he was the advertising manager for Koch Engineering Company, Inc.

Questions and comments on *The Copywriter's Handbook* may be sent to Mr. Bly % *The Copywriter's Handbook*, Dodd, Mead & Company, 79 Madison Avenue, New York, NY 10016.